The Politics of 1992

Beyond the Single European Market

D1120744

The Politics of 1992

Beyond the Single European Market

Edited by

Colin Crouch and David Marquand

Basil Blackwell

ISBN 0–631–17521–0

First published 1990

Basil Blackwell Ltd.
108 Cowley Road, Oxford, OX4 1JF, UK.

Basil Blackwell Inc.
3 Cambridge Center,
Cambridge, MA. 02142, USA.

British Library Cataloguing in Publication Data
The politics of 1992: beyond the single European market.
1. European Community countries. Political cooperation
I. Crouch, Colin *1944–* II. Marquand, David *1934–*
321.04
ISBN 0–631–17521–0

Library of Congress
Cataloguing in Publication Data applied for

Typeset by Joshua Associates Ltd., Oxford
Printed in Great Britain by Whitstable Litho, Kent.

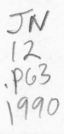

CONTENTS

FOREWORD

As François Duchêne observes in his chapter of this book, the history of the European Community has been marked by a paradox. Its goal was political; only the means were economic. Political union was to be achieved through economic integration. The project has been astonishingly successful. Economic integration has gone much further than anyone could reasonably have expected, and greater political cohesion has duly resulted. In every member state, national politics are inter-twined with Community politics; national institutions with Community institutions. There is scarcely a national minister who has no business to transact in Brussels or Luxembourg, scarcely a policy area in which the Community dimension is of no concern to national actors. At the same time, however, attempts to achieve the Community's political objectives by directly political means have almost always failed. The member states have enmeshed themselves in a network of interdependencies which presses ever more tightly on their freedom of action, but they remain reluctant to acknowledge how much freedom of action they have lost. Still less have they been willing to answer the political questions which their mutual interdependence has raised.

Perhaps the central question now facing the Community is whether the 1992 project to which this book is devoted will provide yet another illustration of M. Duchêne's paradox. The project was born of the belief, widely held in the early and middle 1980s, that the European enterprise had somehow run into the sands; that if existing trends continued, the Community would become less coherent politically and less successful economically; that 'Euro-sclerosis' was eroding the Community's competitiveness in world markets, particularly in the world's markets for the most sophisticated products; that lagging competitiveness would sooner or later spell declining influence; and that something dramatic had to be done to put things right. As before, the 'something' was economic – completion of the internal market: the elimination of the remaining barriers to free competition and free movement across the Community's frontiers; the complex package of practical measures on which most of the chapters that follow are focused. But the purpose of the whole exercise was political as much as, perhaps more than, economic. It had to do with power as well as with wealth. It was to strengthen the Community *vis-à-vis* the two other great trading blocs of the modern world, or at any rate to halt what was seen as an alarming process of relative decline.

As so often in the past, however, the authors of the project were reluctant to address the political and institutional questions implicit in their own enterprise. To be sure, the Single European Act did tackle the single most awkward institutional obstacle to further integration, namely the national veto. It also gave the European Parliament at least the beginnings of a role in Community legislation. But this was little more than patching, albeit essential patching. The underlying assumption was that no fundamental political changes were needed: that, given the necessary patching, the institutional structure bequeathed by the Community's founding fathers was perfectly capable of delivering the practical goods which concerned practical men.

In the half-decade since the Single European Act that assumption has increasingly been called into question. Part of the explanation lies in the logic and dynamic of the 1992 programme itself. That logic has been exemplified most clearly and most dramatically in the debate over monetary union, but other examples seem certain to follow sooner or later. The Thatcherite assumption that the single market, once created, could be left to operate on a kind of automatic pilot was always misconceived. In late-twentieth-century mixed economies – and, for all the excited talk that accompanied it, the momentarily fashionable neoliberalism of the 1980s made only marginal differences to the European mix – politics and economics are inextricably intertwined. The creation of a genuinely single market stretching from the Shetlands to Cadiz and from the Island of Rhodes to the Dingle peninsula is bound to have immense political repercussions, some of them unforeseeable. Community institutions will find themselves dealing with a whole range of issues which used to be settled by national institutions. To put it at its lowest, it is not self-evident that the Community's existing institutional structure is strong enough to bear the weight which these developments will place upon it.

De-regulation has already been shown to mean in practice re-regulation, as the chapter by Campbell, Barnes and Pepper in this volume shows; only the most extreme neo-liberals are really willing to contemplate such things as a complete lack of control over lorry drivers' working hours between intervals of sleep. The examples can be multiplied many times over, and as they accumulate they amount to the establishment of new, European-level regimes to mediate between actors in the free economic market and those wider consequences of their actions that do not enter into their own profit and loss accounts.

What form will these regimes take? Will they follow a particular national pattern, as did the great wave of Napoleonic innovations that embodied modernisation in an earlier Europe? Or will they be distinctively new? Whatever happens, their construction will be a major instance of political action, strategic decision-making, in the grand manner. The project will certainly be more intrinsically political than the bureaucratic exercises in harmonisation that constituted the former European Economic Community's attempt at unifying standards in member countries.

A second major source of politicisation concerns the so-called social dimension. There is a real anxiety among the representatives of work forces in northern Europe that a general relaxation of national regulatory standards will enable the high standards of protection that they have won over decades to be undermined. Health and safety in the strict sense were always to be excluded from the single market project, but many more subtle forms of undermining remain possible. Indeed, such has been the aim of some of the authors of the 1992 exercise. Many battles remain to be lost and won on this field, but the point is that labour and its political organisations have mounted a counter-attack, and have seen the scope for erecting new labour and social policy institutions at a European level where some had seen only institutional destruction. And thus it comes about that some of the voices opposing most shrilly moves for wider European integration on behalf of national sovereignty do so, not so much to protect national standards, as to have them eroded by a completely international competition that is beyond the scope of regulation of the kind that now seems possible through the EC's institutions.

A European monetary system must sooner or later mean reasonably uniform fiscal policies, which must sooner or later lead to congruence, if not actual convergence, in substantive policies financed by public expenditure. If European-level policy constrains how much in aggregate we are able to spend, we should all be expected to consider whether our particular national policy regime is as cost-effective as the others. (For example, if, as is possible, the British National Health Service is among the most efficient ways of financing public health care, will other countries within the Community not come under various forms of domestic pressure to imitate it?) Again it is clear that new fields are being opened for political debate and choice, but also that we have as yet little idea what particular patterns will emerge.

Europe, nations and regions

The fact remains however that for the foreseeable future, and with the exception of many, perhaps most, members of such groups as the Basques, Scots, Northern Irish Catholics and Flemish Belgians, the existing nation state remains the main focus of both the political loyalty and the political competence of the great majority of citizens. There are paradoxes here for most political forces. International business is the set of interests that possesses a political competence that can most easily transcend national boundaries, yet the conservative political forces with which business interests are primarily associated are those most in need of national symbols to render themselves attractive. Labour interests that in theory, as argued by Otto Jacobi in this volume, have a particular need for cross-national solidarity, have particular difficulty generating a political competence at cross-national levels.

Defined by the outcome of largely pre-modern wars and therefore following a geo-political pattern based on an outmoded military technology, not those of modern economic relations, nation states continue in their stubborn, incoherent way to defy such ostensibly more rationalistic and powerful forces as capitalist market relations and the politics of class.

Nationality has a logic of its own: the absence of any sustained period of settled national boundaries does not prevent either Germans or Irishmen from speaking of the *re*unification of their claimed countries.

In fact the nation state does not mean the same thing to all persons within even western Europe. For some (the English, French, Spanish) it is a durable, proud centralised phenomenon that has attracted fierce loyalties despite (or perhaps because of) fissiparous tendencies from 'prisoner' minority nations. For others (Belgians, Dutch, Portuguese) it is a small unit, the viability of which can be explained only in terms of the desire in past centuries of some big states to prevent others from claiming certain territories. For Germans and Italians it is a relatively recently structured unit, in at least the latter case containing among its regions probably more heterogeneity than is found among the separate nation states of Scandinavia.

What will the future of this inchoate group of units be as the European entity of which they are part acquires more decision-making importance and seeks to generate its own loyalties? For some purposes the relevant units for political solidarity cross state boundaries (as for example the group of regions of various nation states, within and without the EC, that share interests in that they all border the Adriatic). A struggle for focuses of identity and loyalty of a distinctive kind will be another of the profoundly political features of the new Europe.

Little Europe and greater Europe

But all this is still only the beginning of the story. Much more important than the logic and dynamic of the 1992 project itself are the changes which have taken place in the external environment since the Single European Act and the Cockfield White Paper were drawn up. The wave of revolutions which swept through eastern Europe in the second half of 1989 demolished the European – and perhaps even the international – order within which the Community was born and grew up. No new order has yet replaced it, and it will take time for one to emerge. But some of the building blocks which will have to be incorporated in whatever new order eventually appears are already taking shape. It is clear that a united Germany, significantly larger and richer than the other member states of the Community, will be easily the strongest power between the Atlantic and the Soviet border. It is clear too that the new democracies of central and eastern Europe will face enormous economic problems, and possible that they will be a prey to irredentist nationalisms of all kinds. It is probable that – like the new democracies of southern Europe ten years ago – they will see Community membership as both an economic and a political lifeline. It is at least conceivable that the Soviet Union will unravel, and that an unknowable number of more or less fragile successor states will also be knocking on the Community's door, certainly for aid and perhaps even for membership.

Will this leave Russia even more clearly set on the path that it has in fact been treading for many years: maintaining its position of importance by surrendering influence over increasingly independent, economically viable lands and replacing them by extended sway over more backward areas? This was the course taken earlier by that last doomed European empire, the Hapsburg, the upheavals of whose eventual collapse are still part of central Europe's instability. Here again, working out relations with this new Russia will demand politics of a strikingly strategic and innovative kind from the countries of western Europe, and for many if not most aspects of it they will have to act together at a Community level.

None of this could have been foreseen when this volume was planned. Still less could it have been foreseen when the Single European Act was agreed. Yet it now forms the context within which the 1992 programme has to be assessed. It no longer makes sense to focus attention on the sedate and cosy little Europe of the Six, the Nine or even the Twelve; on the Europe of Monnet and Schuman, of Heath and Pompidou or even of Schmidt and Giscard. The crucial question is how little Europe is to relate to a much wider and potentially more turbulent Europe, which includes Warsaw, Prague, Budapest and, for that matter, Kiev, Moscow and Leningrad as well as Paris, Brussels and Bonn. No one can possibly tell what the answer will be, but two things seem reasonably clear. One is that the economism of the original Monnet approach to European integration is now out of date. The questions that cry out for answers now belong unmistakably to the sphere of high politics which the Monnet approach sought to circumvent, and cannot be addressed through the back-door of economics. The second is that – partly because of this – the institutions created in pursuit of the Monnet approach are unlikely to prove adequate to the tasks with which they will have to deal.

This is not to say that the 1992 programme is no longer important. The antithesis between 'widening' and 'deepening' which has been seized upon by British opponents of a more integrated Community is a false one. Without the impetus which 1992 gave to its own integration, little Europe would have been in no state to face the challenges posed by the upheavals in the east. So, far from weakening the case for faster economic and monetary integration in the Community, the emergence of a united Germany in the centre of the continent, together with a train of impoverished and insecure new democracies on her eastern border, makes it even more essential to knit the economies of western Europe together as rapidly as possible. The most probable alternative to the 'deeper' Europe sought by Mitterrand and Delors is not the comfortable, loose-knit, 'wider' Europe of so much insular British imagining. It is a fragmented or at least fragmenting Europe, haunted by new versions of the fears and rivalries which have torn it apart so often in the past.

What is true is that the argument has now shifted to a different plane. As

Margaret Sharp points out elsewhere in this book, the question that preoccupied the authors of the 1992 programme was how to make possible the emergence of 'firms of a size to compete with the IBMs or Toshibas of this world' – and how, having done so, to make sure that they could not abuse their market power. That question still matters, but it is no longer the most important one. The crucial question is how to ensure that little Europe discharges its responsibilities to the greater Europe beyond its borders: how to create a dynamic and prosperous internal market in the west while at the same time offering the east a better prospect than that of becoming a reservoir of cheap labour.

* * *

In the above we have dwelt on the wider view of the implications of the single market, and several of our authors offer varying approaches to this same question. Lord Cockfield, who was the original author of the policy, leaves us in no doubt that the '1992' package should be seen as part of a larger project of European integration; a similar view is taken by François Duchêne, who has been involved in the development of the European Community since the very early years. Otto Jacobi presents a trade union view of a topic that has often been described, and criticised, as solely a businessman's vision. Hans Kastendiek and Jonathan Story consider, from rather different perspectives, the problematic encounter between the drive for integration and the strong nation state traditions of western Europe.

It is also important however to think about the detailed workings of the immediate policy package of the single market legislation. Dieter Biehl's discussion of fiscal federalism tackles an issue sufficiently large to be considered part of the general vision, but the other papers here examine specific sectors. Margaret Sharp considers European co-operation in advanced technology; Francis McGowan energy policy; and Campbell *et al.* the more detailed experience of policy implementation in the fields of transport and public procurement.

* * *

Since its foundation in 1930, *The Political Quarterly* has tried to explore issues of emerging public importance in both Britain and elsewhere, mainly but by no means exclusively from a left-of-centre point of view. It does this primarily through its regular quarterly pages, but also through occasional conferences and seminars or, as in the present case, through a book devoted to a question of particular topicality and importance.

C.C.
D.M.
The Editors,
The Political Quarterly

THE REAL SIGNIFICANCE OF 1992

LORD COCKFIELD*

In the European Community, the accepted phrase was 'The Completion of the Internal Market'. But in France it was described as 'The Great Market' and in this country 'The Single Market'. But increasingly everywhere the shorthand of '1992' tends to be used. I have in general stuck to the Community phrase—'the Internal Market'—in this article, but it needs to be borne in mind that this is the same as what is called the 'Single Market' in this country.

By 1992 the Community will be exactly 40 years old. It was founded not as commonly supposed by the Treaty of Rome which was signed in 1957 but by the Treaty of Paris in 1952. The Treaty of Paris set up the first of the Communities, the Coal and Steel Community, and it foreshadowed clearly and specifically the creation of an Economic Community which indeed followed in 1957. In law there are three Communities—the Coal and Steel Community, the European Economic Community (the 'EEC') and the European Atomic Energy Community ('Euratom') but we tend to bracket all these together as the 'European Community' and this is the terminology I will follow. But the fact that in *law* they are separate Communities, although the Institutions have been merged, is of considerable importance and is a valuable precedent in relation to the present dispute over Monetary Union which would almost certainly require a separate 'Community' and a separate Treaty in much the same way.

If one is to understand the Community one must understand its roots and its motivation. The Community was founded in the immediate aftermath of the second of the Great Wars which devastated Europe in the first half of this century. Its objective was the preservation of peace in Europe and in that it has been entirely successful. The Atlantic Alliance—NATO—was directed to the maintenance of peace between the super powers and thus to preventing a conflict which might have seen Europe as the battlefield on which that conflict was fought. But it was the Treaty of Paris and the Treaty of Rome which preserved the peace *between* the

---

* The Rt. Hon. the Lord Cockfield was Vice-President of the European Commission from 1985–88. He is regarded in Europe as the architect of the Single Market programme '1992', having originated it in 1985 and having driven it through to the point at which it was accepted by the heads of government as 'irreversible'. Lord Cockfield was a Minister at the Treasury from 1979–82 and a Member of the Cabinet from 1982–84, first as Secretary of State for Trade and then as Chancellor of the Duchy of Lancaster.

This is very much a personal account of the origins of the Programme for the Completion of the Internal Market—'1992' as it now tends to be called—its motivation and its importance in the development of the Community.

1

nations of Europe whose differences and divisions had been the source of so much bloody conflict over the centuries.

The very first of the treaties, the Treaty of Paris, opens with the words:

CONSIDERING that world peace can be safeguarded only by creative efforts commensurate with the dangers that threaten it.

And it goes on to prescribe the forms that these 'creative efforts' should take:

RESOLVED to substitute for age old rivalries the merging of their essential interests: to create, by establishing an economic community, the basis for a broader and deeper community among peoples long divided by bloody conflicts; and to lay the foundations for institutions which will give direction to a destiny henceforth shared.

The motivation underlying this approach was the conviction that the causes of war lay in economic rivalry and that by substituting economic co-operation for economic rivalry the causes of war would be removed. So the Community started life endowed with a determination to achieve economic union; indeed many people argue political union as well.

Progress, stagnation and renaissance

In the early years rapid progress was made. But in the 1970s that progress slowed down and virtually came to a halt. The reasons for this were manifold—the nationalistic attitude of General de Gaulle, the enlargement of the Community to include new member states, some of whom did not share the visions and objectives of the founding treaties: and perhaps most important of all the recession of the 1970s sparked off by the oil price increases. This was the era of 'Europaralysis', 'Eurosclerosis' and 'Euro-pessimism'. But gradually as we progressed into the 1980s and emerged from the recession the slumbering giant began to stir. There were calls for the 'Relaunching of the Community'; there was the signing of the Solemn Declaration on European Union at Stuttgart in June 1983; and building on this progress the meeting of the heads of government of the member states at Fontainebleau in June 1984. The Fontainebleau Summit solved—so it was thought—all the outstanding problems of the Community—restraining the cost of the CAP, the introduction of budget discipline, a progressive increase in 'own resources' and agreement on a formula for the British budget rebate. There is something depressingly familiar about this catalogue of problems and the high hopes of their solution. Within a few years the spectres were to return to haunt us. But for the moment, however briefly, all was reason and light. The way was clear to 'relaunch the Community'.

Relaunching the community: the birth of the programme for the completion of the internal market

It was in these circumstances and in this atmosphere that I accepted the invitation to go to Brussels and with the specific intention that I should take charge of the 'Internal Market'. I doubt whether anyone at the time realised its true potential and that the Programme for the Completion of the Internal Market was to become one of the turning points in the Community's history. But I was perfectly clear in my own mind that if I was to go to Brussels it should be to do a job which was really worthwhile. Not a negative job, such as controlling Budget expenditure, however important: but a constructive job which would contribute positively to the building of a more prosperous and more united Europe.

I had started work well before I went to Brussels. Nevertheless we succeeded in drawing up what was to be described as the programme for 'Completing the Internal Market' with what in retrospect seems, and indeed was, remarkable speed. The new Commission came into being on 6th January, 1985. The programme was presented to the heads of government in the form of a White Paper on 14th June of that year and was endorsed by them at Milan on 28th and 29th of the same month. The term 'White Paper' is of course entirely British—a clue for future historians to its origin. I doubt whether any such major reform has ever been launched and approved with such speed and it was a remarkable tribute to the Commission Services and to my colleagues who co-operated with me. But what really mattered was that we were on our way.

The concept of the 'Internal Market' goes back to the treaties themselves and in the early days much progress has been made. But, as I have already indicated, that progress came virtually to a halt in the 1970s. When Europe awoke from its slumber, work was resumed with the establishment of the Internal Market Council in 1982 and it met for the first time in January 1983. At that time I was the UK Secretary of State for Trade and responsible for the field of policy covered by the Internal Market Council. But the work was fragmentary and insufficiently focused. It seemed to me that two things were absolutely essential. First we needed a detailed programme, and more importantly that programme had to be a 'complete' programme—that is we should seek to remove *all* the barriers which divided Europe, not make a few improvements here and a few improvements there. Not a question of picking out 'priorities' but of doing the complete job. Second it was essential that the programme should be set in a time frame—without the discipline of a timetable there would be slippage and failure. That is the reason for '1992'. It has always surprised me that so little interest has been shown in why '1992' was chosen. The answer is this. A 'Commission' lasts for four years. Individual Commissioners can be reappointed: most are not. Each Commission is very much a separate entity and the lifetime of a Commission is both a useful measure and a useful planning period. A single Commission could not possibly complete a programme as ambitious as the Internal Market programme. But to take more than two Commissions would lead to successive Commissions 'passing the buck' from one to the other. So 'two Commissions' it had to be: and 'two Commissions' it was. Starting in 1985, the programme was scheduled to be completed by the end of 1992.

There was also precedent in support. The Treaty of Rome provided that the Customs Union—the foundation stone of the Community—should be established over three periods of four years. It was completed in ten years—ahead of time. What our precedessors had been able to do nearly thirty years ago we should I felt be able to do better today. So this time it should be two periods of four years, not three.

The White Paper setting out the Programme for the Completion of the Internal Market is important not just because it detailed some three hundred legislative measures which were needed but also because it was and remains one of the best expositions of Community policy, Community philosophy and Community aspirations. I would in this article quote only one passage and that from the *Conclusion*:

> Europe stands at the crossroads. We either go ahead—with resolution and determination—or we drop back into mediocrity. We can now either resolve to complete the integration of the economies of Europe; or, through a lack of political will to face the immense problems involved, we can simply allow Europe to develop into no more than a free trade area.
>
> The difference is crucial. A well developed free trade area offers significant advantages: it is something much better than that which existed before the Treaty of Rome; better even than that which exists today. But it would fail and fail dismally to release the energies of the people of Europe; it would fail to deploy Europe's immense economic resources to the maximum advantage; and it would fail to set aside the aspirations of the people of Europe.

It is nearly five years since I wrote those words: looking back now there is not a single word I would want to change.

At the time few people thought we would complete the programme, or complete it on time. But progress was such that before I left the Commission the heads of government were able to declare at Hanover in June 1988 that the programme was now 'irreversible'. Interestingly this was the target and in this precise phrase that I set my colleagues when I first launched the programme: namely that by the time we left Office the programme should have reached the stage where there would be no turning back. The concept was incorporated in specific terms in the Single European Act which requires the programme to be completed 'progressively over a period expiring on 31st December, 1992'. The future is no longer in my hands but I have no doubt that my successors will discharge the duty laid upon them by the Single Act.

The 1992 programme was of great importance in itself. But what was perhaps even more important was that it gave the Community new hope, a new sense of purpose and a new prospect of achievement. The Community had come alive again.

4

The Single European Act

The adoption of the 1992 programme was followed very rapidly by the negotiation of the Single European Act at Luxembourg in December 1985. The immediate motivation of the Single Act was to provide for the introduction of majority voting in the Council of Ministers on Internal Market matters. This was absolutely essential if the programme was to succeed and to succeed on time. It is interesting that our own government tried to block it but was outvoted—an important precedent for the future. Important also for another reason. What lay behind the United Kingdom government's opposition was a fear of loss of 'sovereignty'. But once it was clear that the Community would go ahead anyway, the government decided with as good grace as they could muster to fall into step. And when the United Kingdom assumed the Presidency of the Council in the latter half of 1986 they discovered a somewhat belated enthusiasm for the Single Market—or at least for those aspects of it with which they agreed.

While it was the Internal Market programme which provided the trigger for the Single Act, the opportunity was seized to cover a whole range of policies which had been agreed in the Solemn Declaration of Stuttgart, including not least economic and monetary union and social policy. This particular piece of history is very important in relation to the present stance of the United Kingdom government on these matters.

What at first sight might appear to be a very modest part of the Single Act, in fact is of great significance for the future. Not only did the Single Act deal with important issues of *economic* union: it also took the first formal legal step towards *political* union. 'Political co-operation in the field of foreign policy', as it is technically described, had grown up over the years on an informal basis. The Single Act provided a legal basis for this development and nominally a separate institutional framework. But the Ministers who are involved in 'political co-operation' are precisely the same foreign ministers who constitute the 'General Affairs Council' of the Community (which itself is commonly called the 'Foreign Affairs Council') and the 'Institutions' of political co-operation *de facto* but not *de jure* form part of the Commission's services.

It is very important indeed to make the point that this *de jure* separation of 'political co-operation' (i.e. foreign policy) from the rest of the Community did not primarily reflect an attempt to curb the growth of the Community or of Community competence, although there might have been an element of that present. The substance of the matter is that it followed precisely the pattern set when the Community was first established. The Community, as I have already said, is in law three Communities each with its own separate legal base in its own treaty. Equally 'political co-operation' has its own legal base in the Single Act. This precedent is very important when we come to future major developments in the Community, for example economic and monetary union. Thus

5

monetary union both in fact and in precedent requires a separate treaty or legal base. It follows that the only course open to our own government if it continues in its outright opposition is to stay outside. It cannot prevent the other members of the Community adopting a new treaty creating a monetary union. If the precedent of what happened over the Single European Act is anything to go by, it could well be that at the last moment, outvoted and facing the reality of isolation and self exclusion, our own government will back down. We have a long and sad history of too little, too late, but not quite.

An assessment of the importance of the 1992 programme

There are two specific features of the 1992 programme which are sufficiently important to deserve particular mention. The two are in fact linked.

The new approach to standards

The first is the 'new approach to standards'. Technically 'standards'—that is the standards mainly applying to manufactured goods—are voluntary but much legislation on health and safety, consumer protection and the environment is based on compliance with standards. Standards therefore are critically important to the free circulation of goods, member states frequently blocking the import or use of goods which do not comply with their own national standards. The original approach in the Community to this problem was one of harmonization, item by item. This was not only cumbersome and time-consuming but was impossibly slow. As part of the Internal Market programme we developed what was called 'the new approach to standards'. Based on the principles set out in the judgement of the Court of Justice in the Cassis de Dijon case, the new approach limited legislation at the Community level to specifying the 'essential requirements' only. Writing the detailed standards was left to the national standards-making bodies; and provided these standards complied with the 'essential requirements' there would be a legal right of free circulation throughout the Community. In the first of the new style directives, that dealing with pressure vessels, the legislation extended to five pages only. Under the old approach some ten directives each of about fifty pages would have been needed. It was a massive reduction in bureaucracy and red tape and an enormous delegation of power to the member states. So many of the criticisms made of the Community—and of the Commission—in this particular field are based on a situation which has long since ceased to exist.

Services

The second specific feature of the 1992 programme relates to the way services are dealt with. The treaty deals specifically with the freedom of movement of services as well as of goods. Nevertheless the position at the time that I joined the Commission was that much more progress had been made on 'goods' than on 'services'. Partly the reason lay in the fact that the majority of member states tended to be much more restrictive in controlling or regulating services than they were in the case of goods and, as a result, agreement on common rules at the Community level was much more difficult. But also, it is very easy to see a lorry stopped at the frontier but not a banking service. The first and the cost it involved was obvious, the second was not. It was to meet this problem that the Internal Market programme was structured in the way that it was. Not in the conventional way of looking separately at the freedom of movement of goods, of persons, of services and of capital; but by looking at the barriers to the freedom of movement, whether those barriers affected, in particular, goods or services. What emerged from this was that the barriers to the freedom of movement of services were essentially the same in kind as the barriers to the freedom of movement of goods: in the case of goods differences in standards or specifications, in the case of services differences in regulatory and prudential requirements. And if the analysis was the same, so too should be the solution. Just as with goods 'the new approach to standards' envisaged Community legislation restricted to essential requirements; and provided national standards met those essential requirements there would be a legal right to freedom of circulation. In the case of banking services, for example, the 'essential requirements' (e.g. on capital and solvency ratios) should be laid down at Community level and, provided the national rules complied with those 'essential requirements', there should be freedom of circulation throughout the Community. The approach has proved remarkably successful and the establishment of a single European banking market is one of the great achievements of the Internal Market programme; incidentally immensely to our benefit in this country.

Other policies

The Internal Market programme—'1992'—does not stand on its own. It was made clear in the White Paper that competition policy, transport, science and technology, regional and social policy, the environment and consumer protection were all closely related policies which needed to be developed in parallel with the Internal Market programme if the full benefits of that programme were to be achieved; and if the programme itself was not simply to be accepted, but be supported by all member states and all sections of the community—not least by workers as well as management. But one thing I would not accept, and I was supported by the

Commission as a whole, was that progress on the Internal Market should be linked to progress on other policies, particularly regional and social policy. Linkage would simply be a recipe for delay and manoeuvre. If the Internal Market programme were allowed to go ahead unfettered it would in fact provide both the catalyst and the stimulus for progress elsewhere. And so it has proved. There is a very valuable lesson here for other areas of policy in the Community. Policies should support one another; success should stimulate progress elsewhere; but slowing down progress in one area to allow others to catch up is sacrificing tangible benefits in one area for mere expectation elsewhere.

Future policies

Not only is the Internal Market programme the key to Europe's prosperity and the foundation on which the other policies of the Community are built, it is also the road that leads the way to the future development of the Community—a road clearly signposted in the Solemn Declaration and in the Single European Act—namely European union. After the Single Market will come the single currency; and after the single currency will come the single economy; and after the single economy will come the European union.

In his speech at Zurich in which he said 'we must build a kind of United States of Europe', Churchill said:

> We know where we want to go but we cannot foresee all the stages of the journey.

We do indeed know where we want to go and we have committed ourselves to it. We cannot see all the stages of that journey, but the first stage of the journey—the Single Market—is now nearing completion. It is not too soon to start taking the first steps in the next stage of the journey— namely monetary union. And when that stage reaches the point where progress is 'irreversible', we should be planning the next stage, namely economic union. That is the way progress is made: that is the way we will achieve our ultimate goal. To proceed in this way is a true blend of vision and pragmatism—knowing clearly where we want to go and proceeding there in a deliberate and progressive fashion. Taking one step at a time but knowing where each step takes us. Learning by experience as we go along, refining and modifying our plans as we go but never losing sight of our objective or allowing our determination to weaken. That we can succeed in this way is the real significance of '1992' and the Internal Market programme.

LESS OR MORE THAN EUROPE? EUROPEAN INTEGRATION IN RETROSPECT

FRANÇOIS DUCHÊNE*

THE European Community was born in 1950 of political motives. In the forty years of sometimes painful grind since then it has gradually acquired political weight, at home and abroad. Yet all the efforts in the specifically political areas of union which have punctuated its history have produced failure or marginal results. This is the central paradox in the history of the European Community so far. And as with all paradox it must mean that the conventional terms in which the question is, and historically has been, posed somehow, somewhere, no longer apply. To unravel the paradox means opening a window on a changing world.

Jacques Van Helmont, in *Options Européennes*,[1] has stressed that the necessary and sufficient cause of European integration moves has been concordance between the United States, France and Germany. This alone has made 'Europe' more, and possibly less, than European.

At first, after the war, the United States banked on an international system based politically on understanding with the Soviet Union and materially on a dollar standard replacing sterling and the *pax britannica* as the foundation of an open world economy. This vision broke down in less than two years. Growing competition with the Soviet Union focused on Germany was an obvious reason. But another, less conspicuous, was that early assumptions about the effort the United States would have to make to encourage recovery in Europe proved, in the biting winter of 1946–47, far too optimistic. The possibility of a material and political collapse of western Europe, with Stalin as residuary legatee, hove all at once into sight. The result was that well before the Korean war the United States began to see both the economic recovery of Germany and its military contribution to western defence as vital to the European, and by extension world, balance. However, once the US moved in that direction, it had to reckon not only with the opposition of the Soviet Union, discounted as

---

* François Duchêne was press attaché to the European Coal and Steel Community, 1952–55; director of Jean Monnet's Documentation Centre of the Action Committee for a United States of Europe, 1958–63; director of the Institute of Strategic Studies, 1969–74; Director of the European Research Centre, University of Sussex, 1974–82.

[1] Van Helmont, Jacques, *Options Européennes 1945–1985*, Commission des Communautés Européennes, Brussels-Luxembourg, 1986.

beyond the pale, but with that of an ally which also saw itself as a prime victim of German aggression: France. This was delicate, for France was, for geographic reasons if no other, the base of any western continental system. How to satisfy Germany without dissatisfying France became the major American dilemma.

The issue for France was the obverse of the American. Taking the total defeat of Germany in 1945 as their first opportunity to shape central Europe since the lost battle of Leipzig of 1813, the French started the post-war years by trying to revive a fragmented Germany of 'regions'. When that proved a pipe-dream, they tried to extract the Ruhr from the rest of Germany and get it neutralised, restrained or otherwise controlled, ultimately by the Americans. To improve France's relative position in coal and steel against the Ruhr, they also annexed the Saar 'economically'. All this was a Gaullist rerun of the Poincaré policy of the 1920s. It had two basic flaws. It depended on German weakness, but Germany, even truncated, was potentially stronger than France. And it fuelled the reciprocating engine of hostility between French and Germans. It has been said that America forced the German problem on France and so was the hidden hand behind the European Community. Sooner or later the French would have had to face the problem of Germany's superior potential anyway.

The Schuman plan of 1950 broke out of the impasse not so much by reaching a deal between France and Germany as by pointing beyond them both to the common goal and larger context of a united Europe. The aspiration to unity in Europe had other roots than the Franco–German quarrel. It was a natural expression of war-weariness. It was also an obvious response for citizens of *ci-devant* great powers to the sight of power slipping into other hands. This ensured a wide and fervent degree of support for the Schuman plan on the continent. Yet all this should not conceal the fact that when France proposed the plan expectations of European union were winding down. Not having been harnessed to a practical policy, they were running out of fuel.

The Schuman plan succeeded in making a policy of necessity because it accepted the political logic of the option it opened up. It was not a new idea. It had been proposed in many quarters on both sides of the Atlantic. But it had always been censored by a series of unstated objections. What these were can be seen from the choices the Schuman plan had to make in order to take shape. One was to slip the leading strings of links with Britain. Because of her world-wide ambitions and post-war distrust and disdain of the continental Europeans, there was no chance Britain would agree to unite with them. Nor, however, would she like them to do so without her. Therefore, a French policy based on the *entente cordiale* as insurance against Germany precluded European integration. Britain had to be disconnected. Even more breath-taking, it had to be replaced by Germany. This was an enormity six years after Nazi occupation. Acceptance of it was explicable only in terms of total weariness with the waste since 1914. More, it meant accepting equality with the Germans. Equality was the basis of trust in a new relationship. It was, of course, this promise of escape from ostracism that made the Germans the most enthusiastic 'Europeans' at the time. But equality was fragile without a common task. There had been much talk of customs unions since Marshall aid began. The proposals had all come to nothing because they fell foul of French protectionism in particular. The Schuman plan narrowed the field to coal and steel. To pick out a couple of basic sectors like this was, in economic theory, absurd. But, politically, it conjured up visions of Europeanising, and so taking out of the sphere of national competition, the industries most associated with the waging of war. The last novelty, which capped the rest, was to accept that if anything had to be pooled there must be effective decision-making mechanisms and no national vetoes. Emotionally, the European Coal and Steel Community (ECSC) which emerged from the Schuman plan in 1952 was the first step to a European union. Mechanically, it provided the minimum rules of 'supra-national' action which made it possible to mark off the Community from a conference of nation states. The Schuman plan created the political model on which all subsequent Community European development has been based.

The plan displays from the start some of the cardinal themes of the story since. One of the most striking has been American support for European integration which has suffered eclipses but never quite denial. The contrast between the old code of dominant states, *divide ut impera*, and the American zeal, at times far greater than that of the locals, for union in Europe is itself a sign of a partial but fateful shift in post-war outlooks. The anomaly of American behaviour, in classical terms, has usually been glossed over on the grounds of America's interest in balancing Soviet power in Europe, which is true as far as it goes. But it does not account for the enthusiasm of the endorsement of union. Here again it is too simple to ascribe this to infatuation with America's own myth of genesis, or to America's then being so powerful it could not conceive of European competition. In fact, its leaders could and did envisage just that. They nevertheless endorsed 'Europe' because they considered that societies which became wealthy and democratic would have more in common than in competition; and probably also that a collective system was too unwieldy to deviate much from moderation. As this suggests, American policy was based to a considerable extent on a sense of identity with Europe. Latin America has clearly not basked in the same benevolence. This reinforces the sense that policy to western Europe expressed a new conception of interest, in which confidence in the force of compatible and communicating social and economic processes carries more weight than traditional statecraft.

Another aspect of the European Community from the start was, as with all major political movements, many-sided ambiguity. From the American and French points of view, it was, and is, a policy to anchor the Federal

Republic and prevent Germany from playing power games between East and West. Both countries, in the search for a stable Europe, have been pursuing what is at once a Soviet and a German policy. At several crucial junctures there has been a *de facto* alliance between America and France in the pursuit of European integration. From the French point of view, it was, and is, a policy for limiting the costs of weakness relative to Germany. European Community entangles the bilateral relationship in a multilateral net, meshed together by common rules of law and decision-making. From Germany's point of view, Community has provided her with respectability and friends, as well as with political reassurance in case relations with the United States fell short. As German cold war chancellors argued, 'we need America more than America needs us'. It has also allowed her to reassert economic preponderance without arousing hostility. Finally, from the point of view of all the Europeans, it has offered hope of self-affirmation *vis-à-vis* the superpowers. Policy, like water, tends to seep into all the vacant spaces, and the European one has tended at different times to stress one or other of all these possibilities.

The Korean war broke out just as the conference on the Schuman treaty opened. This brought the hidden pressures for German rearmament into the open. The United States insisted on it and it was the case, even from the French point of view, that if all the other Europeans had to rearm, the Germans could not be left to pocket the supplier's profits without making a contribution too. Yet German national rearmament was too much for the French five years after the war. The European Defence Community, first proposed in public by the French prime minister René Pleven on 24 October 1950, and received at first with no enthusiasm by the United States, who saw it as a delaying tactic, was a military adaptation of the Schuman approach to an otherwise insoluble dilemma. Its very authors had serious initial doubts about the European Army. But it also opened up new options. Nothing affected national sovereignty more closely than defence. An army had to have a political as well as military command. So the Six founding states decided to set up a European Political Community to provide a political roof and a European President for the European army. The Dutch threw in an article calling for a Common Market. For a while it seemed as if European integration might lead towards a skeleton federation in the classic image; not that this image has much warrant in history.

The vision came crashing down with the French Assembly's refusal to ratify the European Army treaty on 30 August 1954. From that moment on, political federation, as such, has never been on the Community agenda. In fact, the federal element in all European integration plans was cut to the bone. In the circumstances, the question arises why integration revived enough to set up the European Economic Community (EEC). At the time many thought it would not. There seem to have been two converging reasons why it did. The first was that just as the rejection of the EDC did not remove the issue of German rearmament from the agenda,

12

diverting it back into Nato as the Americans had originally envisaged, so the setback to European integration did not eliminate the post-war search for freer trade in western Europe speeded by rapid economic growth. This was the eve of Europe's 'economic miracles', the springtime of mass consumption. In Germany and the Benelux countries, even in Italy, options for a next step forward in cooperation, including a free trade area, were considered. If they were not serious competitors for a common market conceived as a new Community this was because of the desire to buttress Franco–German reconciliation and keep hopes of unity alive as a condition of political stability. It was appreciated that even in France economic integration did not arouse the contrary passions unleashed by the European army. French protectionism, strong in Parliament and even stronger in the civil service, barred the way to a Common Market at first. The French initially seemed to prefer Euratom, which proposed Community action in a field where they were ahead of the Germans and so need not suffer the inferiority complex that hampered them in other fields. But the Dutch proposed, the Belgians and the Italians supported, and the Germans insisted on, a Common Market as the condition of any European *relance*. In France, a minority of key individuals (including, as it later turned out, de Gaulle) thought it necessary to the country's own prospects of lasting revival. In contrast, French nuclear ambitions, stirred up by that state-within-the-state, the Commissariat à l'Énergie Atomique, thoroughly undermined Euratom. In the end the French, instead of setting the agenda, as in the Schuman plan and EDC, accepted that of Germany and Benelux.

In short, the nation states were already far more self-assertive than five years earlier. The ECSC's 'executive' had been called the High Authority. That of the EEC was only the Commission. The new modesty symbolized the shift in the balance toward the governments. Yet the system had to work. The French and Italians built a series of economic safeguards into the common market which had to be operated by the Community institutions and so, as it happened, reinforced them. The Commission retained unique responsibility for initiating proposals, and, when it did so, majority procedures often removed the individual state's right of veto in the Council of Ministers. This has ever since marked the minimum demanded by all those who want an effective Community.

Nevertheless, the limits of this right became evident in the nineteen-sixties. The return to traditional inter-state norms is associated with de Gaulle. He was responsible for the crisis in the Community in 1965–66 which led to the *de facto* reintroduction of the national veto as the norm in decision-making. Yet some of this was implicit in the treaty of Rome itself. It demonstrated a constant principle of the Communities. Majority voting has been confined to ensuring that the basic agreements reached between the member states are carried through. It has never amounted to a federal licence for the Community institutions, through autonomous legislative powers, to extend their own areas of competence. For example, the voting rules of the EEC were clear and constraining as regards the introduction specifically of the customs union. They were not constraining at all in areas which the Rome treaties proclaimed to be part of the Common Market but on which the member states had not committed themselves in negotiation. The Common Market treaty provided for common policies on agriculture, transport, money, taxes, subsidies, approximation of laws, social affairs, and so on, but envisaged no majority voting to set them up. Some duly proved a dead letter, others were implemented in bits, and the agriculture common policy came in only after a series of showdowns in which de Gaulle annually uttered awesome threats.

When the newly established EEC began to open up the common market early in 1959, the impact was tremendous. This was partly because businessmen, now they were convinced the new system was here to stay, made a self-fulfilling prophecy of the customs union. The tide of trade ran so strongly in that dawn when it was bliss for 'good Europeans' to be alive, that the more romantic (like Paul-Henri Spaak, one of the major begetters of the Rome treaties) thought an economic union would rapidly follow and itself provide the springboard for political union soon after. This belief was widespread.

It was not de Gaulle alone who put the brake upon such expectations. It was the discovery that, in the medium term at least, the customs union simply did not compel the expected economic union, meaning common European policies. Agriculture's Europeanisation promised more, but more did not follow. In the central industrial sphere, few policies, and no real Euro-corporations, emerged. It was American multinationals, not European ones, who showed zeal to treat the customs union not merely as an exporting opportunity but as a unified production base. The state-aided or supervised sectors, and those which depend on public procurement, including most branches from energy and transport to the 'advanced technologies', remained focused on the state. Far from producing economic union, the first stage of the common market was the halcyon period of what Raymond Vernon dubbed 'national champions', the large firms in each country actively subsidised by the state to conquer world markets. This became even more overt in the recession of the 'seventies than in the long boom of the 'sixties, but in essence the outlook, on this cardinal point, remained constant for the first two decades of the customs union.

What de Gaulle did add was an ideological excuse for such developments. Yet even here he was not alone. The determination of the French to become a nuclear power, consummated under the Mollet and Gaillard governments from 1956 to 1958, meant violating the principle of equality on which the Community was founded; demanding privileged status for France; and changing the rules she herself had earlier defined. De Gaulle made a virtue of all this. But it both antedated and survived him. It has been a recurring feature of French policy within the Community. The Community was created to safeguard the French from a more-than-equal

Germany. But recurrently they have tried to exploit their position as its initiators to claim more-than-equal status themselves. The risks of playing games with Germany should have been evident all along. Nonetheless, France, inside the Community, has been subject to temptations parallel to those of Britain outside. Naturally, this did not leave France's partners unaffected. Bureaucracies were glad enough to regain vetoes while protesting righteously at de Gaulle's violations of European virtue. He certainly mobilised the reaction to integration, and this was important. But the resistance of national states, systems and societies was wider and deeper than any accident of personal policy or charisma.

Despite all this, the effect of the customs union was massive enough to turn Europe from Utopia into some kind of reality, however imperfect. The idea of European union did not die. There were a series of *relances* and reforms. The first came when de Gaulle left the scene in 1969. With his long shadow lifted, three proposals were launched: economic and monetary union (EMU) by 1980, diplomatic cooperation between the member states baptised 'political' cooperation, and British entry into the Community. Four years later, in 1974, the French president, Valéry Giscard d'Estaing, advised by his new foreign minister, Jean Sauvagnargues, proposed the revival of majority voting under the terms of the original Rome treaty, along with a European Council of the heads of state or government, the transfer of direct taxing powers (already vested in the High Authority of the Coal and Steel Community twenty years before) to the European Community, and the election by universal suffrage of a European Parliament which would be accorded greater powers to supervise the Community budget. Four years later still, faced with the evident failure of EMU to materialise, Helmut Schmidt as chancellor of the Federal Republic and Giscard as French president launched the European Monetary System (EMS) to ensure exchange rate stability between members of the Community at a time of wild variations in the parities of the Deutschmark and dollar. Together, all these reforms did produce changes, but not in the depth for which some at least were designed. The attempt of Sauvagnargues to reinforce majority voting, though rooted in the very terms of the Rome treaty, was blocked at once by the newly recruited British on the strength of the misnamed Luxembourg 'compromise' imposed by de Gaulle on his partners in 1966. When Sauvagnargues left office in 1976, Giscard made no attempt to salvage the reform. The governments were happy to live with an intergovernmental system so long as their own purposes were still vested in pushing their 'national champions' on world markets. Matters were made worse by the nationalist responses to the energy crisis of 1973–74 and by the high inflation it aggravated. As usual, when great social and economic strains pull imperfectly cemented systems apart, there was a tendency to fall back on established loyalties and pyramids of authority, which were overwhelmingly national and, in bad economic times, bred protectionism.

15

Such weaknesses were magnified by the magnetic attractions of the Community on European countries looking in on the club from outside. The very fact that it was built on a special relationship between France and the German Federal Republic, which reversed the conventional wisdom of decades, shifted the balance in Europe and beyond. This was evident from the first when Italy and the Benelux trio could not stay outside a Franco-German arrangement. But the turning point was the establishment of the EEC. The British knew this meant the appearance of a grouping in Europe to which the United States would pay more attention than to them. They did all they could to prevent its emergence. When they failed, amid much ill-temper, in the late 1950s, there was little left but to join what they could not beat. Harold Macmillan duly applied in 1961.

At this point, one of the major strategic divisions in the concept of European integration came for the first time fully to the surface. Before de Gaulle came to power in Paris, the school which dominated the European policy had moved along a trajectory which led straight to the idea of Atlantic 'partnership' between the United States of America and the uniting states of Europe propounded in John F. Kennedy's famous address of Independence Day, 1962. It was not really a school of European integration, or not only such a school, because the shadow cast by such thinking went well beyond the continent and was represented by small but dominant minorities on both sides of the Atlantic. On the American side, the idea had been propounded a dozen years before by the under-secretary of State, James Webb, in guidelines addressed on 24 September 1949 to David Bruce, the chief of the Marshall aid mission to France, and was not new even then.

> The world today requires the development of new and probably radical methods dealing with economic and political problems which respect no national frontiers ... The ultimate objective is the provision of machinery for dealing effectively with such problems on a world-wide basis. In the near future, progress depends upon developing means for dealing with specific problems among a small number of nations most directly concerned and gradually building outwards from such nuclei.[2]

This view was enunciated in terms still broader than those of the Kennedy oration in a statement issued by the Action Committee for the United States, led by Jean Monnet, on 26 June 1962; that is four months before the Cuban missile crisis propelled Kennedy into *détente* with the Soviet Union.

> The Action Committee considers [proclaimed the statement] that the economic and political unity of Europe including Britain and leading to a partnership of equals between Europe and the United States alone will make it possible to

---

[2] *Foreign Relations of the United States 1949*, US—GPO, Washington D.C., Vol III, p. 666.

consolidate the West and to create the conditions . . . for a lasting peaceful settlement between East and West.[3]

In this view, British entry into the Community was the pivot between integration seen in purely European terms and the creation of a new context for dealing with the problems of the world and for reintroducing Europe into the circle of great powers. Significantly, the Action Committee's statement gave attention not only to East–West affairs, but to the formulation of Western macro-economic and Third World policies as well.

At the time, this was crystal-gazing into a crystal innocent of de Gaulle. His interdict on British entry into the Community in 1963 was the starting point of an alternative policy where he sought to establish an autonomous position between East and West and open up possibilities either of a Franco-German tandem under his direction (so long as it put no constraints on his freedom of action) or of a Franco-Russian tandem to control Germany with or without the United States. This policy was doomed from the start. De Gaulle might just have been able to assert leadership of the Community had he been prepared to play by its rules. But he was far too concerned with his own room for manoeuvre to do that. For the rest, unlike the Bismarcks of this world, he proposed policies unrelated to his power. His strategy could only exist because there was no danger of France's own security being undermined, since she was covered by the US–German alliance. But this same alliance made it impossible for him to break loose from the system or to drag Germany from her moorings. His revolt against Atlantic orthodoxy slowly ground to a halt. It is arguable that he left office because of the frustration of his foreign policy.

However, frustration worked both ways. When Britain joined in 1973, the Community had in many ways lost its impetus. In such a context, constant expansion of membership was akin to running to seed. Country after country in Europe was anxious, like Britain, not to be excluded from the table where decisions vital to itself might be taken. Decision-making, none too easy between six member states, became ever more difficult with nine, then ten and later twelve, and no halt in sight. Decisions in the Council of Ministers became ever more tortuous to fit growing numbers of special interests. The prestige of the Commission as the supposed purveyor of policy initiatives suffered. Belief in the political potential of the Community waned. It was an ingredient in the 'Europessimism' that became the fashion, for wider reasons, after the second energy crisis of 1979–1980.

Once again, the question is where the Community found the resources to stage a revival in the second half of the 'eighties. A number of strands

[3] *Comité d'Action pour les Etats Unis d'Europe, 1955–1965*, (collection of Action Committee declarations and resolutions), Fondation Jean Monnet pour l'Europe, Lausanne, 1965, pp. 113 & 117.

are clear, even if their relative importance is less self-evident. One of them, salient in the lean years, was the sheer weight of interests vested in the Community. On average, the member states carried on half of their world trade with one another. Despite the gaping holes in common policy-making, and its obvious weaknesses even where it applied, as in agriculture, it would have been painful to unwind. The weight of mutual commitments even meant that there were limits to the exercise of the national veto. As David Owen explained to a Committee of the House of Lords when he was foreign secretary, every member state was so beholden to the others for favours in the system, that it could not possibly block all compromise. The resulting 'package deals' in which all the goodies were bartered, were clumsy and unsatisfactory, but not unworkable. Politically, too, as the joint initiatives that came from the French and Germans demonstrated, they had too much invested in their special relationship to be willing to erode what they had achieved together.

It is often claimed, in the Community's rhetoric of alarm, that what cannot move forward must sooner or later fall back. Yet the corollary—that what cannot fall back presumably at some point has good chances of moving forward—has in practice been more in evidence. For, as new problems arise, and as long as the Community offers 'European options', in Van Helmont's phrase, when national ones fail, they provide an opportunity. Such options came together, for a number of reasons, in the middle 'eighties.

One was that Germany became less willing to be the unquestioning lieutenant of the United States after the success of Brandt's *Ostpolitik* in 1972. This, and the advent of Gorbachev in 1983, brought out a phenomenon which at first favoured European integration. So long as Europe remained divided, improved German prospects in eastern Europe had a remarkable effect on the policies both of the Federal Republic and of France. The Germans, faced with the hope of greater freedom of manoeuvre, but aware of the anxieties this creates, have tended to give assurances of Western loyalty by support for progress within the European Community. Nato is not so appropriate. It is military in a time of rising pacifism. It already provides what Germany wants from the United States, security, and can hardly offer more. The Community is more open-ended and Germany is in Europe. The effect on France has been the mirror-image of this. Faced with the prospect of the Germans recovering power and elbow room, the French suddenly rediscover the vital importance of European integration. The games with national 'independence' suddenly lose their attractions and are replaced, as in Mitterrand's presidencies, by intense preoccupation with 'Europe'. Alliance with Britain is a theoretical alternative. It was no accident Pompidou let Britain into the Community during Brandt's *Ostpolitik*. But Britain, too, obviously has an off-shore mentality; is too liable to put America first, to offer a solid link. That leaves the Community. The French consensus on reinforcing Europe today is as closely linked to Gorbachev and the East

German revolution as the European *relance* of 1969 was to the *Ostpolitik*.

Luckily, from the Community point of view, this has coincided with a major change in the economic climate. The failure of the policies of national champions to provide reassurance against the Japanese have convinced both the major European industrialists and governments that if they persist in national mercantilism they will be demoted far down the ladder of world competition. Policy-makers have been driven to try to turn the EEC into that effective 'single market' which failed to materialise in the 1960s. As the Commission's programme of almost 300 regulations to take effect by 1993 suggests, this means not just free trade but a common regulatory context. At the same time, the fight against inflation has driven the states to quasi-German policies of monetary rigour. The turning-point was Mitterrand's decision of 1983, after a brief Heathite dash for growth, to shadow the Deutschmark. Since then, the continental European Community has been almost a macro-economic unit under the leadership of the Bundesbank. Two further factors have also played a part. The first is that if the Community has always been a tangled skein of diverse influences, these have one of the features of a ball of wool—they form a surface to which new objects are apt to stick. Thus, the growth in the salience of environmental issues and of regional ones as a result of extension to the poorer South, neither of which can easily be dealt with nationally and both of which have strong lobbies, has created a new set of activities in which the Community has a relatively open field and limited competition.

Second, in the new mood of urgency, the very danger of enlargement, that it weakens the ability to make decisions, has also had the effect of reinforcing rules for taking them. The direct cause of the Single Act of 1985 was the fears that unless majority voting were really introduced into the Community in order to introduce the single market before 1993, a Council of Ministers of twelve countries would never be able to take the necessary decisions. To this extent, the entry of Spain and Portugal has been a catalyst. Again, it has to be noted that the voting only applies to the measures to set up the agreed Single Market. But this is so wide that the Commission president, Jacques Delors, has announced that eighty per cent of economic law-making in the Community states would have to some degree to pass through the European institutional process. This represents a quite new level of political shaping power.

This brings one back to the paradox noted at the outset. The European Community could not be what it has become without its political aura. This has been vital to its sense of identity and purpose. Yet its achievements have been overwhelmingly economic. The inability to encompass political union has apparently been the great failure of the integration movement. In reality, it may have been its saving strength. To take an example: the stubbornness of Franco-German differences over defence policy and the lack of real willingness on either side to achieve common

19

ground in this quintessentially 'political' domain, has usually been ascribed to the contrasts, especially since de Gaulle, between the two countries' attitudes to the United States. On this view, the American protectorate over western Europe has been the ultimate obstacle to European political union. Yet it is doubtful whether the prospects of political unity would have been a whit easier without the United States. The history of attempts at political federation is almost uniformly dismal, from ancient Greece to the German Bund. The United Provinces and Switzerland seem more convincing. But the Netherlands were long held together mainly by the domination of Holland. Switzerland had five wars between the 'confederate' cantons in as many centuries. Unity really came only after Napoleon had swept through them, and even then had to await a further flurry of civil war in 1848. It is hard to cite a single example of rapid, spontaneous federation between long settled peoples, still less between former great powers without a common language.

Why, then, has the European Community been able to climb up the back stairs to a kind of political identity? A possibly temporary convergence of need in America, France and West Germany on the German question has been a necessary factor, but certainly not a sufficient one. The major reason has probably been the decline of military influences and the corresponding rise of economic ones in international affairs. In a system where the use of force is constrained by nuclear deterrence, even its indirect employment to exert political advantage is demoted. Gorbachev renounces conventional war because of the risks of damage to lethal, though civilian, installations such as nuclear power reactors. Soviet conventional military superiority in Europe is *ipso facto* devalued. The British and French stick like leeches to their nuclear deterrents. Can anyone seriously claim these have delivered political dividends to compare with those of the Yen or the DM? In such conditions, are the military assets of the superpowers really more decisive than the civilian successes of Germany and Japan? The more deterrence works, the more it shifts power, meaning the ability to act, to civilian factors of which economics is not the only one, but the most integrated into government, persistent, flexible and pervading. As a result, the development of the Community as a huge and relatively coherent economic entity, despite obvious weaknesses and incompletion, has already begun to deliver some of the political magnetism associated with 'great' powers. Had it not been forced to work through the dispersed and subdivided economic medium, European union might never have been the catchment area it has proved.

The European Community, then, in its own way reflects the same upgrading of the power of civilian forces in parts of the world ruled by nuclear deterrence as Germany and Japan have done. On the other hand, the Community obviously lacks the cohesion of a Germany or Japan. However fast its competences are spreading, however elaborate the single market may prove after 1992, the Community will fall short of union in many respects so long as it remains without a central banking system, and boasts only sherds of common fiscal, social, law and order, defence or foreign policies. It has been showing signs of inching forward in some of these resistant core areas. But if reunification captures the essence of German attention and new candidate members that of the Community, its recent political magnetism may prove short-lived. It can remain an economic reality in the Thatcher mould. Before 1914, a number of German economists, like Gustav von Schmoller, argued for a European customs union.[4] With the old north German *Zollverein* in mind, they hardly thought that would cramp the Wilhelminian style. Social forces are more democratic today; economic government is more pervasive; and the pressures on Europe from the world will continue. All the same, when a system's strongest component reduces the investment in it, its future as a political focus is hardly assured.

In short, the earthquake in eastern Europe is probably the moment of truth for the Community. Everything depends on how the transition to a new system is secured. At this point, the Community issue becomes subsumed, as in fact it always has been, in the fate of the international order around it.

The Soviet Union has now restated its old theme: a reunified Germany must be demilitarized. In any case, a reunified Germany must transform, if not end, the alliances. Presumably, the future lies with arms control agreements and economic cooperation in a spreading European Community and between 'East' and 'West'. Even so, if no other measures are taken, a political wedge would be driven between a concentrated Germany and the rest of a diluted Community. The US would find it hard to keep a toe-hold in Europe, which may well be the reason for Washington's sudden rediscovery of political 'partnership' with the Community. Central and eastern Europe would be dominated by the Soviet–German dialogue. If the weather there turned variable, it could easily veer to direct competition between a dynamic, civilian Germany tempted to recall the frontiers of 1937 and a defensive Soviet Union, with deep nationality problems, that remains the regional military power. If all that is implied in Gorbachev's idea of a common European home, it could prove as fragile to future trouble as the old 'concert of Europe' which some still appear, very oddly, to regard as a model.

One must hope that is a worst case. Nonetheless, it is not enough to cheer the extension of democratic values to eastern Europe if one connives at throwing away the elements of international contract, or government, which have just begun to form a framework. East–West agreements are not an extension of cold war but a beginning of international contract, particularly if they spawn common agencies, and must be pursued as such. If all the recently freed societies of eastern Europe cast eyes upon the Community, that is because it has already created a rule of

---

[4] Fischer, F., *Krieg der Illusionen*, Droste, Düsseldorf, 1969. I am grateful to Anthony Hartley for pointing this out.

law where every member's vote is heard. To ignore the needs of either, whatever the rhetoric, is to deny a new stage in international regulation. A deepened, as well as gradually broadened, Community, including a re-unified Germany, could generate security; it would be far too collective to pose the threats of a centralized state, to Moscow or to anyone else. True, it might attract dissident Soviet nationalities. But those problems will be posed anyway; and the many-headed character of the Community would be a guarantee against abuse of opportunities. In fact, one of its functions would be to close the period of unruly nationalism unleashed by the French Revolution. It would be a leading substructure of a system of which the US and USSR would be others. It would constitute a major unit of the codified, contractual third of the world. German reunification and the emancipation of eastern Europe require that the Community be strengthened for the general good.

ELEMENTS OF A EUROPEAN COMMUNITY OF THE FUTURE: A TRADE UNION VIEW

OTTO JACOBI*

HISTORICAL experience and theoretical insight has taught and made it a basic component of trade union knowledge that the joining together of workers into trade unions was the decisive step away from the isolated impotence of the individual to the organized and powerful politics of the many. The union is more than the sum total of its members; the association of workers puts combined resources in their hands and rewards them with the fruits of solidarity and common action. And so it is with Europe. For a long time it was divided, splintered and contentious. It tore itself to pieces in nationalist and imperialist rivalries; it reduced itself to ruins in the two world wars of the twentieth century. With colonialism and its contemptuous fall into fascist barbarism, Europe has shown the miserable face of its Janus-head. And with Stalinism, it pulverized one of its great ideas and utopias, that of socialism.

Europe nearly killed itself. Almost a half century ago it suffered its 'zero year'—as the French social scientist Edgar Morin[1] has expressed it. Can Europe, like the phoenix, lift itself out of the ashes and establish a new life? Can the last four to five decades of relatively peaceful (in any case, non-warring) development be the harbinger of a new era in European history, whose basic law is the cooperation between all parts of Europe to the mutual benefit of all its peoples, rather than destructive rivalry? Can Europe come together in a community of the future which avoids the mistakes and errors of the past?

We can state the problem in reverse and ask whether Europe, in view of the challenges of the third industrial revolution, is equipped for the looming Copernican turning point. Unless we are being deceived by the signs all around us, we are living in a phase of epochal changes; we are witnesses to historical breakthroughs and global ruptures. As the leader of the German metal-workers has said: 'We are experiencing nothing less than the feverish hours of history. New existing dangers have sprung into

* Dr Otto Jacobi was at the Institut für Sozialforschung, and now works as a free-lance social scientist in Frankfurt am Main. His principal research topic is industrial relations in Europe. This paper is based on a lecture given at a Conference to commemorate the 40th anniversary of the Youth Organization of the West German Public Service Union (ÖTV) in Stuttgart, 24–26 November 1989.

[1] Morin, E., 1988, *Europa Denken*, Frankfurt/Main (*Penses l'Europe*, Gallimard, Paris 1987).

23

being, old values and institutions have lost all credibility.'[2] The developmental dynamic of modern society is being seized upon by all Europe and has, to some extent, brought forward volcanic upheavals pointing to the future. These have been accompanied, however, by historically retrograde counter-tendencies of a right-wing conservative and nationalistic sort. Nonetheless, this dynamic is dissolving the old certainties and social environments. It is leading to disenchantment with ideologies and putting into question all forms of governing which are illegitimate from the democratic point of view—whether it be in the plant or society, in political and social organizations or institutions of the state.

A new technical age, the harbingers of ecological collapse, socio-structural change and differentiation and a multiplicity of individual life styles and demands for self-realization have all combined in a violent collision with the traditional structures of West European capitalism and East European socialism. In this regard, the chairwoman of the German public-service union (ÖTV), M. Wulf-Mathies,[3] has written that the pluralization and individualization of life styles has led to a weakening of the binding force which holds together a collective identity, and that a common class position is not playing the same role in building solidarity as it once did. But this is not turning solidarity into a meaningless historical formality within the trade union movement. Indeed, the need for a social structure is even greater in an individualized society: 'Only through understanding and solidarity can greater freedom for all arise from differentiation and individualization.' When Wulf-Mathies points out that 'the need for understanding' has grown 'exponentially', then she has formulated a watchword for the future of the continent and the globe.

If we add the fact (as many observers say we should) that the decisive feature of the third industrial revolution is an 'exponential growth of global interdependence', then the task before all of us—with the trade unions in the lead—is clear: We must create the elements of a European community of the future which provides the foundation for political–economic unity and a democratic–social–cultural identity and which shifts the necessity for global cooperation to the centre of daily consciousness.

A first answer (albeit incomplete and unsatisfactory) is the 12-nation single European market. Nonetheless, it must be vigorously pointed out that the economic potency and the politically energizing effects of this partial European integration have the greatest significance for the future of the entire European continent. Any person who still believes that the EC 'Europe of Twelve' is preoccupied with its mountains of butter and meat and its lakes of wine and milk, exhausted by endless haggling over agricultural prices, straitjacketed by an inefficient bureaucracy, is

[2] Steinkühler, F., 1989(a), 'Zeiten des Umdenkens', address to Trade Union Conference in Berlin, 1989.
[3] Wulf-Mathies, M, 1989, 'Das heutige Fuhrungspersonal der bundesdeutschen Gewerkschaften und zukünftige Anforderungen am Beispiel ÖTV', address at Ruhr-Universität, Bochum, on 6 July 1989.

mistaken. The reorientation of a structurally conservative agricultural union into a future-oriented economic and technological community powered by a spirited leadership has been in full-swing for some time. Euro-sclerosis is a thing of the past because—however incompletely—two basic principles for a Europe of the future have been taken to heart: no single European country is in the position to carry out the structural change with national structures alone. According to Franz Steinkühler, Chairman of IG Metall,[4] 'For some time now it has not been possible to solve the central problems of our societies with a national yardstick'. And further: no single European country is capable of assuming a hegemonial position and unilaterally imposing its own interests. In this sense, the Christian Democratic Minister President of Baden-Württemburg, Lothar Späth, has said, 'Either everyone together will lead the struggle for survival in the next century, or each will lose it on his own'.[5]

To repeat this clearly: Only a united Europe can assemble the economic, scientific and technical resources needed to exploit the opportunities and guard against the risks involved in this epochal process of change. The single European market is a politically conscious, economically parochial reaction to this problem-laden situation and is betting on the synergistic effects of supranational cooperation of its member countries.

If the trade unions are to strive for a better Europe, then they must free themselves from the unjustified, numbing fear of a Europe allegedly dominated by capital—an excuse uttered by those too lazy to think and who often consider themselves to be especially progressive. The trade unions have to transform themselves into willing, cooperative organizations which collect, coordinate and bring to life their scattered resources and potential, instead of bemoaning their future destiny. If they are willing to use the shortcomings of the single market to their advantage, they will find a growing field of action open to them and heretofore unrecognized opportunities to shape conditions and events.

The imperfections of the 'Europe of Twelve' consist in the following: it comprehends only half of Europe; it is only an economic community; and it pursues interests characterized by a too narrow-minded Eurocentrism.

The Hungarian author György Konrád is right on the mark when he writes: 'A United States of West Europe is not possible. Only a United States of Europe is possible.'[6] What is lacking with a 'Europe of Twelve' is the neutral and East European half; what is lacking is political unity and cultural identity; what is lacking is the recognition of global responsibility.

In spite of this, the European Economic Community has established new standards. In addition, the neutral countries have effectively

[4] Steinkühler, F., 1989(b), 'Chancen humaner Zukunftsgestaltung gegen Kapitalmacht und Sozialdumping', in Steinkühler, F., (ed.), *Europa '92—Industriestandort oder sozialer Lebenstraum*, Hamburg, p. 19.

[5] Späth, L., 1989, *1992—Der Traum von Europa*, Stuttgart, p. 207.

[6] Konrád, G., 1988, *Antipolitik—Mitteleuropäische Meditationen*, Frankfurt, p. 15.

announced their claim to participate, and political developments in the eastern half of Europe have unleashed many expectations and hopes for ending state-bureaucratic straitjacketing. All parts of Europe must be able to freely grow together and, at the same time, remain open to world-encompassing cooperation.

It might be somewhat exaggerated, but the heart of a certain German sociologist's argument contains more than a grain of truth: 'World history has started in motion at a breathtaking tempo, and Europe is its engine.'[7] Only now is the question no longer to be avoided: What exactly holds this Europe together? Despite all the differences and diversity, a sufficient supply of common interests and identities obviously has to be gathered together in one common fund which can provide the scaffolding for cooperative collaboration. To this must be added an immediate second question: what contributions did the workers' movement make in the past and what contributions do the trade unions of today have to offer? Without a doubt, there is an irresistible movement towards supranational structures in Europe. But the political content and the direction of problem-solving are not set. So, it is even more important that the trade unions work out a European perspective and take part.

European diversity and identity

The French historian Braudel liked to point out that historical research is nothing but 'the interrogation of the past in the name of the problems and curiosity of the present'.[8] When one tries to understand what Europe is, one is struck by an overwhelming diversity. Europe enjoys a hetero-geneous cultural heritage nourished by competing ideas and antagonistic theories. Europe does not have, and has not had, a hegemonic centre. It has always been polycentrically divided into rival metropoles, each with its own specific political, economic and cultural attractiveness.

It is obviously of decisive significance for European common interests, characteristics and identities that—as Edgar Morin especially emphasizes—'trans-European waves' in a 'Maelstrom of reciprocal actions' or a 'permanently boiling dialogue' have allowed for a unique, uninterrupted collision of ideas, theories and dreams. 'European culture does not only suffer its differences, conflicts and crises; it lives from them. ... European genius does not just lie in diversity and change, but in the dialogue within this diversity which ultimately effects change. ... Expressed in another way: That which is of greatest importance to the

[7] Lepenies, W., 1989, 'Europa als geistige Lebensform', in *Die Zeit*, Nr. 44, 27 October 1989.
[8] Braudel, F., Duby, G. and Aymard, M., 1987, *Die Welt des Mittelmeeres*, Frankfurt (*La Méditerranée*, Flammarion, Paris, 1985), p. 7.

existence and evolution of European culture is the fruitful collision of differences, antagonisms, and competing and complementary forces.'[9]

Out of these conflicts and differences have arisen powerful forces of destruction, colonial expansion, social exploitation—in short, the miserable side of the European Janus-head. But, out of them have also sprung the progressive inventions, discoveries and political-social innovations which constitute the friendly face and which, in the wake of the suffering of its 'zero hour', can now become the basis for a better Europe. A noteworthy aspect of Europe's periods of turbulence is the fact that the newer spirit has established itself in the cities, 'veritable hornets' nests', modern and inventive;[10] historical experience which trade unions long ago should have put to use in forging a European political perspective.

At the risk of grossly oversimplifying, might I dare list a few examples of European virtue and progressiveness? Rationalism, science, technology and industrial capitalism is one group of European inventions; others include enlightenment, humanism, secularism, tolerance, democracy and the social-welfare state. Freedom of thought and the figure of the intellectual as a restless poser of problems always finding joy in contradiction have played a role in the emergence of a 'Europe of individuals' and a 'continent of reflection'.[11]

It is with a healthy dose of effusive enthusiasm that I say the value of all European culture is concentrated and embodied in modern democracy. Democracy is the game-rule, whereby differences of opinion and opposing interests are settled in a civilized manner, without forgoing the stimulating effect of confrontation and conflict. The democratic game-rule says that democracy has no inherent truth at its disposal, but merely organizes the struggle between various contending 'truths'.

Put more sharply, this means that all fundamentalisms which evade democratic discourse are to be resisted in an uncompromising fashion. All religious, nationalistic and ideological fundamentalisms have brought forward their own specific methods of suppression and book-burnings. One early victim was the Italian poet Dante Alighieri, who was forced into exile, and whose books were publicly burned in Rome. Later it was the workers and the many intellectuals who sympathized with them who became the victims of fundamentalist vengeance under capitalist–imperialist systems, as well as under that perversion of socialistic ideas, Stalinist communism.

Trade unions, with their impatience and perseverance, can proudly lay claim to having made an essential contribution to the modern democratic project. With the rights won through struggle to wage strikes and carry out negotiations; with their advocacy of social and industrial democracy; with

[9] Morin, E., 1988, *op. cit.*, p. 128.
[10] Braudel, F. (ed.), 1989, *Europa: Bausteine seiner Geschichte*, Frankfurt (*L'Europe*, Flammarion, Paris, 1987), p. 20.
[11] Konrád, G., 1989, 'Europa der Individuen', in *Die Neue Gesellschaft*, Frankfurter Hefte, Nr. 7, July 1989, Bonn.

their struggle for universal voting rights, equal educational opportunities and a solidarity which transcends parochial worlds; with all of this, the free trade union association has played a leading role in bringing about an enlightened and democratic daily life and made decisive contributions in shaping the phenotype of political culture in Europe. Structures for working out compromises have been established which can be well described by the English expression 'capitalist democracy'. In a more self-confident way than in the past, the trade unions should take up the successes gained through struggle as the starting point for its participation in the launching of a united Europe. They can find support for this in the early Euro-political visions and utopias which were bound up with trade union ideas: the anti-royalist republicans, the anti-authority democrats, the anti-military pacifists, the anti-centralist federationists, and the anti-national Europeanists. The leading ideas of Kant, Hugo and Mazzini (to name just a few) emphasize the great tradition of European thought as an international movement for democracy and freedom.

If the trade unions recall their liberal traditions, if they take note of the fact that international cooperation is a basis for multiplying organizational, intellectual and, above all, political–strategic resources, then it should be possible to refrain from certain ideas. We are speaking of those ideas which have become dear to us but which, unfortunately, have also lost their 'enchantment' through such events as the 'dramatic decline of socialist utopias in East European countries'—oftentimes with immense repercussions on the western labour movement. Replacing them with the democratic concept of manifesting one's power through better alternatives would mean sparing no pains when it comes to the challenges of the third industrial revolution and offering future-oriented solutions to problems. A traditional strategy of total (and therefore simple) counter-proposals will not just do justice to the conditions of an ever more differentiated and complex world. What is called for are convincing, intelligent and democratic counter-proposals which would be a match for the strategies of governmental, political and business opponents. The field ought not to be abandoned to them. As willing participants in European affairs, the trade unions must acquire the competence characteristic of a practical and democratic alternative. This is a prerequisite for survival.

Half of Europe, Europe as a whole

The 'Europe of Twelve', the association of the politically and economically most advanced countries of Europe, will remain a mere torso if it persists in its current status as a centre of gravity limited to West Europe. Should it prove incapable of transforming its powerful attractive force on the other parts of Europe into an offer to participate freely and equally in the shaping of Europe as a border-spanning, multi-cultural unit, then the momentum towards a confederative European Union will be retarded and perhaps even lost. Only European integration marked by the joint action of all political, economic and military blocs can lead to the generation of creative impulses.

As for the neutral countries organized in the EFTA: first, due to the significance of their democratic and social-welfare character, they are an indispensable part of the newly-emerging Europe. Secondly, their integration poses no serious problem since there is already a significant interface with EC-Europe with respect to political–cultural and economic–technological affairs.

The situation is quite different with Eastern bloc nations. They are the unwilling satellites of the Soviet Union, kept on a short leash within its alliance, but are straining to break out. The costs of the past are truly immense: Deformed in terms of political institutions, backward with respect to economics and technology, ecologically exploited—these countries face a towering wall of problems, largely inherited. The lagging of these countries is so great that closing the gap can become the starting shot for bloc-straddling cooperation. In their own interests, the rich West European nations must show an unprecedented and exemplary readiness for equal burden-sharing among all European countries in order to eliminate the deformities of the eastern half. To avoid any misunderstanding: we are not speaking here of a modernization programme with the transfer of technology at its heart, but rather modern, democratic societies which are capable of learning and which can carry out course corrections with the aid of trial-and-error mechanisms systematically built into the system.

The German sociologist Hondrich has quite rightly focused attention on the paradox that the industrial capitalist countries, because they felt threatened and challenged, have learned more (and thereby profited) from the 'socialist experiment' than the Stalinists who clung to the error of thinking it possible to have a dynamic economy and Prussian disciplines in one social entity.[12] This erroneous road cannot be remedied within the system itself (the events of 1989 are not an 'industrial accident', but a systemic crisis), given that an 'all-powerful state bureaucracy' has been trained to the point of total incapability through corruption and 'barracks discipline' and has allowed the motivation and learning capacity of the individual to atrophy. Decades of frustration cannot be made up for in a short time. If we are to prevent the earlier Stalinist tutelage from being replaced by the tutelage of the (expansionist by nature) western capitalist system and promote the 'growing together of the parts of Europe, however contradictory that may be',[13] (and see Voigt[14]), the systems must be

[12] Hondrich, K. O., 1989, 'Chancen des Scheiterns', in *Der Spiegel*, 37/1989, Hamburg.

[13] Brandt, W., 1989, 'Wenn Europa wieder zusammenwächst', in *Die Zeit*, Nr. 47, 17 November 1989.

[14] Voigt, K., 1988, 'Mitteleuropa—Ein Konzept mit unklarer politischer Substanz, ein Raum mit wechselnden Grenzen', in Papcke, S. and Weidenfeld, W. (eds), *Traumland Mitteleuropa*, Darmstadt.

opened up through cooperative efforts on both sides—including especially those of the trade unions. There is not much they can contribute to the overcoming of antagonism between the military blocs, but they can play a substantial role in reducing political and social tensions. Free trade unions, wage autonomy and the right to strike, the power to shape social and company affairs—all these constitute a treasury of experience which the western trade unions can make available to those in Eastern Europe. The trade unions in the East and the West can build up a social-security partnership serving their own mutual interests and the interests of Europe as a whole. Should they succeed in making such an innovative quantum-leap by cooperating across the boundary separating the two blocs, they will have gained an important foundation stone for a socially and politically modern society on its way to becoming tomorrow's Europe.

In the West, one all too frequently forgets the historical fact often pointed out to us as a warning, for example, by Leszek Kolakowski: 'So long as the eastern peoples of Central Europe have good reason to feel that they have been torn by force from their historical continuity, Europe will remain ill.' This is a diagnosis that Germans should be able to understand especially well. It is also true with respect to the question of national unity of the German people that a solution of whatever kind is only thinkable as a component part of an overall future European order; thus, the preamble of the basic law of the Federal Republic of Germany explicitly refers to national unity in the context of a 'united Europe'.

As the Christian Democrat Lothar Späth has emphasized, the 'Europeanization of the German desire for unity' must be expressed in the readiness to confer 'the sovereign right to develop foreign and security policy' upon supranational European institutions. In view of the fact that the FRG will also be a beneficiary of the EC association in the future, and that the Germany of two states can possibly expect to enjoy the most advantages flowing from an all-European cooperative relationship, everything depends on the integration of the German question into a Europe-wide concept. Only through the voluntary surrender of national rights of sovereignty can the ground be pulled from under our European neighbours' fears of a revival of German strivings for hegemony.

It is nothing short of historical irony that the Germans, who violated the world with two world wars and the holocaust, have developed the Federal Republic into a comparatively modern society with a high productive capacity and which in many respects acts as a locomotive for Europe. The trade unions also see themselves and the social nets built up by them as a model.[15]

Europe (West), which extended such a generous hand to post-war Germany (West), can accept (West) German contributions to European integration and the sharing of intra-European burdens without worry so

---

[15] Steinkühler, F., 1989(a), *op. cit*.

long as processes of de-nationalization continue to be pushed forward in a cautious but decisive way—including especially by the trade unions.

Europe as a self-interest bloc, or part of a world society

Not infrequently we hear that Europe can find peace and ensure its future only by remaining equidistant from the western hegemonic power as well as the eastern one. There is talk of a political–cultural, socio-economic European power bloc which would be up to the competition of the others.

Such ideas find representatives especially among EC European political leaders. Europe's chances are rated relatively favourably with regard to competition with the other socio-economic poles, if it brings into play its specifically European advantages, its 'gentler ways': individuality *vis-à-vis* the Japanese-led bloc; social-welfarism and industrial democracy *vis-à-vis* the US; and democracy and freedom *vis-à-vis* the Soviet-dominated bloc.

In a very similar way, IGM chairman Steinkühler hopes that the strengthening of the EC will provide a 'counterweight to the neoliberal and neoconservative trends emanating from the US and Japan'.[16] The prospects for being able successfully to compete in the field of innovations is also judged favourably for the economy and enterprises of the EC.

In his book *The Rise and Fall of the Great Powers*,[17] Paul Kennedy comes to the conclusion that the EC, as the representative of Europe, can mature into the fifth world power. While he foresees a decline in the position of the US and the Soviet Union and envisions an improvement in the role and status of Japan and China, Europe remains a 'mystery' to him. Surmounting its disunity and division would be a prerequisite for rising to a position of world power.

I think it is advisable to face up to the hard realities confronting us: a Europe which is capable of acting as a world power and defending its own interests is vastly preferable to a fragmented Europe which is treated as the plaything of foreign power blocs. Particularly in view of the expected loss of hegemony by the USSR and the US, the idea of an EC-led Europe filling this power vacuum is extremely seductive.

But the result of this would be nothing more than an additional power bloc. Would it not be much better to give up the idea of Europe as a new world power and instead take up the concept of Europe as a preliminary stage or model on the road to a government of global interdependence?

By this, I mean the very same thing as that which the representatives of the large democratic parties are saying—even though they belong to opposing camps: 'Europe as an economically strong, culturally mature,

[16] Steinkühler, F., 1989(b), *op. cit.*
[17] Kennedy, 1989, *Aufstieg und Fall der grossen Mächte*, Frankfurt (*The Rise and Fall of the Great Powers*, Random House, New York, 1987).

enlightened power which marshals its forces for the well-being of humanity, challenges others through its example—that is the indicated path. Europe as an economically or even militarily hegemonic power is unnecessary, threatening to peace and stability. Europe as a sharing, helping and balancing power, on the other hand, as an example of globally responsible freedom, is more necessary than ever in order to guarantee peace for all peoples and peace with nature.'[18] In nearly identical fashion, the Italian communist Napolitano (1989), referring to the North-South reports authored by Social-Democratic politicians Brandt and Brundtland ('Towards one nation' and 'Our common future'), points out most emphatically that we are dealing with truly planet-spanning problems: from climactic catastrophe and energy supply to the debt crisis and political and social oppression. In view of the complex interconnections between all parts of the world and the capacity for mutual injury and destruction, in view of our experience that the rich countries will not be able to enjoy their good fortune so long as the others are living in misfortune and darkness, he proposes that we think of Europe as a preliminary stage of a world government, a government of global interdependence.[19]

Here, we can only repeat what was said about the sharing of burdens among all European countries. In its own interests, Europe—with trade unions as the representatives of the social-welfare viewpoint—must respond to the exponentially growing demand for understanding, capacity for compromise and a balancing of interests with an exponentially greater preparedness for global responsibility. The message, therefore, is: if Europe remains stubbornly fixated on its own interests it will short circuit and pass up those opportunities that lie in granting aid on an altruistic and selfless basis. Looked at from a certain perspective, 'selflessness' is a superior strategy to 'selfishness' as a form of insurance, since the world can only survive as a whole and humanity can only survive as a world society. A utopia which is making itself felt, a vision for Europe which is long overdue, must be concretized and carried forward without being deterred by setbacks.

Capitalist and social-welfare Europe

With respect to the EC Europe of Twelve, we are obviously dealing with a capitalist economic project. But to conclude from this that what must prevail is the 'dog-eat-dog nature of the marketplace—a Europe dominated by capital has to result'[20] is a premature way of seeing things. If there

[18] Späth, L., 1989, *op. cit.*, p. 359.
[19] Napolitano, G., 1989, *Oltre i vecchi confini—Il futuro della sinistra e l'Europa*, Mondadori, Milan.
[20] Lang, K. and Sauer, J., 1989, 'Wege zu einer europäischen Tarifpolitik, in Steinkühler, F. (ed.), *Europa '92, op. cit.*, p. 213.

is talk of falling back into Manchester capitalism—as is also the case among some high-ranking trade unionists—then the wrong signals will be flashed across the field of trade union politics as a consequence of insufficient analysis and mental exertion; and one need not wonder why the international trade union movement is at a standstill.

So that the trade unions can free themselves from such crude clichés—which, incidentally, have never been of any use as agitational slogans—some hard facts about our opponent would be in order. Only a few of the employers' difficulties can be sketched out here, but they prove nonetheless that their problems are no less substantial than those of the unions. Generally speaking, in epochs characterized by structural changes in society and the rupturing of global trends, even capital is compelled to act under conditions of changed circumstances and uncertain prospects for the future. And it is forced to draft new business strategies which conform to the claims for broader freedom by people who, at least in Europe, are always becoming better educated, more highly qualified and politically aware. Why should capital be any more successful in this than the trade unions with their long tradition of a great movement for freedom? Another fundamental problem facing employers is the fact that they are competitors in the marketplace; structurally speaking, an extraordinary and significant impediment to cooperation across sectoral and national boundaries. In other words, there are sharply conflicting interests within the camp of capital.

In connection with Europeanization and globalization, the employers supposedly enjoy the advantage of being able arbitrarily to leave their national points of production and invest in foreign countries. Even though this has recently brought them the reproach from trade unions of being 'a brotherhood without a fatherland', it is not really such a definite advantage. Capital, too, is embedded in its national history; it is an engine of socio-economic and political culture of each country. One of the factors determining the behaviour of the employers is the particular stage of capitalist development peculiar to the national economy and the way in which labour and industrial relations are regulated with regard to company personnel and the trade unions. A survey of the employers' associations in Europe, for example, would show that they are just as diverse and colourful as the unions. In other words, the employers face significant difficulties in their efforts to shape a 'Europe of capital' through cooperation across the boundaries separating nations and societies, economies and economic sectors, cultures and various developmental stages.

These comments are made in order to dispel the dramatic fears of a Europe dominated by capital—but, in no way are they intended as an 'all-clear' signal. If the trade unions continue to huddle in fear like a rabbit before a snake, then the 'Europe of capital' could more or less come into being as a self-fulfilling prophecy.

We must emphatically advise the trade unions to stand by their successes: political, social and industrial democracy as well as the democratization of education, organizations and daily life have indeed not led to socialist utopias. But they have allowed the emergence of a restrained capitalism which has provided freer and more social life opportunities to a greater number of people than ever before. In the struggle to advance beyond their defeats, the trade unions have time and again proved their tenacity, imagination, inventive spirit and capacity for learning—vital qualities in achieving better social conditions. Nothing argues for the fact that these attributes have been lost and that the unions must submit to the domination of capital in Europe.

Considering their historical development, the certainly not insignificant barriers which stand in the way of the trade unions in the working out of European political perspectives lose their horror. Discouragement is not called for—in spite of the complexities which must be mastered by a supranational trade union politics. Let us examine two major difficulties.

(a) *The national orientation of the trade unions*: Despite all the programmatic professions of international solidarity, it cannot be overlooked that unions arose in the context of the specific historical developments of their respective national capitalisms and are bound up with a national labour force through the representation of their demands and needs. What is true for the employers is even more true for labour and its trade union organizations: they are rooted firmly in their respective countries by means of a common national mentality and deeply embedded in their political and institutional structures.

The real difficulty is not national peculiarities, but conflicting national interests. These bring together employers, employees, trade unions and governmental authorities—including political parties—into a common national community rather than separating them on a class basis and organizing them into united, multinational, antagonistically opposed blocs of capital and labour as taught by Marxist theory. In more pointed terms, this means that the unions run the danger of becoming junior partners to their respective national economies, economic branches or home-based transnational corporations. In this sense, we are often dealing today with competition between trade unions over jurisdiction, production and jobs rather than solidarity stretching across borders.

One example of a narrow-nationalist view of an objectively existing conflict of opposing interests is the complaint raised by West German unions about 'social dumping'. What is meant by this is gaining economic advantage by means of strategies aimed at lowering wages and the cost of social benefits. But what is overlooked, on the one hand, is that this undercutting provides a comparative advantage in competition to the less developed national economies, and on the other hand, that it is merely the counterpart of the undercutting carried out by the high-tech/high-wage countries on the basis of technological and training advantages.

This problem is already putting a strain on trade union cooperation between the member states of the EC. With the addition of the East

European countries, this problem-mix will be greatly compounded. The trade unions are being ever more urgently faced with the task and confronted by the demand to muster up the readiness and competence required for a multilateral balancing of their interests. To develop an international association capable of such an altruistic, selfless and denationalized representation requires sound knowledge about the various diverging interests involved as well as a high degree of confidence in the credibility of neighbouring trade unions; it requires political and social imagination and will not be possible without an experimental spirit and a willingness to risk unavoidable detours and false paths, dead ends and setbacks.

(b) *The splintered nature of trade unions*: As heirs of the various national capitalisms which emerged in the context of imperialist rivalry—and also due to the political division of the workers' movement, such as the antagonism between blocs following World War II—the trade unions are today confronted with splintered organizational forms and a patchwork of legal regulations and institutional arrangements which make multinational cooperation even more difficult. A couple of examples might suffice in illustrating how extremely varied the structured system of industrial relations actually is. We are dealing with unitary and politically partisan trade unions; the principle of industrial association (one plant, one union) versus the multiple-union plant; the lock-out is allowed in West Germany and has become a valued weapon of the employers, but in some other countries it is illegal; the German works constitutional law has very little in common with the Italian factory council or the British 'shop-steward'.

Although this list could go on forever, we can bring some systematic order to the confusion. First, the middle and northern European model of unitary, non-partisan trade unions, which are organized according to the principle of industrial association and characterized by a high degree of centralization, juridification and institutionalization, have proved themselves in the last fifteen years to be comparatively resistant against erosion tendencies despite high unemployment and structural changes. It can be shown by means of examples from these countries that robust and socially innovative trade unions which are used to thinking in macropolitical and macroeconomic terms can exercise a more consolidating and stimulating effect on the efficiency of their national economies. Thus, a successful Euro-capitalist economy and a successful trade union association interact in a more symbiotic way—they are not mutually exclusive. Looking to the future, we can formulate the following thesis: The more developed democratic rights are, the greater the economic efficiency and possibly even ecological rationality.

Second, from this point of view, the exact opposite can be said with regard to the countries of East Europe. Degraded to the role of transmission belts for the ruling party and state bureaucracies, the trade unions have atrophied to the point of having no independent existence and thereby have contributed to the economic sclerosis of their countries. These unions have no future.

Third, the Anglo-Saxon trade union model, with its fragmented, particularized and factory-centred character, has proved to be capable of little resistance when exposed to tendencies of erosion and decline. Union-free zones and union-free labour relations are spreading; membership losses are significant; competition both within and among the various trade unions is gradually taking on the character of a ruinous displacement contest. If the British unions now turn to continental Europe, then it appears as if they can expect a Euro-political perspective to have a positive influence on their overall situation and interests. In reverse fashion, the continental unions could learn from the factory-centred nature of their British counterparts.

Finally, in the western and Mediterranean countries of Europe where 'political unionism' prevails, trade union losses of power caused by an unfavourable labour market have been met by political support measures taken by friendly governments or by budgetary actions revealing governmental sympathy. Whether the frequently observed emergence and expansion of plant or professionally centred levels of organization can be maintained will depend on the ability of the traditional trade union associations to draft new political concepts and restrict their rivalry (that of the politically partisan trade unions) or even redirect it in an innovative manner. The singular feature of 'political unionism'—specifically to create anew the balance between competition and cooperation among rival organizations through the permanent willingness to compromise and balance the interests of the various trade unions—is of inestimable value for European-wide cooperation.

Everything depends therefore on making use of the specific advantages of each of the three western trade union models with great organizational and political imaginativeness. A European trade union entity, not as a gigantic organizational unit in the sense of 'one big union', but rather as an interactive network of trade union organizational diversity, has a good deal of difficulty to overcome. But such an entity does obtain clear relief through the positive economic effects to be expected, especially for the southern and East European countries. Finally, however, it lives from the perspective of a future community, for which it is necessary to draft joint projects and alternative solutions. The trade unions can and must participate in the historical journey into a post-national and post-imperial Europe. I will conclude with a statement by Victor Hugo: 'Nothing is so powerful as an idea whose time has come.'

EUROPE'S FUTURE: WESTERN UNION OR COMMON HOME?

JONATHAN STORY*

EUROPE of the 1990s is being transformed by the EC's internal market programme and President Gorbachev's *perestroika*. The thrust of Gorbachev's policies points towards a pan-European state and market system, whose geographical centre-point is Berlin. It implies the development of a special relationship between a restructured Russia and a united Germany. The vision is of an extended 'European Community of the 21st Century'.[1] The thrust of the EC's internal market strategy points to political and market integration, whose geographical centre-point is Paris. It is predicated on consolidating the coalition of states in the European Community (EC) through a further development of its central institutions. As Commission President Delors stated, 'in ten years' time, eighty per cent of economic legislation—and perhaps tax and social legislation—will be directed from the Community'.[2]

In 1985, the main features of Europe were not too dissimilar from those of the early post-war years.[3] Europe's division seemed set in stone. Stalin's territorial annexations and his suspicions of Western motives had: ended the wartime Grand Alliance; led to Germany's and Europe's division; and was a crucial factor in the creation of the two hostile alliances under the dominance of the United States and the Soviet Union. Monopoly party rule and centralized planning systems were clamped onto the satellite states. Political pluralism and market economies prevailed in Western Europe. Interdependent among each other and with the rest of the world, the states were particularly sensitive to changes in the global balance of power. Their common affairs were managed through a complex diplomatic system, centring on three clusters of institutions: the European Communities; the North Atlantic Treaty Organization (NATO); and the European Conference on Security and Cooperation (ECSC) between the 35 signatory states of the 1975 Helsinki Final Act. The contrast, half a decade on, is startling. Major changes are under way on the world stage.

* Jonathan Story is Professor of International Politics at INSEAD (the European Institute of Business Administration). His recent articles include 'The Launching of the EMS: An Analysis of Change in Foreign Economic Policy', which appeared in *Political Studies* (XXXVI, 1988) and 'La Communauté Européenne et la Défense de l'Europe' published in *Studia Diplomatica* (Vol. XLI, No. 3, 1988). He is currently working on a study of Spanish external relations.

[1] *Financial Times*, 7 July 1989.
[2] *Financial Times*, 7 July 1988.
[3] Guy de Carmoy, Jonathan Story, *Western Europe in World Affairs: Continuity, Change and Challenge*, New York, Praeger, 1986.

They impinge critically on Europe. Simultaneously, the European Community (EC) is engaged on the path to closer political and market integration. Germany, too, is moving to unity, while the Soviet Union is undergoing revolutionary changes. As the cold war recedes, the post-war alliances are either disintegrating or undergoing profound transformation, prompting a symbiosis of the two Europes: 'the real Europe', as President Mitterrand wrote, 'that of history and geography'.[4]

Europe in 1990

Europe's position in world affairs in 1990 is markedly different from that of 1985. For forty years, Western Europe had evolved a complex polity, integrating the United States. But three sets of changes have altered the arrangement. First, Japan's emergence as the world's second largest and most dynamic economy exerts a crucial impact on the United States, the Soviet Union and the European Community. Second, the EC's enlargements, including first Britain and then Spain, have altered its structure and functioning. Finally, the slow changes in world politics affecting the United States and the Soviet Union have altered the setting of the Federal Republic in Europe.

The 1980s had opened with an accentuation of the United States military build-up, and a conflict between an expansionary fiscal and a tight monetary policy. Interest rates jumped. The federal deficit ballooned and corporate investment picked up. The solitary US boom of 1982–85 rescued the world from depression, but was followed by the rapid growth of the United States as the world's main debtor. Japan became the US' prime creditor, thereby cementing a competitive industrial and financial duopoly across the Pacific. Trade relations soured with the US Congress' passage of the Fair Trade Act in 1988, inspired by a prevalent Nippophobia. The new thinking in President Bush's Washington holds that little is to be gained in negotiations with Tokyo.[5] Rather, the solution to the United States' competitive problems lies through arms cuts, and a redeployment of US technological, financial and human resources from containment of the Soviet Union to confronting the Japanese challenge on consumer markets. This means seizing the olive branch tended by President Gorbachev in Europe. The tone was set in Bush's foreign policy speeches of April and May 1989.[6] Japan received bare mention. The new

---

[4] François Mitterrand, *Réflexions sur la Politique Extérieure de la France*, Paris, Fayard, 1986, p. 71.

[5] The main source for this argument is the best-selling book by Karel van Wolferen, *The Enigma of Japanese Power: People and Politics in a Stateless Nation*, London, Macmillan, 1989.

[6] The five speeches are: 17 April 1989, on Poland; 2 May, on the Americas; 12 May, on welcoming back a reformed USSR into the world order; 21 May, on the emergence of a united Europe; 24 May, on the eclipse of communism, *Wireless File*, United States Information Service.

38

goal of US foreign policy is declared to be 'the integration of the Soviet Union into the Community of Nations'. This was conditional on the extension of political, market and individual freedoms into Eastern Europe, as well as steps towards political pluralism and human rights in the Soviet Union. 'The United States welcomes the emergence of Europe as a partner in leadership.' Such a Western Europe acts as 'an economic magnet, drawing Eastern Europe towards the commonwealth of free nations'.

Japan's impact on the Soviet Union is no less dramatic. Starting in the late 1960s, Japan's mixture of 'administrative guidance' and highly competitive markets launched the nation into a vigorous assault on the lead electronics sector. The Japanese challenge hit US and European producers in the late 1970s, and left the rigid Soviet economy standing. Chief of Staff Marshal Orgakov's blunt criticism in 1984 of Soviet technology for not being able to provide up-to-date weaponry provided an indication of the dimensions of the economic restructuring required of the Soviet Union if it was to join the new industrial revolution under way in the world economy.[7] The Politburo's March 1985 election of Gorbachev as Secretary-General launched the Soviet Union on the path of 're-structuring'. His aim was reform of the inherited apparatus in order to create a 'socialist state of law'. The main stumbling block was the party's 'leading role', articulated in the Soviet Union's Constitution. The stirring of national and religious demands in Russia's multi-ethnic empire in turn fostered Russian chauvinism, threatening the Union's cohesion. Tensions were aggravated by disastrous economic conditions. Only a legitimate government issuing from multi-party elections could take the necessary decisions. Hence Gorbachev's success in early 1990 in suspending Article 6, ending the party's monopoly on power, was a major step to reform. But the key decisions such as freeing of prices and rouble convertibility lay ahead. Without such changes, the Soviet Union is, by export structure, a developing country: 'Upper Volta with missiles', in Helmut Schmidt's dismissive phrase.

Japan's trade practices have been a central motivation in the European Commission's efforts since the late 1970s to extend its reach over the internal market, as a pre-requisite to its negotiating from a position of strength with Tokyo. By contrast to Western Europe's complex political and market interdependence, the post-war development of Pacific Asia has been predicated on unequal access to OECD markets by mercantilist states and societies. Little attention was paid by Tokyo to EC complaints, which were rarely followed by effective action to reduce trade imbalances. There was also the consideration in the early 1980s of low growth and high unemployment, compared to the United States and Japan. A Pacific economy, hinging on Tokyo and San Francisco, was threatening to

[7] On high technology as a key consideration for *perestroika*, see Marshall Goldman, *Economic Reform in the Age of High Technology: Gorbachev's Challenge*, New York, Norton, 1987.

displace the centre of world political and economic gravity from its post-war Euro-American moorings. Japan's corporations, furthermore, were driving European competitors into the nooks and crannies of the crucial North American markets. They were a major factor in the EC's 1984–85 relaunch.[8] The central components of the strategy were outlined by Commission President Delors in his January 1985 inaugural speech to the European Parliament: a strengthening of Commission powers; the elimination of all remaining internal barriers to trade by 1993; and joint EC research projects. Relations with the Ministry of Industry and Trade (MITI) were upgraded and intensified. Delors' meeting in July with Prime Minister Nakasone signified that a key dimension of the new internal market policy was to place EC external trade relations on a stronger footing: the member states, Delors was quoted as saying, could now 'speak with one voice'.[9]

A second set of factors changing the EC's environment has been the prolonged period of enlargement from the original six founding states to nine, ten and twelve. The Rome Treaty of 1957 had set a number of targets, together with a detailed timetable to achieve the customs union and to dismantle internal tariffs and quotas. The timetable was completed in 1968, while the Commission became involved in a never-ending series of trade negotiations with outsiders seeking to preserve access to EC markets through applying for membership, association status or preferential trade arrangements. The negotiations spanned the period from 1969 to 1985; absorbed EC energies, disrupted the compromises of the 1960s on which the partial trade and farm policies of the EC had been based; and accentuated the trend to a reinforcement of the Council of Ministers in EC mechanisms. The principal innovation, alongside the setting up of the European Political Cooperation (EPC), was the creation of the European Council in December 1974, involving the heads of government and state directly in EC affairs.[10] It has patronized direct elections to the European Parliament; the launching of the European Monetary System (EMS); the enlargement negotiations, especially with Spain; the reforms of existing policies in 1984–85; the launching of the '1992' programme; and the Single European Act, finally ratified by all member state parliaments in June 1987, that records the extension of majority voting to key areas of the 1992 programme. This extension registers the fact that any perpetuation of the previous tendency to use the veto indiscriminately would have brought the EC of Twelve to a grinding halt.

---

[8] Delors' version of the relaunch is to be found in his preface for 1992: *Le Défi*, Paris, Flammarion, 1988. (French version of the popularized Cecchini report.)

[9] *Le Monde*, 21–22 July 1985.

[10] See Simon Bulmer, Wolfgang Wessels, *The European Council, Decision-Making in European Politics*, London, Macmillan, 1987. Also, Alfred Pijpers *et al.*, *European Political Cooperation in the 1980s: A Common Foreign Policy for Western Europe?* Dordrecht, Martinus Nijhoff, 1988.

Spain's entry negotiations, opening in 1979, dragged on until the dual changes in government in Bonn and Madrid in the winter of 1982–83. France was the main source of resistance. Spain's entry threatened the delicate equilibrium in EC farm markets, as well as US and Moroccan interests. But early 1983 witnessed a further lurch in the EC's internal weighting towards Bonn, at Paris' expense. In alliance with the new Socialist government in Madrid, the Christian Democrat–Liberal government in Bonn pushed hard for Spain's cause in the EC. At the Stuttgart European Council, Chancellor Kohl linked the availability of new financial resources for the EC budget in an enlarged Community to ratification by the EC members of the new accession treaties. The talks then languished until the French Presidency of early 1984, when Mitterrand embarked on his redeployment of French domestic and European policy. Mitterrand's full substitute policy, announced in two key speeches in early 1984 in The Hague and at Strasburg, was European unity.[11] This implied prior agreement on control of EC farm surpluses, bilateral negotiations with Madrid to wrap up entry negotiations by March 1985, and support for the internal market programme. Spain's entry helped loosen up the EC's decision-making, stimulated EC institutional reforms, and widened the internal market. Above all, a special relationship has been created between Bonn and Madrid. The Federal Republic came to account for three quarters of Spain's trade deficit. Spain's European diplomacy, supportive of German,[12] was rewarded during the German EC Presidency in early 1988: Kohl agreed to increase German EC budget contributions by nearly 50 per cent, involving a doubling of the EC's regional funds by 1993. A key objective of the Madrid government was thereby secured, to ensure as large a flow of public or private funds into Spain as the trade barriers came down.

The British government also came round to support the new EC initiative. With reform of the farm policy underway, and EC enlargement negotiated, there was the chance to promote free market deals as a positive contribution to EC integration. Indeed, by introducing deregulation to the centre of EC activity, the new policy would go well beyond the old negative freeing of trade between states to a direct attack on non-tariff barriers, as the heart of the continental states' mercantilism. While this would lead to inevitable resistance by continental producer interests, whether of conservative or social democratic orientation, it would place British foreign policy in line with domestic practice. A free market policy at home would become the inspiration for British policy in the Community, while keeping free hands for the conduct of foreign policy in the

[11] 'Le Reveil de l'Espérance Européenne', The Hague, 7 February 1984; 'Une victoire de la Communauté sur elle-même', Strasburg, 24 May 1984, in François Mitterrand, op. cit., pp. 267–297.
[12] See Felipe Gonzalez' speech in Bonn to the Deutsche Gesellschaft für Auswärtige Politik, 'Spaniens Beitrag zur Europäischen Integration', Europa Archiv 20.42 (1987), pp. 569–576.

world arena. The Community, as Prime Minister Thatcher stated in her Bruges speech in September 1988, is a practical means to 'achieve international cooperation between independent sovereign states'. Europe is a family of nations, incorporating the peoples of eastern Europe, and 'that Atlantic Community—that Europe on both sides of the Atlantic—which is our greatest inheritance and our greatest strength'.[13] Yet the negotiation of such a complex process, whereby member states enter a mutual disarmament pact on non-tariff barriers, would require a strengthening of EC federal powers. The internal market policy necessarily revives the debates of the 1960s, but in the EC's new context, between the advocates of a Europe of the states and those inclining to more federal powers for the Community.[14]

A third set of factors impinging on Europe has been the evolution in the Soviet Union affecting Germany. Germany's division and the Federal Republic's key role in NATO and the EC ensure a particular sensitivity to its national situation. This has been most changed by the policies announced by Gorbachev at the CPSU 27th Congress in February 1986, when he declared with respect to eastern Europe that 'fundamental reform is necessary'.[15] No mention was made of the concept of 'proletarian internationalism' that had been deployed to justify the Warsaw Pact's military intervention in Czechoslovakia in 1968. The content of Gorbachev's 'common European home' evolved with time. It was further elaborated in his visit to Prague in April 1987, when he proposed 'the peaceful development of European culture which has many faces, yet forms a single entity'. In his book, *Perestroika*, published that autumn, he added that 'we do not seek to impose our view on anybody'. In his United Nations speech of December 1988, along with a renewed emphasis on the common interests uniting humanity, he announced a unilateral withdrawal of 50,000 Red Army troops from the German Democratic Republic (GDR), Czechoslovakia and Hungary. Finally, in June 1989, Gorbachev in Bonn signed a document pledging the right of all people to self-determination: 'everyone has the right to choose his own political and social system'.[16] No Soviet troops stirred when the revolutions of November and December 1989 swept aside the 'fraternal' regimes in the GDR, Czechoslovakia, Bulgaria, and in Romania. A breach was opened in the Berlin Wall, and in the inner-German frontier on November 9. These momentous changes paved the way to the extension of pluralist demo-

[13] *Financial Times*, 21 September 1988.
[14] On British foreign policy, Christopher Tugendhat, William Wallace, *Options for British Foreign Policy in the 1990s*, London, Routledge, 1988.
[15] On Gorbachev's 'new thinking', and the 'common European home', Lilly Marcou, *Les défis de Gorbachev*, Paris, Plon 1988; Karen Dawisha, *Eastern Europe: Gorbachev and Reform: The Great Challenge*, Cambridge, Cambridge University Press, 1988; David Holloway, 'Gorbachev's New Thinking', Robert Legvold, 'The Revolution in Soviet Foreign Policy', *Foreign Affairs: America and the World*, Vol. 68, No. 1, pp. 66–81, 82–98.
[16] *Financial Times*, 14 June 1989.

cracies into eastern Europe, including in East Germany. They have paralleled changes in the party system, and a shift to a more fluid electoral arena in the Federal Republic.[17] At the time of writing the next general elections are planned for end of 1990, and they promise to be the most intense in the history of the Federal Republic, where the overriding issue is German unity.

The kernel of Gorbachev's 'new thinking' in foreign affairs is disarmament, and relief from the burden of military expenditures, estimated as equivalent to about 18 per cent of a GNP not much larger than Italy's.[18] Security in an interdependent world was to be achieved by arms reduction, rather than their accumulation. 'Sufficiency' and 'defensive defence' describe the new policy. Gorbachev's disarmament offensive was launched in February 1986, with dramatic proposals to rid the world of nuclear weapons in three stages by the year 2000; to withdraw the US and Soviet fleets from the Mediterranean; and for the denuclearization of Europe, along with the 'total withdrawal of foreign troops from the territory of other countries'. While President Reagan showed US determination to remain a Mediterranean power with the bombing of Libya in April, he lent a more ready ear to Gorbachev's acceptance of his earlier proposals to withdraw intermediary range missiles in Europe. Washington overrode objections from Bonn, Paris and London that Western Europe was thereby more exposed to the deployment of Soviet military power. But the way was cleared for the Washington Treaty of 8 December 1987, between Gorbachev and Reagan.

The Treaty represented a major event in the history of nuclear weapons.[19] All missiles with a range of between 500 to 5,500 kilometres were to be destroyed within 3 years. For the first time the Treaty included extensive verification procedures. The resulting climate of confidence facilitated a spate of agreements on chemical weapons; the resumption of discussions on strategic arms cuts; and conventional arms talks between NATO and Warsaw Pact members opening in Vienna in March 1989. At the May NATO Council meeting in Brussels, the Western allies agreed to postpone modernization of nuclear weapons, pending progress on conventional arms. President Bush, under pressure from Congress on the budget, proposed an ambitious programme to accelerate mutual cuts in armaments. The rapid changes in Europe in the subsequent months allowed Bush and Gorbachev, at their meeting off Malta in December, to

---

[17] See Gordon Smith, William Paterson, Peter Merkl, *Developments in West German Politics*, London, Macmillan, 1989.

[18] Assume a Soviet *per capita* income of 2000–4000 dollars. The lower range yields a mythical GNP equivalent to 4 per cent of the world total, as measured in the World Bank Development Report, 1989. The higher range yields 8 per cent. Italy's is about 6 per cent, assuming reliance on Italian public accounting.

[19] *Politique Etrangère, 1/88. Le Traité de Washington*. The whole volume is dedicated to the Treaty. It includes a short overview of the EC's internal market. Philippe Moreau Defarges, '1992: Non-événement? Echéance Décisive?', pp. 173–182.

speak of a new treaty limiting conventional arms in Europe, ready for signature by 1990. The prospect is of a withdrawal of some US,[20] and allied, troops from Germany, accompanied by the elaboration of a new security system for Europe as a whole, within the context of the Helsinki Final Act.

Europe's renewed centrality in world affairs in 1989 was tokened by the itineraries of world leaders. Gorbachev visited London, Bonn, Paris and Rome, prior to his meeting off Malta in December with Bush. Bush's interest in Europe was underlined by his three visits to Brussels and Bonn in May, Paris in June, and Malta and Brussels in December. In part response to Gorbachev's active diplomacy, the President also visited Poland and Hungary in July. In January 1990, Japan's Prime Minister Kaifu made a ten-nation trip to Europe, while his party political rivals opened tentative negotiations with Moscow for an eventual settlement of the major issues which have divided Japan and the Soviet Union since 1945. But the focus of all this diplomatic activity is Germany. Progress on disarmament promises to demilitarize international relations; allows for a significant redeployment of resources to alternative uses; and points to the elaboration of a pan-European security system. The United States seeks an intimate, but more balanced relationship with the new Europe. The central and eastern European states are embarking on the arduous task of creating pluralist states on communist ruins. Gorbachev has started the Soviet Union on a revolutionary path of restructuring. The declarations of peace between the United States and the Soviet Union leave Japan diplomatically isolated and trapped in economic struggle with Euro-America. The symbiosis of the two Germanies, accelerated by the spread of pluralism into East Germany, is creating another Europe, whose geographical heart is Berlin.

'Europe 1992': uncertain destination[21]

'Europe 1992' was launched in the international conditions of 1985–86. It was also future-oriented, supported by multiple motivations, and sanctioned by reference to the general interest of the Community to break down internal barriers to trade. Yet it remains a multi-state strategy to modify the operations of markets, and therefore its introduction may conflict with domestic political imperatives; bump into the sovereign aspirations of the states; be tied by the states into ever wider spheres of activity; and must contend with an unstable political and market environment. '1992', as understood in Brussels, is also not the only horizon

[20] *Financial Times*, 2 February 1990. President Bush's proposal is to reduce US and Soviet forces to 195,000 each in their respective 'central zones', allowing 30,000 US troops to redeploy to other NATO member countries.

[21] Andrew Schonfield, *Europe: Journey to an Unknown Destination*, London, Penguin, 1973.

available in Europe. Alone, and as a policy process, '1992' may not lead anywhere in particular. Indeterminacy of outcome is inherent to a policy process, where singleminded focus on the EC agenda is constantly endangered by shifts in domestic preferences or changes in the international setting.

The vision of a 'Europe without frontiers', centred on Brussels, was designed as a means to overcome stagnation. It is future oriented, and a programme to meet the multiple demands of its participants. But it is also based on a set of newly agreed rules, a timetable, and an overall goal to achieve a more efficient internal EC market. It was nurtured in the Europe inherited from the early post-war years. That Europe was not only divided into two, three, twelve or sixteen. Besides the disparities of geography, religion, language and regime, there are at least five political Europes.[22] There was the Europe of Brussels, with the headquarters of NATO and the institutions of the EC. There was the Europe of Russia's satellite states, vulnerable to the pull of Western Europe. The neutral and non-aligned countries, with their western institutions and markets, straddled the diplomatic fence in East–West relations. Many of them belonged to the European Free Trade Association (EFTA). European Russia, representing only one-fifth of the Soviet Union's geographic area, held the bulk of the population and economic resources. The United States, geographically isolated from Europe by the Atlantic Ocean, was nonetheless omnipresent militarily, economically and culturally.

The new EC vision is above all a political programme to harness the twelve national states of the EC to a common task for the future. European publics are offered wider horizons than national introversion. But the main target of the programme is the world of business. As the Commission states, a key condition of success is 'the credibility of the process, the assurance that in the medium term the environment will undergo a transformation that will oblige all firms ... to adopt a European strategy'.[23] The process involves a combined effort to fashion business expectations by acting on political impediments to a more efficient continental-wide economy. It is an experiment in levitation whereby businesses are invited to consider that even if the programme is not implemented in all its legislative guises, competitors may assume that it will be, thereby requiring risks to be taken as if the internal market was a near certainty. Not least, the whole programme is a media phenomenon, with a date—1992—which holds the promise that something significant is going to happen by December 31 of that year. It thereby resurrects the Community method to write a detailed timetable, holding a deadline over the heads of government to which all manner of expectations may be pegged.

---

[22] Jorge Fuentes, 'Hacia un nuevo concepto de la seguridad europea', *Politica Exterior* (Madrid), Vol. III, No. 13, Autumn 1989, pp. 122–134.
[23] Economie Européenne, Commission des Communautés Européennes, 1992: *La Nouvelle Economie Européenne*, No. 35, March 1988, p. 21.

The origins of '1992' lie in a prolonged campaign by the Commission to revive the Community. It has sought to harness the multiple motivations at play to launch a determined attack on non-tariff barriers; to promote a series of EC-wide technology programmes; and to strengthen its negotiating position as the EC's representative in trade relations with outsiders.[24] While the states were embroiled in the early 1980s in discussions on reform of agriculture and the enlargement to Spain, the Commission's principal allies were European businesses, particularly those represented in the Round Table of European Industrialists. The European Parliament militated for an EC federal constitution. To these were added the states, with their own particular motivations. The new government at Bonn in 1983 established its EC credentials at the Stuttgart European Council, where the European heads of government subscribed to a Solemn Declaration on European Union, indicating an intention to extend EC domains into 'the economic and political aspects of security', as well as into the cultural or foreign policy areas.[25] The Benelux countries stayed loyal to their traditional attachment to the ideal of European union. The British government saw an opportunity to promote free market ideals as a positive contribution to the common enterprise. Italy looked for a more determined lead from Brussels as a means to promote reforms at home, while welcoming the culmination of Spain's lengthy entry negotiations to the EC as providing a new impetus to Community affairs.[26] But the major change in attitudes towards the EC was registered in France: whereas in the 1960s and 1970s, French diplomacy and public opinion had been wary at any loss of national independence, the early 1980s revived a policy in favour of European integration. The European Community came to be seen as the only effective means to escape stagnation; to counter the Pacific challenge; to satisfy the changing composition of the French electorate towards the pro-EC centrists; and to develop a more satisfactory partnership with the Federal Republic.[27]

Though the ground had been laid, the EC's relaunch began with the conclusion of Spain's lengthy entry negotiations in March 1985. In June, the Milan European Council voted by majority to hold an intergovernmental conference to modify and extend Community powers written into the Rome Treaty of 1957. At the Luxemburg European Council in December, another majority vote was cast in favour of an international

[24] Wayne Sandholtz, John Zysman, '1992: Recasting the European Bargain', *World Politics*, Vol. XLII, No. 1, October 1989, pp. 95–128.

[25] See Helmut Kohl, *L'Europe est notre destin*; *Discours actuels*. Présentation et traduction de Joseph Rovan, Paris, Edition de Fallois, 1990.

[26] Prime Minister Craxi at the Madrid ceremonies on Spain's membership: 'The wills and new energies joining us will have a multiplier effect and will stimulate us to confront our new objectives', *Le Monde*, 14 June 1985.

[27] See Stanley Hoffman, 'Mitterrand's Foreign Policy, or Gaullism by any other Name', in *The Mitterrand Experiment* (ed. George Ross *et al.*), Cambridge UK, Polity Press, 1987, pp. 294–305.

conference to modify the Treaty of Rome. The Single European Act (SEA), finally ratified by all member states' parliaments in June 1987, both amends the original treaties and incorporates into it the institutions and practice that have developed alongside. It strengthens the Commission; upgrades the role of the Parliament; and reinforces the Community as a negotiating partner for third parties. But the states retain their legislative power in Council. The Act also enshrines in Article 8A a commitment of the states to achieve 'a progressive establishment of the internal market by December 31, 1992'. The aim is the reduction of non-tariff barriers, 300 of which are listed in the June 1985 White Book. The process is expedited by resort to the new procedures, encapsulated in the SEA, and by the broad application of the principle of mutual recognition.[28] The principle, derived from EC law, holds that a good may be freely exported to another member state when it has been produced and commercialized in accordance with the regulations of the exporting country.[29] Thus the kernel of the internal market programme is to facilitate competition between public policies, and in all possible areas of business activity. It is a compact to reduce non-tariff barriers among the member states. The new approach is predicated on diversity of the European state system in that it seeks to use rather than be blocked by it.[30] It represents a shift towards a policy for a federation of distinct states, rather than an effort to impose harmony as a step to a single state.

'Europe 1992' may be understood as a state strategy ostensibly aimed at making markets operate more efficiently, but enacted in a multi-state Community whose member states are sovereigns. Such a definition places changing and therefore intermediate limits on the range of issues on which agreement between the member states is possible, and points to the constant significance of national constituencies in EC deliberations. The programme abounds with examples, where the new Brussels procedures and legislative activism contrast with the strength of traditions, nonetheless exposed to change through the policy. Customer loyalty to Germany's quality standards, elaborated in the Deutsche Industrie Nörmung (DIN), is unlikely to be shaken by the new policy for EC standard harmonization, that outlaws national standards based solely on quality criteria. Similarly,

---

[28] In January 1990, of the 279 measures in the White Book, 152 have been adopted by the Council of Ministers. Of these, 88 should have been implemented by the states. Only 14 have been by all 12 states. *The Economist*, 20 January 1990.

[29] On the legal origins of 'mutual recognition', see Christian W. A. Timmerman, 'La Libre Circulation des Marchandises', in Trente Ans de Droit Communautaire, Collection, 'Perspectives Européennes', Commission des CE, 1982, pp. 283–285; 295–296. Also Jean Claude Masclet, 'Les articles 30, 36 et 100 du traité CEE à la lumière de l'arret "Cassis de Dijon", Cour de Justice des CE, 20 Février, 1989', Revue Trimestrielle de Droit Européen, Paris, 1980. No. 4, pp. 611–634; A. Mattera, 'L'arret "Cassis de Dijon": une nouvelle approche pour la réalisation et le bon fonctionnement du marché intérieur', *Revue du Marché Commun*, Paris, No. 241, November 1980, pp. 505–514.

[30] For a contemporary discussion, Helen Wallace, Adam Ridley, *Europe: The Challenge of Diversity*, London, Routledge and Kegan Paul, 1985.

moves to establish a single financial services market contend with well-entrenched practices to protect firms from foreign takeover. Labour markets remain decidedly subject to national laws and practices. Not least, there are strong currents of resistance in the states to 'Europe 1992', and concern at Brussels centralizing ambitions.[31] The programme's progress, therefore, has inevitably rekindled the debate of the 1960s: the proponents of a Europe of the states, championed by the British Prime Minister, insist that the national states alone have democratic legitimacy and international standing. By contrast, the proponents of a federal Europe seek a strengthening of parliamentary control to lend greater authority to EC decisions.

The states' many reservations about alternative paths to union trace out ahead of time where the internal market could break down. The creation of an internal market would mean the incorporation of national defence procurement within the EC domain. A single market for defence procurement, though, would require a Community-wide consensus on a European security strategy. Such a consensus is a pre-condition to the selection of criteria for the choice of weapon systems.[32] Similarly, as the bounds of the internal market extend into all areas of economic activity, the need for stable monetary conditions becomes more pressing in order to secure a predictable environment for business operations. That implies an attempt to keep exchange rates stable; liberalize capital movements; and reduce national autonomy to conduct macro-economic policy,[33] through the move to monetary union and the creation of a European System of Central Banks. But the Bundesbank is reticent to abandon monetary powers to an unproven entity, while the German public is more than reserved about a European currency substituting for the Deutschmark.[34] Technology policy is hampered by the states' reluctance to provide funds, and by disagreements over their use. Fiscal policy remains subject to the veto, based on the principle of representative democracy whereby there is to be no taxation without representation. The power of this principle is evidenced in the Commission's failure to win support for its proposals to approximate value added and savings tax differentials between the states. France, with Britain, opposed the first in 1988; the Federal Republic ditched the second in early 1989. Not least, the creation of the internal market is hampered by differences over relations with non-members, as exemplified in the inability to agree on the treatment of non-member

[31] SOFRES polls for *Le Monde* showed that 55 per cent were not favourable to 'Europe 1992'. *Le Monde*, 13 May 1989. Repeated polls on German opinion over the past decade show a decline in support for the EC. See Simon Bulmer, William Paterson, *The Federal Republic of Germany and the European Community*, London, Allen and Unwin, 1987, Chapter 5.

[32] I have elaborated on this theme in 'La Communauté Européenne et la Défense de l'Europe', *Studia Diplomatica*, Vol. XLI, No. 3 (1988), pp. 269–279.

[33] See the Padoa–Schioppa report, *Efficacité, Stabilité, Equité*, Paris, Economica, 1987.

[34] 'Interview avec le président de la Bundesbank', *Le Monde*, 23 May 1989.

country firms in access to the Community procurement markets; in the failure to complete the EC automobile markets; or on the intra-EC differences revealed in late 1989 on the matter of the EC's future relation to the German Democratic Republic (GDR). The Federal Republic insisted on its association, or early entry to the EC, once political pluralism had been instituted, following the elections there on 18 March 1990. The problem was resolved by 'East Germany's' disintegration into five Laender, and the extension of the Federal Republic eastwards.

The counterpart to the states' reservations is their being bound in harness with the Commission to achieve the internal market programme. The evolution of the Community's constitutional practice engages them in the process reinforcing the EC's federal dimension, as evidenced by: the expanded area for majority voting; the reinforcement of the European parliament's powers; the growing body of jurisprudence from the European Court of Justice; the possibilities for the Commission under the SEA to deploy its powers of proposition, and of negotiation with non-members; and, not least, the growing importance of the intragovernmental conference as a device to extend the Community's competences. The states seek to shine in the EC firmament, for the benefits they may bring at home; but their pursuit of particular concerns pulls the Community into ever wider areas of policy, requiring the deployment of Community powers and possible further amendments to the Rome Treaty. Expectations are aroused in the business communities of Europe, that may not be deceived with impunity. Lobbying activities grow. Outsider concern of an exclusive drive to union engenders a scramble to influence insiders to speak on their behalf. France does so for the French-speaking African countries; Spain for Latin America; or Britain for Japan. The spirit of spill-over lives.

Trapped in the Community process between their reservations and the widening arena of EC activities, the states have agreed informally to bind themselves to a timetable. Yet '1992' is an open-ended undertaking, introduced in a world polity whose structure is undergoing fundamental changes. It is not the only vision on offer. Gorbachev and the Pope both refer to 'a European Community of the 21st century' whose boundaries stretch into eastern Europe, the Ukraine and European Russia. Prime Minister Thatcher's vision of a Europe of the states, inclusive of the United States, corroborates Gorbachev's definition of Europe as 'a community of sovereign democratic states with a high level of inter-dependence'.[35] Chancellor Kohl declares his goal as the unity of Germany, in a united Europe: 'Our aim', he stated in January 1989, 'is the [EC] European Union as model and keystone of a peace order including the whole of Europe, because—let us not forget: Europe is much more than the European Community.'[36] Gorbachev won Mitterrand's accord,

[35] *Le Monde*, 2 December 1989.
[36] H. Kohl, *op. cit.*, p. 309.

accompanied by Anglo-American reservations, on the holding of a Helsinki conference in 1990 on the future of European security. Official timetables for the 1990s stretch at the outer limit into the next century, inviting the question whether the Europe of the year 2000 will resemble in any way that of 1990.

France's Europe

A driving force behind the new policy is France, formerly the champion of the states' veto right in EC affairs and of national independence within the Atlantic alliance. The constant theme in French policy on Europe is Germany. There have been two formulas. The first sees Germany's defeat and division as an ideal chance to take the political initiative as the central state in Western Europe.[37] Historically, it is predicated on the United States policy of containment. The main preoccupation has been to bind the Federal Republic westwards, accompanied by gusts of anxiety that West Germany may be losing its Western moorings and edging closer to the Soviet Union. This has meant tightening relations with the Atlantic allies in order to ensure the continued presence of the United States in Europe. In the 1950s it was paralleled by efforts to promote federalist institutions within the European Communities, contributing to the initial success of the EC in the early 1960s. The Soviet Union functioned as ideological enemy and objective ally: the rhetoric of the cold war provided the cement for Western policy, while the Soviet Union's military presence in the GDR consecrated Germany's division.

The second formula holds the Federal Republic as the indispensable partner in building a European coalition of states, whose joint cooperation strengthens their negotiating position with non-members without restricting their sovereign rights to pursue independent national policies.[38] The counterpart has been acceptance of the Federal Republic's autonomy in domestic as in foreign policy, and implicit support for its constitutional commitment to achieve national unity. The statist principle is exemplified in the Franco-German Treaty of 1963 that set the mould for the development of inter-governmental cooperation in foreign policy, and for the creation in 1974 of the European Council, involving the heads of state and government directly in EC affairs. This closer Europe could accommodate the multiple ambiguities of Europe in the 1970s. The Federal Republic's *Ostpolitik* was embedded in partial diplomatic accords between the wartime allies; Bonn was the major partner in promoting

---

[37] Guy de Carmoy, *French Foreign Policies, 1944–1968*, University of Chicago Press, 1970.

[38] Edward Kolodziej, *French International Policy Under de Gaulle and Pompidou. The Politics of Grandeur*, Ithaca, Cornell University Press, 1974; Haig Simonian, *The Privileged Partnership: Franco-German Relations in the European Community 1969–84*, Oxford, Clarendon Press, 1985.

European Parliamentary elections, in the launch of the European Monetary System, and in relations with the United States and Japan. But the Federal Republic's non-nuclear status underpinned its psychological reliance on the United States' extended deterrence, while the Helsinki Final Act brought the Soviet Union and eastern European countries into a pan-European diplomatic network.

Germany's changed setting in the 1980s, and French concern about the evolution in German public opinion, has prompted a third variant: France and the Federal Republic are bound in 'a community of fate'.[39] That requires development of the bilateral relationship in the context of the 1963 Treaty and a strengthening of the federalist aspects of the Community, in harness with the states in Council, beyond the context of containment or détente. A return to the first ran the risk of stimulating a German national sentiment of frustration at unfulfilled hopes;[40] a return to the second was impossible, as the ideological competition between the two Europes in the 1970s had presented the party-states with a challenge that they could not match.[41] Their only response to Western pluralism in the early 1980s was one of political repression and economic stagnation. France's new policy on Europe developed empirically, but with a prevalent theme: better to promote the complex interdependencies of Western Europe that have been built up over the past forty years than to allow the nationality principle to become triumphant in Europe and Germany. France's concerns have taken a number of forms: French security policy has moved closer to NATO, without sacrificing the principle of independence in the determination of nuclear weapons policy; successive governments have promoted 'Europe 1992' as the best means to galvanize the French economy, reduce German mercantilism, and bind the Federal Republic westwards; France above all champions the proposal for a European System of Central Banks. All forms hinge on Germany and are therefore conditioned by the changing circumstances affecting Europe.

A prime concern of Moscow remains the prevention of a tightly structured Western European security community. Gorbachev's disarmament campaign, rising in crescendo as Paris, London and Bonn in 1986 and 1987 edged towards organizing a European pillar in the Atlantic alliance, met with initial rejection. But his proposals in February 1987 to dismantle intermediate range missiles in Europe, as separate

---

[39] The expression is Chancellor Kohl's. See Mitterrand, *op. cit*., pp. 104–105. The background to this change in French attitudes, Ingo Kolboom. 'Unsicherheiten in der Deutsch-Französischen Sonderbeziehung', in *Die Internationale Politik: 1983/1984*, München, Oldenbourg, 1986, pp. 146–159.

[40] German public opinion polls consistently recorded a four-fifths support for eventual unity, while registering a single figure belief in its feasibility.

[41] On the structure of competition between the two Europes in the 1970s, Christopher Royen, *Die Sowietische Koexistenzpolitik gegenüber Westeuropa: Voraussetzungen, Ziele, Dilemmata*, Baden-Baden, Nomos Verlag, 1978.

items from discussions on the US and Soviet central arsenals, were listened to attentively in Washington. Pressure was brought to bear on the NATO allies, particularly Bonn, to agree. Kohl reluctantly conceded. Washington then had Bonn renounce part possession of short range nuclear weapons based in Germany. As French and British nuclear weapons were for national use only, and it was clear that the United States willingness to spread a nuclear umbrella over the Federal Republic in the event of a crisis was a fiction, the only way left for Bonn was to seek reinsurance in a new relationship with Moscow. In July 1987 President Weizäcker visited Moscow; the East German leader, Secretary-General Honecker, visited the Federal Republic in September; and by December the Washington accords were signed, opening up the prospect of a Europe after the cold war.

One proposal emanating from the crisis in East–West relations in the early 1980s was to strengthen the European pillar in the Atlantic alliance. European governments would be seen to be more responsible for their collective security by their public opinions, and less vulnerable to the changes in the climate of relations between the United States and the Soviet Union. A mutual opening of arms markets, and more joint procurement, would reduce the burden of military spending. This was the spirit in which the 1983 Stuttgart European Council's Solemn Declaration on 'the economic and security aspects' of EC affairs came to be included in the SEA. The impetus to forge closer defence ties was reinforced in 1986–87, when Washington and Moscow edged towards their agreement to remove intermediary weapons. France succeeded in resuscitating the West European Union (WEU)—a somnolent appendage of the Atlantic alliance—when its seven members produced a joint statement in October 1987 entitled a 'Platform on European Security Issues'. The platform reiterates the principles of NATO strategy in its emphasis on nuclear deterrence. Two months later the Washington Treaty undermined the psychological support in Germany for deterrence: the withdrawal of intermediary weapons from German soil in three years left very short range weapons, whose use would devastate Germany in the event of war. Spain and Portugal entered the WEU in 1988.

Fears of German neutralism have conspired with the changes in the nuclear policies of the powers to modify the style of French security policy. The substance of national policy has not been altered.[42] Mitterrand backed the Kohl government in 1983 on the installation of Cruise and Pershing missiles, in the event of a failure in Western negotiations with the Soviet Union for a balanced arms reduction. The military provisions in the 1963 Franco–German Treaty were revived, and given shape in January 1988 with the setting up of a Franco–German Defence and Security Council to be chaired by the French President and the German

[42] See Fondation pour les Etudes de Défense Nationale, *La Politique de Défense: Textes et Documents*. Présentation par Dominique David, Paris, 1989.

Chancellor and to be attended by their defence ministers and chiefs-of-staff. A 4,200-man Franco–German brigade has been constituted. But they have scarcely flourished. Franco–German relations have been deprived of their post-war anti-Soviet cement, as the party-states have been swept away in eastern Europe and the Warsaw Pact has become a ghost of its former self. Competing national industrial interests have militated against any move beyond partial collaboration on new joint projects. Above all, Mitterrand has moved back since the Washington Treaty to the purest rendering of de Gaulle's nuclear doctrine. 'The mission of France', he declared in October 1988, 'is not to assure the protection of other European countries.'[43] The creation of a European pillar within the Atlantic alliance would have to wait until 1992–93, and the completion of the internal market.

Successive French governments since 1981 have seen the European Community as the means to galvanize the French economy,[44] to open up German markets, and to bind the Federal Republic westwards. As expressed in a contemporary foreign policy report, 'European integration has become a *sine qua non* condition for a *modus vivendi* with the German question.'[45] For France this spelt a major change in policy direction. French domestic and foreign economic policies were to be made more compatible with those of the Federal Republic, whose position as the determinant of Western European policies and performances has been confirmed in the interest rate war with the United States in the early 1980s. 'In the EC, no national macroeconomic policy may diverge upwards from the average without long term damage to the national interest.'[46] This meant acceptance of the growth rate permitted by German economic policy, while lifting domestic constraints on corporate performance. In 1984, the government began to deregulate financial markets in order to reduce corporate reliance on bank debt; the privatization of state properties then extended the capital base of French corporations and strengthened the ability to deploy and ally on an international scale.[47] In parallel, President Mitterrand announced France's renewed emphasis on EC integration in the French EC Presidency of that year, and cleared the way for the '1992' strategy by setting the stage for Spain's entry.

[43] *Ibid.*, pp. 316–326.

[44] 'Memorandum sur la Relance de la Communauté Européenne', Bulletin des CE, No. 11, 1981, pp. 100–109; also 'Quelle Stratégie pour la France dans les Années Quatre-vingt', La Documentation Française, Paris, 1983, pp. 131–163. In September 1983 the French government presented to the other member states a document, 'Une Nouvelle Etape pour l'Europe: un espace commun de l'industrie et de la recherche', Europe Documents, No. 1274, *Agence Europe*, 16 September 1983.

[45] Kaiser, Merlini, de Montbrial *et al.*, *La Communauté Européenne: déclin ou renouveau*, Paris, IFRI, 1983, p. 59.

[46] Michel Albert, *Un Pari Pour l'Europe*, Paris, Seuil, 1983, p. 64.

[47] Philip Cerny, 'The "Little Big Bang" in Paris: financial market deregulation in a dirigiste system', *European Journal of Political Research* 17 (1989), pp. 169–192.

An EC compact to negotiate the reduction of non-tariff barriers offers an additional opportunity for France to deal with its principal economic weaknesses. The persistent complaint of the past decade has been the deterioration in the bilateral trade deficit with the Federal Republic, accounting for over 140 per cent of the total deficit with the rest of the world.[48] This is aggravated by the fact that the industrial sector became a net importer in 1987. Arms exports have fallen off, along with oil prices and the ability of Gulf countries to buy. Weakness on the external accounts is underlined by the slight decline in world market shares to around 5 per cent, compared to the Federal Republic's 11.5 per cent. French capital goods production covers half of industrial final demand.

The EC internal market policy, emphasizing the fragmentation of markets as the common cause of Eurostagnation, offers an easing of market access, through the EC's more flexible policy on standards; its help in contesting procurement markets; the financial services' programme easing of the protectionist devices inherent to national corporate finances; or the parallel development of an EC transport policy.[49] In all these areas, the Federal Republic's 'social market' practice has buttressed protectionist practices. 'Europe 1992' acts as a stimulus to liberalization policies in Bonn.[50] Bilateral channels provide additional means to negotiate the eventual opening of German energy markets to French nuclear-generated electricity; the development of high-speed trains; or the highly contentious work-sharing involved in the Airbus consortium. The French presidency in late 1989 took notable pride, after the Economics Ministry in Bonn overrode anti-cartel authority objections to the creation of the armaments giant, Daimler–Benz–MBB, in the creation of a more effective EC competition law. The Commission, from September 1990 on, has sole power to block large Community mergers between companies with a combined turnover of 5 billion ecu, where 250 million ecu of each company are in the EC.[51] Brussels powers in this crucial area are likely to be augmented in the future.

Yet France's fling with liberal market ideas remains partial. The state élites continue to occupy the senior echelons of government and business. Managements have built defences against hostile takeovers. Nationalized companies account for 30 per cent GNP. Mitterrand, since 1988, has stalled the 1986–88 conservative government's drive to privatize. The

---

[48] Figures in. Bilan de 1988: l'Expansion Inattendue, *L'Année Politique, Economique et Sociale en France, 1988*, Paris, Editions du Moniteur, 1989, pp. 493–494.

[49] A federalist view on the internal market as requiring a transfer of powers to the Community in order to mitigate national mercantilisms in Dominique Bocquet, Philippe Delleur, *Génération Europe*, Paris, François Bourin, 1989; a jaundiced view that the nationality principle will win, Alain Minc, *La Grande Illusion*, Paris, Grasset, 1989.

[50] Kenneth Dyson, 'Economic Policy', Simon Bulmer, 'The European Dimension', in Gordon Smith, William Paterson, Peter Merkl, *Developments in West German Politics*, London, Macmillan, 1989.

[51] 'EC ministers hand Brussels the power to vet large mergers', *Financial Times*, 22 December 1989.

corporatist agricultural sector accounts for about one quarter of total exports, while large swathes of services benefit from tax breaks or special interest rates. The traditional concern to moderate the pace of change imposed through free markets is evidenced in the French position on the EC's external trade policy. French diplomacy regularly takes the lead in Brussels as champion of protectionist stances in international trade negotiations: most notably, the French, with Italian and Spanish support, resist Commission proposals for an EC-wide quota on Japanese automobiles against an abandonment of national quotas; a similar alignment has recurred in the discussions on procurement, or banking, with France arguing for reciprocal access to non-member markets in exchange for the opening of EC markets. France's dream of a protectionist coalition including the Federal Republic is as recurrent as it is illusive.

Finally, France's growing weakness compared to the Federal Republic is expressed in the decline of the franc, relative to the Deutschmark. Following the devaluation of the franc in August 1969, a first attempt was made at monetary union in the EC. National autonomy would be restricted by a joint commitment to fixed exchange rates. This would require close coordination between governments in the setting of budgetary policy. An initial attempt in 1970–73 ended in failure, when divergent national economic policy conditions and the US dollar policy conspired to move the world towards a system of floating exchange rates. France suspended the link with the Deutschmark in January 1974, with successive attempts to repeg at a new rate. The opportunity came in the winter of 1977–78 when the Federal Republic faced US and British demands for reflation, revaluation or both. German industrialist concern to preserve price competitivity on world markets met French farm demands for stable exchange rates within the EC as an essential element of the annual price review, setting EC producer prices.[52] The result was the launching of the European Monetary System (EMS). It amounted to an organization of stable, but adjustable, exchange rates. The original commitment to move to a pooling of central bank reserves was postponed *sine die* in 1980.

France's motive for joining essentially amounted to acceptance of the argument that a common discipline on exchange rates would impose a convergence of domestic economic policy on German preferences. But the Bundesbank moved abruptly in February 1981 to extremely tight monetary policies, and condemned President Mitterrand's moderate reflation of 1981–83 to failure. Mitterrand's crucial decision was to keep the franc within the existing exchange rate constraint. The Bundesbank became Europe's *de facto* central bank, leaving other central banks with little alternative than that of negotiating occasional adjustments, with the

[52] See Marcello de Cecco, 'The European Monetary System and National Interests', in *The Political Economy of European Integration* (ed. P. Guerreri, P. Padoan), London, Harvester Wheatsheaf, 1989, pp. 85–99.

burden falling on the weaker currency country. German business benefited by the permanent undervaluation of the Deutschmark, a growing trade surplus, and low interest rates. Other European economies were tied to the growth path of the German economy, with a 1 per cent GNP average from 1981–1987. The Finance Ministry and the Bundesbank stonewalled against demands from the United States and OECD Europe for reflation. The turning point came in 1987–88: counter-cyclical actions by the leading Western central banks following the stock market crash of October 1987 flooded cash into the international circuits, kept interest rates down, and galvanized the world economy. Oil prices were on a downward trend. In 1988, the German and EC economies lifted to growth rates of 4–5 per cent. In June, a deal was cut at the European Council at Hanover whereby France and Italy agreed conditionally to liberalize all capital movements by 1 July 1990; and Germany acquiesced in a mandate for a report to study the means for achieving monetary union.

France has thus emerged as the champion of monetary union. The idea is simple: the best way to reduce policy dependence on the Bundesbank is to join it. It is an indication of Mitterrand's determination to give the EC, and France, the means of its ambitions for 'Europe 1992'. His horizons give an idea of his agenda. Re-elected in 1988 with a large majority, Mitterrand's mandate runs until 1995. General elections are dated for 1993. The internal market, and the deregulatory policies accompanying it, are to remain the new imperative for France, along with the creation of a European 'social space', environmental policies, and monetary union.[53] A report, presented at the Madrid European Council in June 1989, proposed monetary union in three stages, with a federal scheme for a European System of Central Banks (ESCB).[54] At the Strasburg European Council of December 1989, an accord was reached whereby the EC pledged support for the German people to 'refind unity through free self-determination', and the German government agreed that a new inter-governmental conference—in the manner of 1985—be held prior to the German elections in 1990, with a view to incorporating monetary union into the Treaties.[55] That, in turn, means a reinforcement of the federal dimensions in EC institutions.

EC federalism, in short, has grown in attraction as a strategy for France. Nuclear weapons may not be shared; indeed, France's national nuclear policy keeps Bonn at arm's length on matters of European security. The internal market, enacted through the Brussels mechanisms, promises to attenuate German mercantilism. But the thrust of French policy is to take the royal way to union through the creation of a European central bank. The principal factor prompting France into this championship of the

[53] La Documentation Française, le Dixième Plan, 'La France, l'Europe: Le Plan, 1992'.
[54] EC Commission, 'Comité Pour l'Etude de l'Union Economique et Monétaire', Rapport sur l'union économique et monétaire dans la Communauté Européenne.
[55] 'Les Douze acceptent que le peuple allemand retrouve son identité', Le Monde, 10–11 December 1989.

Community's development is the dynamics of change between German domestic politics and Europe's setting that have gathered force over the past decade. Only a more federal Europe, with stronger central institutions, may contain an increasingly powerful Germany.

Germany and Europe

The three major policies for the 1990s—Gorbachev's *perestroika*, Bush's 'new Atlanticism', and '1992'—all converge on Germany, altering its domestic political balances and international setting. Common to all three is the changing structure of world politics, evidenced by the rise of Japan and of Germany. Japan provides the EC with a continued inspiration to build a continental economy, and is pushing the United States to reach a settlement in Europe, thereby releasing resources for non-military uses. An end to the cold war brings with it the prospect of a single Germany; it is only through the equal curtailment of sovereignties in a strengthened EC that the western (and eastern) continental neighbours of a united Germany would feel comfortable.

The promise of disarmament from 1986 on, coupled with the first moves to decompression in eastern Europe, found Germany particularly receptive. The cold war tensions of the early 1980s had alerted public opinion to the risks inherent to NATO's deterrent policy, based on the threat of nuclear retaliation. Ideas to move NATO to a defensive conventional strategy had come to be widely shared, given fears of Germany as a potential nuclear battlefield. Equally, it was noted that the Washington Treaty meant the removal of nuclear weapons that the Soviet Union feared, while leaving 'battlefield' nuclear weapons, whose use spelt the devastation of Germany.[56] Yet the British and Americans argued that their troops could not be expected to fight for German freedoms without nuclear cover, while the potential enemy enjoyed massive superiority in the European region: 'no nukes', the argument ran, 'no troops'.[57] Germany, in short, was no longer defendable on conditions to which the allies could agree; NATO was an alliance in search of a new purpose. The embarrassment was evident at the NATO summits of March 1988 and May 1989. Chancellor Kohl conceded eventual modernization of NATO battlefield weapons, if progress was not recorded in the conventional arms talks at Vienna. With their rapid progress of the talks in the course of 1989, and the collapse of the East German regime in November, their modernization is postponed *sine die*. The national question has moved to the forefront of German politics; NATO armies bunched on German soil

[56] Senior civil servants and leading party political personalities felt abandoned twice by Washington: in the 1977–78 neutron bomb affair, and over the intermediary nuclear weapons, by President Reagan. See Joseph Rovan's introduction to H. Kohl, *op. cit.*, p. 32.

[57] International Institute for Strategic Studies (IISS), *Strategic Survey, 1988–1989*, Oxford, Nuffield Press, 1989, pp. 79–82.

have lost a clearly definable enemy, and run the risk of being perceived as occupation forces rather than as allies.

Fortuitously, the Washington Treaty of December 1987 was followed by the Federal Republic's tenure of the EC's sixth month rotating Presidency.[58] Here was a chance to reassure the Community member states that the Federal Republic was firmly anchored to the West. A successful German Presidency, it was hoped, could help revive enthusiasm in the Federal Republic for the EC. As Western Europe's industrial powerhouse, the Federal Republic had much to gain. About 75 per cent of exports are with Western Europe, whence comes about 95 per cent of its trade surplus. The Deutschmark is Europe's lead currency. The Federal Republic had championed Spain's entry to the EC and the EC's internal market policy. It had a vested interest in the creation of a European union.

The German Presidency of early 1988 proved decisive in the launching of 'Europe 1992'.[59] It marked the transition under way whereby Germany's political influence in Europe and the world is coming to match its economic eminence. Bonn was instrumental in negotiating a long term EC budget package, satisfying the demands of Spain for more funds to the poorer regions. Bonn thereby increased its contributions to the EC budget by 40 to 50 per cent, underlining its role as Europaymaster; it pushed through a spate of market opening measures; the German standards institute (DIN) is the main player in the EC's policy for standard harmonization; the German trade union confederation (DGB) provides the main support for the EC's 'Social Charter', aimed to protect acquired worker rights in a more unified market; the German public's sensitivity to environmental issues make Bonn a champion of high standards in the EC, as well as in other fora. The Bundesbank is Western Europe's *de facto* central bank. This resurgent EC under the Presidency of a more assertive Federal Republic burst on the world's attention in June 1988: on 13 June the EC Finance Ministers decided to move to liberalization of capital movements; at the seven power summit of advanced industrial states, held in Toronto on 20 June the EC resisted US pressure to 'eliminate' farm subsidies; at the European Council of Hanover on 27 June the EC political leaders appointed a committee to study a move to monetary union.

The Federal Republic's EC Presidency also recorded a triumph in securing mutual recognition of the EC and the Council for Mutual Economic Assistance (COMECON), set up in 1949 as an equivalent to Western European integration.[60] The two bodies recognized each other,

---

[58] For an assessment prior to the German Presidency, Wolfgang Wessels, Elfriede Regelsberger, *The Federal Republic of Germany and the European Community: The Presidency and Beyond*, Bonn, Europa Union Verlag, 1988.

[59] Peter Hort, 'Eine Bilanz der deutschen EG-Präsidentschaft', *Europa-Archiv* 15 (1988), pp. 421–428.

[60] Jacques Bel, 'Les relations entre la communauté et le conseil d'assistance économique mutuelle', *Revue du Marché Commun* 318 (1988), pp. 313–316.

but the EC's status was underlined by the allowance for COMECON member states to make bilateral trade deals with the EC. The Federal Republic, with Italy, is the country that stands to gain most. Chancellor Kohl's October 1988 visit to Moscow highlighted the economic relationship. For the Soviet Union, Germany and the EC provide 70 per cent of hard currency earnings; Germany is seen as Moscow's key technology partner; its banks have the resources to help in the necessary economic restructuring of eastern Europe. But historical resentments and revolutionary conditions in the East draw sharp limits around what the Federal Republic may do alone; the EC, not a solitary Federal Republic, has the moral authority to condition each newly formulated accord for trade concessions and aid packages to political reforms. The result is that the Community's trade and aid functions have expanded extensively into eastern Europe, and the Soviet Union. They have been reinforced by the decision of the advanced industrial powers at their Paris summit meeting in July 1989 to accept Chancellor Kohl's proposal to give the Commission the task of coordinating western aid for eastern Europe. Besides accords with Hungary and Poland, in November 1989 the EC signed a 10-year trade agreement with the Soviet Union whereby all quotas on imports are to be removed by 1995. The broad aim is to open EC markets to allow the former party-states to earn hard currencies. But competition from low labour cost neighbours will no doubt generate protectionist pressures in the Community member states.

Germany's EC Presidency prompted anxiety in Washington and Tokyo about 'Fortress Europe'.[61] An EC united front, corresponding to the tough retaliatory powers granted the US administration under the new Trade Act, heralded severe transatlantic trade clashes. But Washington's redefinition of relations with Europe has altered the terms of debate: there is the realization that the EC is twice as large an export market for the United States as Japan; that US corporations within the EC stand to benefit by the EC's internal market policy; and that Western Europe has become a crucial partner in opening eastern Europe, and eventually the Soviet Union, to pluralist politics and market systems. In this scheme, the US institutional vision of Atlantic relations—Bush's 'new Atlanticism'—is of a NATO serving as a forum to develop and implement arms agreements; and of an EC, reinforced through the signing of a Treaty with the United States.[62]

For Japan, a resurgent Europe is altogether more problematic. Japan poses European corporations their most severe challenge. The constant revaluation of the yen, and massive investment in capital equipment, have

[61] See, for example, 'Who's Afraid of 1992?', *Newsweek*, 31 October 1988; 'Fortress Europe', *International Management*, December 1988; Jean-Pierre Lehmann, 'Japan and a New World Order: Implications and an Agenda for Europe', *European Affairs* 1/89 (Spring), pp. 41–49.

[62] 'Washington propose de conclure un traité avec la Communauté Européenne', *Le Monde*, 14 December 1989.

moved Japanese manufacturers into headlong rivalry with their German competitors. Hence, one source of German industrial support for a European economic space from which to strike back at Japanese rivals, and a *de facto* interest in the opening up of eastern Europe as a source of cheap, and skilled, labour. German, with Dutch and French corporations, have prompted the Community to develop a more effective armoury of trade policy instruments, such as anti-dumping procedures and local content regulations. That, in turn, has generated pre-emptive inward investment by Japanese corporations, especially into the United Kingdom whose industrial base has been gravely weakened since entry to the EC. The promise is of a Japanese–British industrial alliance that by 1995 has regenerated British-based manufacturing through the expansion of Japanese-owned plants.[63] But the prospect of a US–EC treaty and of Western Europe's central role in eastern Europe has lent new urgency for Japan to define relations on a more assured basis. Prime Minister Kaifu's ten-nation visit to Europe in January 1990 provides a first step: Japan is to be a major provider of financial resources to the emerging pluralist states of eastern Europe. But the success of its engagement depends on cooperative relations with the EC.

The Scandinavian countries and Finland, as well as Switzerland and Austria, are closely tied by industrial, trade and currency relationships into the European economic space, whose hub is Germany. They, too, are pulled towards the Community by the dynamics driving 'Europe 1992'.[64] The EC is their major market. They have impeccable credentials for membership. They are European, pluralist and they have market economies. They enjoy close institutional relations with the Community. They participate in the EC technology projects, and in the EC standards organizations. But they have tended to shy away from membership. One reason is that domestic regulations have formed an essential part of political bargains struck in the early twentieth century between national producer interests, on consensual management of the economy. Alignment on EC regulations spells their unravelling. Only Austria, in July 1989, has drawn the conclusion and opted to lodge its candidature for the EC. Commission policy has been to postpone prospective EC candidatures until after 1993. Another reason is that Moscow in the past opposed the neutrals in EFTA seeking to join the EC, with its ambitions to develop into a tightly knit political, even military, entity. But with Moscow's grip on eastern Europe weakened, and the Warsaw Pact and COMECON mere ghosts of their former selves, Moscow's veto has lifted. Indeed, the former party-states are lining up to join Western European institutions, such as the Council of Europe, and anticipate associate status, even membership

[63] Chris Dillow, *A Return to a Trade Surplus? The Impact of Japanese Investment on the UK*, Nomura Research Institute, London, August 1989.

[64] Helen Wallace, Wolfgang Wessels, 'Toward a New Partnership: the EC and EFTA in the wider Western Europe', RIIA Occasional Paper 28, London, 1989.

in the Community. With such a perspective, the EFTA countries are pressing for an EC–EFTA Treaty by the end of 1990. The hope is to create a European Economic Space (EES)[65] composed of 18 sovereign states, with compatible domestic regulations, and comprising 350 million people. Success in the talks implies extensive domestic adjustments in the EFTA member states; failure of the talks means that the Commission could be flooded by a spate of membership candidacies.

The central novelty in Europe, deriving from the changes in the world balance, is the prospect of German unity. That prospect is of a nation of 80 million people, with a dynamic economy equivalent to about 60 per cent of Japan's but stuck in the heart of the continent. It was endorsed in June 1989 by President Bush's invitation to the Federal Republic as a 'partner in leadership', and by his expression of US support for the right of the German people to self-determination. It was implicit in Gorbachev's 'common Europe home', predicated on self-determination and non-intervention; the Soviet leader's readiness to allow the collapse of the East German regime, and have free elections held there in March 1990; and the Soviet Union's longer term interest in economic relations with the Federal Republic, as expressed in his June 1989 visit to the Federal Republic. Germany's right, etched into the United Nations Charter, is engraved in the Basic Law of the Federal Republic, and reiterated by Western leaders as a promise at the heart of the Alliance. It was the central feature of Chancellor Kohl's Ten Point plan for German unity, announced in the Bundestag on 28 November 1989.[66] 'The way is open', the Chancellor declared, 'for an overcoming of Europe's division and thereby that of our Fatherland.' The Chancellor outlined his policy for inner-German relations; for the creation of a 'confederation or federation' of Germany, 'soon after free elections'; his support for the EC as a 'pole of attraction', that must open to the GDR and to other eastern European countries. 'Only in this sense may the EC become the foundation for a truly global European unification.' A central part in Europe's 'new architecture' is ascribed to the Helsinki process. The need for further disarmament measures was presented as serving the 'condition of peace in Europe, within which the German people in free self-determination may acquire again their unity'. 'Reunification, that means the return to Germany's state unity, remains the federal government's goal.'

This important statement further accelerated the political and diplomatic momentum in Europe. Kohl had consulted neither his coalition partners, nor the allies. He had not included in his Ten Points any reference to Foreign Minister Genscher's statement to the United Nations General Assembly that the Poles 'may be assured that their right to live in secure frontiers will not be placed in jeopardy by German territorial claims'. The wording was included in a Bundestag resolution, adopted by

[65] 'EC and EFTA go back to drawing board', *Financial Times*, 18 December 1989.
[66] *Die Welt*, 29 November 1989.

400 (for) and 33 (against) on 8 November—the day before the Berlin Wall was breeched. Kohl thereby fostered allied suspicion, which in turn kindled comment in Germany to the effect that the Western allies were less than prepared to live up to their commitment under the 1955 German Treaty to support German rights to self-determination. Differences were patched up by a successful Franco–German meeting that set the agenda for the EC Strasburg summit of December. As mentioned, the summit pledged EC support for German rights, against German agreement to hold an EC intergovernmental conference before the end of 1990. Meanwhile, Gorbachev's initial enthusiasm for a dissolution of the blocs waned as events accelerated in Germany.[67] Western allied support for a gradual approach to reunification was confirmed at the NATO summit meeting at Brussels in December. 'German unification should occur', Bush was quoted as stating, 'in the context of Germany's continued commitment to NATO and to an increasingly integrated European Community.'[68] The official Soviet position drew the line at any precipitate change in Europe's structure, and the allied position was to support it. The danger was therefore that Germany's right for self-determination be seen to be sacrificed on the altar of European stability.

The symbiosis of the two Germanies has occurred in 1990, Germany's election year. There are four regional elections—one already won by the SPD in the Saarland—and a general election for December. The key elections were for 18 March in East Germany, and they were taken as a guide to the general elections earmarked for 2 December. Given the flood of emigrants from the former 'East Germany', and the resentments created in the Federal Republic, the political parties were desperate to improve conditions as soon as possible in the five Laender. One after another political leaders abandoned gradualism. Calls for patience were undermined by the speed of events and by the scramble between the parties to position themselves for the forthcoming elections. Kohl's fishing for votes among the right electorate furthermore conditioned his public position on foreign policy, notably his ambiguity on the Oder-Neisse line. The SPD has striven not to leave the national position, as in 1918, to the conservatives. German business is lining up to reconstruct the economy.

Germany's symbiosis is also transforming Europe. After Kohl's Ten Point speech, the Soviet position was that the two Germanies, and their alliances, must stay in place. But the Warsaw Pact lost its ideological substance as the party-states collapsed. Shevardnadze duly proposed German unification against neutrality. In late January 1990, the Soviet delegate to the Vienna talks stated that the Soviet Union was prepared to withdraw all troops from East Germany in five years, on condition that the NATO forces withdraw from the Federal Republic. Finally, the East

[67] 'M. Gorbachev compte sur l'appui de M. Bush', *Le Monde*, 3–4 December 1989.
[68] 'Nato agrees its approach to German reunification', *Financial Times*, 5 December 1989.

German leader, Mr. Modrow, proposed on 30 January a move to a united federal Germany, once the two Germanies had been militarily neutralized. The Poles, with their nightmare of a neutral and unattached Germany, opposed any change in Europe's military structures as premature. The German coalition parties and the SPD, while welcoming Moscow's support for unity, affirmed NATO's position that Germany's unification was not exchangeable for neutrality. Nonetheless, fears were expressed that a change in Germany's status, notably a unified Germany in NATO, could unseat Gorbachev.[69]

With Germany's unification imminent, the prospect is opened of a wider Europe of democratic sovereign states cooperating together. That Europe, in Gorbachev's words, is to be 'a community of democratic sovereign states with a high level of interdependence, of frontiers easily accessible and open to the exchange of technologies and ideas, to contacts on a grand scale between the peoples'.[70] It is expressed in the lengthening list of countries with guest status attached to the 23 nation Council of Europe; the discussions in the Community about trade and aid concessions to former party-states as they acquire political and market freedoms; and in the French support for Gorbachev's idea of a Helsinki conference for 1990 to start thinking about a European Community of the 21st century. Its sudden emergence, though, has revealed the differences among EC member states about Germany.

The Federal Republic's demands for East Germany's association with, or entry to, the EC met with frank reserve. France and the Benelux countries used East Germany as a pretext to postpone *sine die* the intended Schengen accord with the Federal Republic on the free cross frontier movement of people. The hitch was that they were unwilling to grant the Federal Republic that the GDR is not another foreign country. On the EC issue, Bonn pushed for the GDR to be treated as another candidate or member state. Holland objected to bringing the GDR into the EC ahead of Austria, while Belgium switched to championing Austria's early entry. The British Prime Minister was for no enlargement before 1993, and the French were muted. The change in the Soviet position for German unity in January 1990 implies that the former 'East Germany' may enter the EC as a series of Laender in an extended Federal Republic. That would require modifications to the Basic Law, in an all-German parliament; a rearrangement of the weighted vote in a united Germany's favour in the EC; and East Germany's inclusion in the EC regional policy as a backward zone. The advantage would be that East Germany would come under the internal market legislation, so that

---

[69] 'Thatcher says Germans should slow any move toward reunification', *Wall Street Journal: Europe*, 26 January 1990. Notably, the moves on German unity in Moscow coincided with Gorbachev's manoeuvre to shift the basis of his power from party to state.

[70] 'Gorbachev souhaite réunir "des 1990" les 35 membres de la conférence pan-européenne', *Le Monde*, 2 December 1989.

non-German firms could benefit by access to business there.[71] There would also be one German vote, and not two. A wider Europe beckons as a means to dilute Germany's prospective weight in Europe.

Germany's move to unity not only opens the prospect of the EC's widening before completion of the internal market programme: it fundamentally alters Europe's post-war security structures. NATO is fast losing an enemy. Yet NATO demands East Germany's inclusion. If this is to be acceptable to Moscow, NATO must become explicitly Moscow's partner in ensuring European security. One way is to continue along the path to troop reductions on both sides. But that scarcely answers the question of how to incorporate Germany into an all-European peace order, as Kohl desires. Another is for a minimalist NATO alongside a federally strengthened EC.[72] A minimalist NATO means few troops on German soil, a major reduction of nuclear weapons placed on the continent, but an integrated command structure to fulfil NATO's security-sustaining tasks, and to be ready—in the event of a change of direction in Moscow. It reassures Moscow, facilitating a minimalist defence for the Warsaw Pact. A united Germany is bound into a federalist EC, where it is large, but only one among many. This civilian power extends its foreign policy reach into 'the political and economic' domains of security policy, as outlined in the 1987 Single European Act. Not least, such an EC—in a new form of relation with the United States—would both incorporate Germany and form the cornerstone of a wider Europe, including Russia.

Conclusion

The two visions of 'Europe 1992' and a 'common European home', launched simultaneously in 1986, entail two competing strategies for Germany and Europe. France seeks to bind the Federal Republic into a strengthened Community; the Soviet Union has prevented a tightly structured Western European defence organization. This represents the main dividend from allowing political pluralism and market mechanisms to be built on the ruins of the communist party-states in eastern Europe. The West is deprived of an integrating enemy, but the resultant symbiosis between the two Germanies is creating a new Europe, eventually centred in Berlin: eventually, because the contours of Gorbachev's 'common home' may be only dimly perceived. The contours are dim in eastern Europe, where the future must be built on a pre-1945 history, ridden by national and ethnic rivalries, and on a post-1945 nightmare of police states and monopoly power. They are even dimmer in the Soviet Union, whose leaders must invent a new legitimacy if they are to hold together the Tsarist empire after the collapse of 'real scientific socialism'. They are

---

[71] Christian Deubner, 'Une perspective communautaire', *Le Monde*, 2 February 1990.
[72] Ian Davidson, 'A new alliance for a new Europe', *Financial Times*, 2 February 1990.

clearest, by contrast, in Western Europe, where the patient construction over forty-five years of a complex polity provides a sound basis for an uncertain future.

The Western European future might be uncertain, but it is not entirely unknown. European affairs are laden with official or proposed timetables stretching into the future. Most of the major leaders' terms of office stretch to 1992–93, with Mitterrand sailing through to 1995. Kohl is the exception, with 1990 as election year for eastern and central Europe. In East–West relations, a possible 1990 treaty on conventional arms at Vienna sets the stage for a redefinition of NATO's role as the Western forum for disarmament talks and verification procedures. The Warsaw Pact, like COMECON, is now a ghost, though a banquet is laid in 1990 for the 35 signatory states of the Helsinki Final Act to discuss the future of pan-Europe. This rapid evolution in 'the common European home' has prompted France to start EC talks on monetary union before the German general elections at the end of 1990. The Germans are likely to demand an increase in the federal powers of the EC institutions.[73] The date bandied about for monetary union is 1993, after near completion of the detailed agendas for the internal market. Before then, the EFTA states hope for a treaty with the EC to create a European Economic Space. A US–EC treaty would have to be in place for the Republicans to take the political credit in the 1992 general elections. Mitterrand has dated 1993, and the completion of the internal market, as the time to start considering a European pillar in the Atlantic alliance.

There are no certainties that the powerful trends towards a more united Western Europe will win out. Europe stays differentiated within, and in relations between its component states and outsiders. National institutions, traditions and interests remain vigorous, as exemplified by the states' resistance to abandon powers in tax, money, or defence. In each one of the member states there are strong currents of resistance to 'Europe 1992'. They could be readily stoked by ambitious projects for union, threatening to undermine national identities. Major divisions between EC member states plague the development of foreign and commercial policies towards the rest of the world. National currencies ensure that each state is affected in particular ways by oil price movements, or by speculative shifts affecting exchange rate alignments. It has yet to be shown that the Deutschmark's replacement of the former Ostmark is compatible with the difficult move to monetary union in the EC. NATO, one of the pillars of the post-war Western European system, and a centre point for US influence, is losing its old *raison d'être*. NATO aims to incorporate East Germany, while the Federal Republic seeks to bring East Germany into the EC as a part of itself. A minimalist NATO may not be enough to

---

[73] See Kohl's speech in Bonn on the occasion of the hundredth anniversary of Jean Monnet, 9 November 1988; H. Kohl, *op. cit.*, pp. 199–217. He pledged that the 1994 elections would be to a European parliament with 'greatly extended' powers.

reassure Germany's neighbours, while a nationalist Germany could take exception to the presence of any foreign troops on its soil. Germany united may be predominant in an EC that is deeper, wider or both. Germany's political primacy in Europe is coming to match its economic leadership. The irreversible and accelerating inner-German dynamic towards a single German polity accentuates the trend. A multitude of problems attend the elaboration of a pan-European peace system, ending the distinctions between the five Europes, inherited from the early post-war years.

But the probabilities are higher in the immediate future for a Western European union than for a closer pan-European association of states, concerned to ensure peace and to promote trade. Gorbachev's vision of a 'common European home' has yet to be filled out with a pluralist and market content. Acceptance of German unity, under terms yet to be clarified, must be reconciled with the need for a stable European structure within which the German, eastern European and Russian transitions may be played out. The risk for the Western allies was that they sacrifice the German right for self-determination on the altar of European stability. The Western European nightmare is of nationalism as a liberating force sweeping into Germany from eastern Europe, in combination with Japan's example, to recreate an assertive Germany with hegemonial ambitions— close, large, neutral and possibly nuclear—in the heart of Europe. Gorbachev's acceptance of German unity opens the way for a Western incorporation of Germany, in the EC and reformed NATO, in a way not threatening to Russia. As the December 1989 Strasburg EC summit statement declared, German self-determination is to procede 'in the perspective of Community integration'. Furthermore, it received the backing at Strasburg of eleven out of twelve heads of government or state. Such a union is likely to have five dimensions: a strengthening of parliamentary and Commission powers; a move to monetary union, and perhaps some agreement on a European System of Central Banks; the internal market policy; a European pillar in an Atlantic alliance, where the military dimension has lost its former salience; and an EC that extends its foreign policy and security functions, in conjunction with NATO, as the cornerstone for a wider Europe.

The crucial issue determining Europe's emerging shape is timing. The EC could be blown off its internal market course as well, by an irresistible rush to widen, rather than to deepen. That rush may be controllable to the extent that East Germany is merged into an enlarged Federal Republic. Germany's desire for unity is thereby met; Prime Minister Thatcher's interest in completing the internal market first is met; Mitterrand's desire to deepen the EC first is met. The coming EC package—if it matures— must therefore string together German unity, the internal market, money, and parliamentary powers. It is a tall order. The timing was spelt out in President Mitterrand's 1990 New Year's message.[74] The new Europe is to

[74] *Le Monde*, 2 January 1990.

be achieved in two stages. In the first stage, the EC is to be 'the pole of attraction' around which the twelve, and then a future wider Europe is to gather. The second stage is to see the emergence of a 'European confederation in the real sense of the term, which will associate all the States of our continent in a common and permanent organization of exchanges, of peace and of security'. The United States will be allied to the first on a new basis by 1992–93; the Soviet Union will be included in the second sometime in the mid- to late 1990s. But that depends on the unpredictable outcome of Russia's second revolution.

So the conclusion is that as Germany moves to unity, Berlin becomes first the eastern outpost of Western Europe. In the longer term, Berlin and a united Germany have the opportunity of becoming the centre of a pluralist and reconciled pan-Europe.

CONVERGENCE OR A PERSISTENT DIVERSITY OF NATIONAL POLITICS?

HANS KASTENDIEK*

IN many discussions of 1992 it has been taken for granted that the introduction of the single market as a major step towards economic integration will also have a significant impact on national politics in Western Europe. The shift of authoritative decision-making from national arenas to transnational institutions and mechanisms will establish a new power centre to which the member states of the Community have to adjust, however reluctantly in some cases. Subjected to agreed policy objectives (enforceable from above) and responding to increasingly common economic and social pressures from their domestic fields of action (i.e. from below), they will have to apply similar principles of policy-operation and, for this purpose, to adapt their structures of social and political organization. In reaction to the economic competition tightened up by the introduction of the single market, this process will often take the form of a cross-national imitation of those policy-styles and political structures which have proved or promise to be most effective. The combined effects of these multiple pressures for mutual adaptation, it is assumed, have initiated a general trend towards a political convergence.

In this paper, I want to argue that this assumption is precipitate because it neglects an analysis of previous patterns of political change in and across individual Western European countries and misinterprets recent changes in the politics of the Community. Consequently, it does not consider the fact that formerly proclaimed theses of convergence have regularly failed and thus have rather confirmed the alternative view of a persistent diversity of national patterns of politics and society. Nor does it bother about the experience that so far the politics of Western European economic integration have been marked rather by a pronounced political diversity than by homogenization. Instead, the assumption rests on the perception of the introduction of the single market as a qualitatively new situation and combines this view with a functionalist concept of political change according to which economic imperatives determine policies which in turn shape politics. Against this view, I want to argue that the eventual outcome of 1992 may well be determined by the impact of persistently diverse national politics.

* Hans Kastendiek teaches British and American Politics at the Department of English Studies, University of Giessen, West Germany. He is a member of the International Committee for the Study of the Development of Political Science.

For a discussion of these points, my argument will be presented in three steps. First, I shall compare the course of post-war political developments in three countries (Britain, Italy and West Germany) with special reference to the 'convergence versus diversity' theme.[1] Second, I want to propose a reformulation of this theme which is based on a multi-level approach to the analysis of political change. Building on these historical observations and conceptual reflections, I shall finally discuss the politics of the Community and the political dimensions of 1992.

Politics in Britain, Italy and West Germany since 1945

Debates on the 'convergence versus diversity' theme have puzzled comparative analysis again and again. In an account of British, Italian and West German politics I want to demonstrate that these debates have mirrored patterns of political change in Western Europe which have been characterized by a strikingly parallel sequence of development stages and an equally striking persistence of national diversity. The parallelism has been so evident, I think, that we can apply the same periodization of political change to all the three countries,[2] identifying five stages of development:

(i)   1945–1947/48;
(ii)   1947/48–early 1960s;
(iii) early 1960s–early 1970s;
(iv)   early 1970s–late 1970s/early 1980s;
(v)   the 1980s.

The *first stage* from 1945 to 1947/48 was a short period of relative strength of the labour movement and a period of some uncertainty about the prospects of capitalism as an economic, social and political formation. At that time it was taken for granted that the labour parties had reached a status of political equality, if not more. The Labour Party had gained full recognition as a member of the war coalition in Britain, and in Italy the Communist and the Socialist Parties had become respected partners of the *resistenza*. British Labour triumphantly won the election of 1945, and in Italy both the Communists and the Socialist Parties were accepted participants in the post-war governments of national unity. In West Germany, the Social Democrats and the Communists, having been major

---

[1] Although this sample does not represent the entire plurality of national politics in the EC it should be a sufficient basis for a discussion (of the debate) on '1992' which pays some special attention to the 'convergence versus diversity' theme.

[2] For this periodization, see, for example, D. Sassoon, *Contemporary Italy. Politics, Economy & Society since 1945*, Longman, London and New York, 1986; C. Crouch, *The Politics of Industrial Relations*, 2nd ed, Fontana, 1982; and A. Markovits, 'Trade Unions and the Economic Crisis: the West German Case', in P. Gourevitch *et al.*, *Unions and Economic Crisis: Britain, West Germany and Sweden*, Allen & Unwin, London etc., 1984.

opponents of National Socialism, now claimed to be the natural parties of government, whereas the parties on the centre-right still had to be rearranged in programmatic and organizational terms.

The changes in the constellation of political as well as social forces were seen in a wider context. A general trend since the First World War towards an 'organised capitalism' seemed to have been fuelled further by the political organization of the national economies during the Second World War. What was often either stated or expected now was a substantial mutation of capitalism in social democratic terms or even its socialist conversion. These expectations, however, were not met by events. On the contrary: the emergence of the East–West division in European and global politics and the re-liberalization of the national economies from 1947/48 onwards (catchwords: Truman Doctrine and Marshall Plan) marked the beginning of a new stage of post-war developments.

The *second stage* – a long period of conservative and entrepreneurial dominance, supported by economic prosperity and the domestic impact of the Cold War – lasted until the early sixties. The British Labour Party had already lost its drive before it lost the mandate in 1951, staying in opposition until 1964. The West German Social Democrats and Communists lost any major influence on the re-organization of the economic, social and political order. The Communists were already in heavy decline when they were declared to be unconstitutional and were dissolved as a party in 1956. Suffering a series of disastrous election defeats throughout the fifties, the Social Democrats – despite a substantial policy review in 1959 – had to wait until 1966 to become a party of national government for the first time since the 1920s. In Italy, the Communists and Socialists were expelled from government office in 1947. The Communists have been excluded ever since, but the Socialists have participated in centre-left coalitions from 1963 onwards.

In this long period of economic prosperity, conservative dominance and entrepreneurial strength, a whole bunch of convergence theses flourished: the affluent society, the end of class society, the decline of old-fashioned labour parties and the transformation of the West European party system due to the advent of catch-all parties, a new pluralism as a social and political order etc. Each thesis captured, I think, some *general* trends common to the countries considered in this paper. But there remained or even newly emerged quite different national patterns of politics and society. I shall demonstrate this point with regard to the party systems and to the systems of industrial relations.

In Britain, the distribution of electoral strength within the two-party system was relatively balanced as Labour was a potential challenger of the Conservatives even in the fifties. This contrasted with the West German multi-party and later two-and-a-half party system where the Social Democrats were in a clear minority, although they gained access to governmental offices in several states of the Federal Republic. In Italy, the situation was different again: the Christian Democrats were able to dominate a very fragmented party system because the Communists, by far the biggest opposition party, were principally excluded from any coalition building. The national differences were even more significant in the sphere of industrial relations. The British system of 'free collective bargaining', as re-established in the fifties, was highly fragmented and decentralized, poorly institutionalized, hardly regulated by legal provisions, and relatively balanced with regard to the power relations between the 'two sides of industry'. Again the contrast to West Germany is evident: her system of industrial relations was highly centralized, extensively institutionalized and strictly juridified, often – and especially in the fifties – in favour of the employers. In Italy, neither a formalized system of the West German kind nor a network of informal bargaining procedures like in Britain emerged. Preferring a policy of permanent confrontation like their French colleagues, Italian employers skilfully exploited the political set-backs of the labour movement since 1947/48 and also the divisions of trade unions which had organized themselves along party political lines. These specific patterns of industrial relations, I think, help us to explain many differences of social and political developments since the 1960s.

The *third stage* from the early sixties to the late sixties and early seventies, marked the end of the post-war reconstruction of the national economies under the conditions of a booming world market. In all three countries this period started with the confident assumption that a new take-off for economic growth and stability could be achieved by institutional reforms and new policies. By the mid-sixties 'modernization' had become the most prominent catch-word of the economic and political debate, advocated by conservative, liberal and labour parties alike. But it was the labour parties which were most successful in capturing this general mood. Harold Wilson's promise of 'a white heat of technological revolution' is a shining example of the competition for modernization programmes. In a similar way, the West German Social Democrats offered a 'New Economic Policy' which, in its Keynesian inspiration, promised to add sophisticated state intervention to the basically liberal concept of a 'social market policy' which had prevailed in the 1950s. Labour got the mandate in 1964; the West German Social Democrats became the junior partner in the 'grand coalition' with the Christian Democrats in 1966 and then the leading party in a coalition with the Free Democrats in 1969. And in Italy, already in 1963, the first centre-left coalition, led by the Christian Democrats and including the Socialists, was designed for economic reform as well. The proclamation of five year plans in Britain and Italy in 1965, as well as the medium-term fiscal planning agreed upon by the 'grand coalition' in West Germany, all seemed to confirm Andrew Shonfield's studies on the emergence of a 'modern capitalism'. (It is also significant that the title chosen for the German translation was *Geplanter Kapitalismus*, i.e. 'planned capitalism'.)

But all these initiatives failed – with the partial exception of West Germany. In Britain, the technocratic thrust clashed with the persistence of the structural problems of the economy and with the peculiarities of the industrial relations system. It was this constellation which contributed to the emergence of the vicious circle of industrial conflicts and adversary party politics which since then has often been blamed for Britain's problems, a vicious circle which in 1973 and 1974 led to an 'opening up of class divisions and to the emergence of social antagonisms on a scale probably not witnessed since the General Strike half a century ago'.[3] Even in West Germany, where the 'new economic policy' of the Social Democrats initially succeeded in imposing wage restraint in order to achieve economic recovery and a new export offensive in 1967/68, the unions and especially their rank-and-file members developed a militant approach to industrial actions, often tutored by immigrant workers from southern Europe. However, the failure of modernization policies had the most significant consequences in Italy. The immobilism of the political system and even more so the intransigent attitudes of the industrial employers, who insisted on their previously gained prerogatives, blocked any reform of political and social institutions. Such reform was urgently needed because of the rapid transition of the Italian society in the fifties and sixties. The 'hot autumn' of 1969, i.e. the grass-root rebellion of the workers' movement, was an eruption of social and political conflicts which nearly swept away the social and political constellations of the post-war period. For five years or so the trade unions became the major agents not only in the economy but also in the political arena.

Again, academic debates were dominated by a series of convergence theses which now clearly mirrored the divisions in politics and society: centre-right academics stated a general trend towards an overloaded government and ungovernability; liberal authors rather concentrated on a crisis of party government and parliamentarism; the academic left theorized the resurgence of class conflict and a legitimation crisis of capitalism as an economic, social and political formation.

There is no space to discuss the national evidence and non-evidence for these interpretations in a detailed way. I can only state that each of these interpretations has to be carefully qualified and specified for each individual country. In retrospect this is easier than it was at that time, also because most of these far-reaching interpretations were corrected rather soon by factual changes of social and political developments, changes I now want to discuss in the *fourth stage* of my periodization.

From the second half of the seventies until the early eighties in each country under consideration a new configuration of socio-politics developed which was strikingly similar again: a new emphasis on the politics of cooperation and concertation. This was the time of the 'Social Contract' in Britain, the time of the proclamation of the 'Modell Deutschland' which was designed by the German Social Democrats as a model for

---

[3] M. Stewart, *Politics and Economic Policy in the UK since 1964. The Jekyll and Hyde Years*, Pergamon Press, Oxford, 1976, p. 181.

a solution to the economic crisis; and in Italy this was the time of the 'historic compromise' and then of the 'government of national unity' from 1976 to 1979. The Communists, though not a party *in* government, became – as a member of a broad parliamentary coalition – a party *of* government.[3a] Of course, this parallelism led to a further debate on convergence, i.e. to the thesis of a general trend towards a new corporatism, characterized by a close interconnection of the state and the economy and by tripartite bargaining structures between governments, employers and trade unions aimed at the implementation of jointly developed policies.

One of the specifications of the corporatism debate I have found very useful is the differentiation between corporatism as a *strategy* and corporatism as an *institutional order*. In Britain, neo-corporatism as a strategy was even more pronounced than in West Germany because it was designed as *compensation* for the structural deficiencies of the system of industrial relations. But it was precisely the patterns of this system that blocked this strategy. Ironically, in West Germany, the need for a comprehensive corporatist strategy was less urgent than in Britain because the quasi-corporatist structures of the industrial relations system mostly delivered the results which the Social Contract was looking for. In Italy, neither the preconditions for the formulation of a successful corporatist strategy nor the structures which may support such a strategy existed. Italian 'neo-corporatism' was rather an attempt to include industrial bargaining more directly into the very complexities of the *mercato politico*. This term nicely circumscribes the specificities of the Italian political system characterized by a permanent bargaining between and within the major political and social organizations.

The 'trends towards corporatist intermediation', to quote the title of the influential book edited by Lehmbruch and Schmitter, were already reversed when their publication arrived on the bookshelves. From the end of the seventies onwards, *stage five* of my periodization, neo-liberalism and neo-conservatism, gathered momentum. Soon after Mrs Thatcher took office in 1979, the 'national unity' in Italy collapsed. At about the same time the Social-Liberal coalition in West Germany began to stumble when the Free Democrats increasingly urged for a Thatcher-like revision of economic policies and of government policies of industrial relations, preparing the coalition with the Christian Democrats (which was formed in 1982). Initially, in Britain and West Germany, the formulation of another thesis of convergence, i.e. of a neo-liberal counter-revolution, was supported by the outcome of the presidential elections in the USA (1980) and by the introduction of Reaganomics. Since then, however, it has become well recognized that Thatcherism has not been the vanguard of a radical reversion of post-war politics in Western Europe and that the diversity of national patterns has continued again.

[3a] Fee D. Sassoon, *Contemporary Italy, op. cit.*, p. 237.

Dimensions of political change: a reformulation of the 'convergence versus diversity' theme

Both these theses of convergence and of national diversity reflect important aspects of political change in Western Europe. The notion of convergence actually addresses quite similar developments to be observed in several countries but tends to misinterpret cross-national constellations of change as constellations of identical national changes. Theses of diversity rightly insist on the national differences of actual changes but tend to overstate their singularity, if not to assume an autonomy of national political developments. This may suggest that we should find a balance of both patterns of interpretation and dissolve their dichotomy. But as long as they compete in their generalized form, both theses are incompatible. In my view, this competition is unnecessary. It is possible, I think, to relate each thesis to different aspects and dimensions of political change. For an explication of this argument I want to sketch out what may be called a 'hierarchy of political change':

(i) The historical account outlined in the previous section clearly demonstrates the extent to which developments of national politics have been shaped by *cross-national constellations of change*. The impact of economic and political internationalization is evident. All countries, and certaintly those considered in this paper, have to respond in a very similar way to new constellations in world politics, transformations of the international division of labour, changes in the (fortunes of the) world-market, and general trends of techno-economic and socio-political restructuring. We may thus suppose that these developments have meant rather identical *stimuli or challenges for change*.

(ii) Furthermore, there seems to be a clear correspondence between overall changes of cross-national economic and political constellations and *changes in the national formations of political and social forces*. Both in party politics and in the politics of industrial relations, power relations have shifted in a remarkably parallel way. Accordingly, significant shifts in the political course of each country have occurred at about the same times, leading to (and expressed by) similar reorientations of basic approaches to the politics and policies of economic and political development. Hence, at each stage and cross-nationally, very similar *objectives for change* have been formulated.

(iii) However, neither overall constellations nor similar national formations of political and social forces translate to nationally uniform *programmes for change*, as these programmes have to relate to the nationally specific *conditions for change*. Firstly, countries differ in their position in world politics, in their industrial profile and economic strength and thus in their position in the international division of labour. Hence the stimuli for change and the imperatives for adaptation to new challenges may be perceived quite differently, and hence political objectives articulated in a similar way may differ in their power of persuasion from country to country. Secondly, the formulation of actual programmes for change is shaped by the mechanisms of different systems of political and social organization. Thirdly, there might be rather parallel shifts in the formation of political and social forces but, as shown in the previous section, there remain many distinct patterns of concrete power constellations when we compare individual countries.

(iv) Even if roughly similar programmes for change are determined, they may result in rather different *policies for change*, for at least three reasons. Firstly, actual policies may be shaped by 'national policy-styles', defined by J. Richardson *et al.* as nationally distinct '"standing operating procedures" for making and implementing policies';[4] thus a similar objective may be pursued in different ways. Secondly, in each country, a strategy for change may locate the need for policy action at different levels of societal organization (e.g., in one country it may be the industrial profile which is seen as a major obstacle to adaptive change, in another it may be the system of industrial relations or simply the 'excessive power of the trade unions'). But, thirdly, even if the same problem sector is addressed, the sector policies may differ as, in each country, the individual fields of societal organization are interconnected in a specific way (e.g., the labour market and the systems of social insurance, of vocational training, etc.).

(v) However deeply rooted in a society, national forms of politics and policy-styles are by no means invariable, and hence, in analyses of political change, they cannot be treated as independent variables. They have to be constantly reproduced *and*, for this purpose, to be adapted to new policy requirements. But at the same time, they restrict the scope and limit the impact of actual policies for change. This explains why strategies for change are not just policy-centred but politics-oriented as well. In order to achieve the intended policy outcomes, strategies of change aim at a transformation of existing politics. Thus, policies of change are inextricably interlocked with the *politics of change*.

To conclude: the thesis of convergence is most convincing when we consider the emergence of similar problem constellations and the general orientations for economic, social and political change; the thesis of national diversity is most convincing when we consider the impact of national conditions on actual policy-programmes and on the politics of change in individual countries. It seems that in the course of each cycle of the 'convergence versus diversity' debate, at each stage of post-war developments, the focus of attention has gradually moved 'down' the

[4] J. Richardson, G. Gustafsson and G. Jordan, 'The Concept of Policy Style', in J. Richardson (ed.), *Policy Styles in Western Europe*, Allen & Unwin, London etc., 1982, p. 2; see also G. Freeman, 'National Styles and Policy Sectors: Explaining Structured Variation', in *Journal of Public Policy*, vol. 5 (1985), no. 4.

'hierarchy of change' outlined above. We may anticipate the same pattern for the current debate on '1992' which, so far, has very much concentrated on the stimuli and objectives for change and rather underrated the immense problems of its implementation.

Europe 1992: economic integration and political convergence?

What is so significant about the debate on the single market and its political implications is the shift in the perception of the Community. Seen as a 'lame duck' only a few years ago, it is now reputed to be a main asset of the European economy and of European politics. The introduction of the single market, defined as an absolute economic necessity, has been regarded as a starting point of a new dynamic of political integration. This new dynamic has been concluded from recent changes in the institutions and policy-making mechanisms at the level of the EC,[5] but also from the momentum coming from below as the member states have to respond to the quest for an integrated Europe demanded by business and industry as well as to the social and cultural changes resulting from a multitude of integrationist trends in Western Europe.[6] It is this combination of economic and political consequences expected from the introduction of the single market which has created the present 'Euro-fever' and fuelled the notion of a political convergence.[7]

In my attempt to counterbalance the present debate I want to pose the question whether this notion once more interprets a cross-national constellation of change as a constellation of identical national changes. The introduction of the single market and the new dynamic of political integration seem to indicate an *adaptation to new imperatives for change*, in particular to the requirements of a techno-economic restructuring imposed by international competition. The problem is, however, whether these changes necessarily point to a *process of mutual adaptation of national politics*, supported and reinforced through the mechanisms of the EC. The account of post-war development in Britain, Italy and West Germany above has shown that national politics have changed frequently but have maintained their distinct patterns. Thus, the present situation may again prove to be a constellation of *parallel* rather than *convergent* developments, i.e. a constellation of simultaneous changes which may, in

---

[5] See J. Lodge, 'The Political Implications of 1992', in *Politics*, vol. 9, no. 2 (October 1989), and by the same author 'EC Institutions', in *Contemporary Record*, vol. 3, no. 3 (February 1990).

[6] See M.Clarke, 'Britain and the EC. How Britain Has Adapted', in *Contemporary Record*, vol. 3, no. 3 (February 1990).

[7] The present 'Euro-fear', stemming from various critical views of possible implications and effects of the single market, e.g. political centralization, 'social dumping' or increasing regional disparities, seems to be rather an expression of, than a counterbalance to, the 'feverish' debates on 1992.

the geometric sense of a 'parallelism', not dissolve but reproduce the patterns of political diversity. However, for a discussion of these points, it would be precarious simply to extrapolate my former argument. The question at stake is whether, in recent years, (a) a substantially new constellation of change has emerged which (b) demands or at least supports rather uniform changes of national politics.

The prospects of present and future political change in general and within the EC in particular have been concluded from a variety of problem constellations, ranging from the secular trend towards an accelerating internationalization of economic, social, political and cultural relations or the future obsolescence of national politics resulting from impending worldwide environmental catastrophes on the one hand to the more traditional themes of the political implications and consequences of techno-economic change or of the trend towards regional integration on the other.[8] Clearly the third point has been at the forefront of the present discussion. It may have been forgotten that the present 'Euro-fever' did not start immediately after the decision to introduce the single market had been taken in 1985. It did so only when the debate on '1992' became articulated with the public campaigns for a techno-economic and, subsequently, socio-political restructuring as a solution to the economic crisis – campaigns which had gathered momentum in the second half of the eighties.[9]

Former Euro-scepticism: a reminder

In order to assess recent changes in the politics of the EC (and the shift in the perception of the Community mentioned above) it is worthwhile to recall the rather disillusioned accounts of European integration which dominated the discussion only a few years ago. The Euro-scepticism of the seventies and early eighties mirrored the stagnation of the Community and the horse-dealer attitudes by national governments outside and inside the EC institutions. These attitudes dominated the bargaining about individual sectoral policies and were even more documented in the rows about national contributions to the EC budget and the priorities (and receiving ends) of EC expenditure. However, it was not just national egotism which was blamed. The whole integration enterprise was called in question: the Community, it was suspected, might be a case for good weather conditions but is incapable of standing the real test of economic crises. Furthermore, the entire institutional ('constitutional') set-up of the Community was regarded both as inefficient and poorly legitimized as it was characterized by arcane bargaining processes among national governments.

---

[8] For these and further arguments see O. Jacobi's contribution to this volume.
[9] See B. Jessop, H. Kastendiek, K. Nielsen and O. Pedersen (eds), *The Politics of Flexibilisation: Scandinavia, Britain and West Germany* (forthcoming 1990/1991).

By the middle of the eighties, as a result of these experiences, academic analyses had often departed from previous interpretations of integration.[10] Former analytic models had relied on a rather unilinear advance of European politics. By 'sticking closely to the terms of the Treaties establishing the European Communities', they had postulated 'integration as a stage-by-stage process, in which the ultimate target of economic union would be preceded by the pooling of significant national instruments for the management of economic policy', and some of them had woven 'an ingenious political schema around this step-by-step formulation of economic integration, emphasizing the transfer of political loyalties which would accompany a shift in the focus of economic policy-making towards a new centre in Brussels'.[11] Obviously, at that time, neither this functionalist view of European integration nor a federalist interpretation assuming the emergence of a new institutional and constitutional order in the spirit of a European Union fitted to the process and outcome of actual Community affairs. Thus, a more realistic analysis was suggested which had to focus on the uneven and disjointed character of the EC's decision-making, to grasp the intergovernmental rather than supra-national or even federal patterns of EC politics, and even to question the very notion of integration and to possibly replace it by more 'modest' concepts like 'policy coordination', 'intergovernmental cooperation', or 'politics of interdependence'. Not surprisingly, this view – based on a series of detailed policy-making studies presented in the same volume – was very much inclined to stress the impact of national politics and thus of political diversity on the performance and the prospects of the Community.

The problem of diversity even became the central theme of a further study by the author cited, published two years later.[12] The entire argument now revolves on the thesis that, from the very onset, diversity has been the inherent characteristic of the European Communities and has become even more so as a result of the enlargements of the membership in 1973, 1981 and 1986. Therefore, the solution to the shortcomings and difficulties of the EC cannot be seen in attempts to *overcome the heterogeneity* but only in attempts to cater for the requirements of *adapting to this diversity*! Consequently, the various proposals for a revitalization of the Community, discussed by other authors as initiatives for a new dynamic of European integration,[13] appear as 'strategies for managing diversity'.[14]

[10] See H. Wallace, W. Wallace and C. Webb (eds), *Policy-Making in the European Community*, 2nd ed., Wiley & Sons, Chichester etc., 1983, esp. chs. 1, 13 and 14.

[11] H. Wallace, 'Theoretical Perspectives and Problems', in H. Wallace *et al.*, *op. cit.*, pp. 7 and 8.

[12] H. Wallace with A. Ridley, *Europe: The Challenge of Diversity*, The Royal Institute of International Affairs, Chatham House Papers No. 29, Routledge & Kegan Paul, London etc., 1985.

[13] See R. Pryce (ed.), *The Dynamics of European Union*, Croom Helm, London etc., 1987.

[14] H. Wallace, *Europe: The Challenge of Diversity*, p. 29.

Strategies for further market integration are explicitly – and bluntly – included in this argument: 'Attachment to the pursuit of market liberalization implies giving priority to decentralized and efficient competition which preserves diversity.'[15] Seen from the perspective of the present debate on '1992' this is clearly a provocative statement.

The 'natural focus of Community policies', it is maintained, has already 'shifted towards cooperation or collaboration rather than full integration'.[16] The 'very language of policy coordination as distinct from harmonization, let alone integration ... also suggests implementation of agreement by *parallel national action* rather than by *common instruments*'.[17] 'Obviously, coordination has made most progress in those areas where diversity is less great' but it 'has had little impact yet on other areas, such as fiscal policy, where the divergences of national approaches remain considerable.'[18] What has been significant about this development of EC policies and politics is that this kind of decision-making has explicitly recognized the facts of diversity by extensively adopting the policy of differentiation. Several levels of the 'hierarchy of change', outlined in the previous section, can well be detected in this account: 'One of the phenomena which we can observe is a progressive blurring of the edges as the development of policy moves from the more abstract statement of principle to the point of implementation, starting from the Treaties, moving through negotiations in the Council of Ministers to what is often rather nuancé operation by the Commission.'[19] 'British claims for diversity of practice'[20] fit perfectly into this development. Hence, many British Euro-fears have become obsolete, and – this is clearly the main thrust of the entire argument – Britain should be well advised to develop a fully supportive attitude towards the Community.

'1992' or what has changed?

Pronounced as it was, the reported interpretation of the 'pre-1992' Community may have overstated the case. But obviously it reflected (in the double sense of the term) salient features of the EC until the mid-eighties. Thus, the question necessarily follows whether the present debate has neglected a 'realistic' view of the Community or whether the EC has changed substantially and dramatically.

For a discussion of this question I want to comment further on the two major strands in the debate already mentioned in this paper. The first derives the new dynamic of the Community from the observation that the

---

[15] *Ibid.*, pp. 10 and 11.
[16] *Ibid.*, p. 10.
[17] *Ibid.*, p. 53 (my emphasis); see also p. 71.
[18] *Ibid.*, p. 53.
[19] *Ibid.*, p. 23.
[20] *Ibid.*, p. 82.

economic rationale of West European integration has gained a new persuasive power, and argues that this has paved the way for a political redefinition of the EC; the second deduces the new drive of the integration process from a genuine *political* response to the former shortcomings and deficiencies of Community affairs. As the first strand is based on a functionalist interpretation and as the second more or less assumes a trend towards a federalist organization of Western Europe, the two main approaches rejected by the 'realists' have become prominent again. Both share a Euro-optimist view (if not attitude) and therefore do not conflict with each other. On the contrary, in their respective concentration on the economic and political aspects of 1992 they are rather complementary, and thus contribute jointly to the notion that there has been a process of accelerating integration in which the economic and political objectives are directly interrelated, if not coordinated.

The picture becomes more complicated, however, when we look at the initiatives for a revitalization of the Community launched from the early eighties onwards.[21] Again, there was much evidence that Community affairs had developed in a rather uneven and disjointed way. In the course of events the main emphasis of successive proposals for reform shifted from the political to the economic side and vice versa; individual initiatives became watered down in bargaining processes; some initiatives were taken to counterbalance others; and generally there was a propensity or custom to present the final results in the well established mode of Euro-rhetoric. We should also be well aware of the fact that the proclamation of the 1992 exercise in 1985 fits this pattern of ('normal') politics. It should be fair to say that the plan for the 'single European market' (or 'internal market' as it was called in the first instance) hardly presented a new vision of Western Europe. Basically, it was a reaffirmation of the main goals already agreed in the Treaty of Rome in 1957, and accordingly the newly introduced terms actually offered new designations for a long-existing model, i.e. the Common Market. This reaffirmation was important enough when we recall the state of Community affairs of the seventies and early eighties. Although the 1992 plan was linked with changes in EC decision-making procedures (to be discussed below), its main emphasis was on the revitalization of economic integration. In this, it was a deliberate response and reaction to the Draft Treaty Establishing the European Union which had been initiated by Altiero Spinelli and others and was adopted by the European Parliament in 1984.[22]

Spinelli conceded that the integration process had to be gradual and piecemeal. He was convinced, however, that further progress depended on a major reform of the political setting of EC institutions which could

[21] Cf. the edition by R. Pryce, *op. cit.*
[22] Cf. J. Lodge (ed.), *European Union: The European Community in Search of a Future*, Macmillan, London and Basingstoke, 1986; and O. Schmuck, 'The European Parliament's Draft Treaty Establishing The European Union', in R. Pryce, *op. cit.*

not be made step-by-step but had to be designed comprehensively in order to provide the Community with a solid foundation.[23] The main task was to strengthen the European Parliament and the Commission *vis-à-vis* the Council of Ministers as the latter was the most powerful organ of the Community and yet – at the same time – its most impotent institution.[24] It has been responsible for most of the EC's inertia:

> due to the fact that within the Council each minister is there as the representative of his own country. Each minister has a complex national decision-making machinery behind him organised by national administrations, which were themselves created and exist for the purpose of examining all political problems from a national perspective . . . in the Council ten [at that time, HK] ministers meet to decide any European common action and behind each one there is a complex process in which everything that can take the form of a national interest emerges strongly whilst everything that should appear as a European interest remains submerged and shapeless.[25]

It was necessary, therefore, to establish a new power centre, i.e. a more powerful Commission cooperating with and controlled by a more influential European Parliament. In contrast to normal parliamentary logic, this latter must have a genuine interest in having the responsibilities of the exexcutive increased in order to be strengthened itself.[26] Spinelli explicitly rejected projects like the Genscher-Colombo plan of the early eighties which proposed extending the responsibilities of the Council and leaving the whole decision-making procedure unchanged: 'Nobody will ever succeed in understanding why the Council, ineffective in its present tasks, should become more effective if its field of actions were broadened.'[27] As a result of this analysis the European Parliament Draft Treaty, according to the summary given by Spinelli:

(1) broadens the economic and political competence of the Community, and introduces methods which allow successive developments as necessary;

(2) makes the present Commission into a true government within the competences of the Union;

(3) gives Parliament real power of co-decision with the Council in matters of control of the executive, legislation, taxation and budget;

(4) reduces the present excessive powers of the Council and requires a clear composition of the Council, the abolition of unanimous voting, power of co-decision with Parliament in legislative, fiscal and budgetary matters . . .[28]

---

[23] Cf. M. Burgess, 'Altiero Spinelli, Federalism and The EUT', in J. Lodge (ed.), *European Union*, *op. cit.*, p. 181.

[24] A. Spinelli, 'Foreword', in J. Lodge (ed.), *op. cit.*, p. XV.

[25] *Ibid.*, p. XVI.

[26] Cf. Burgess, *op. cit.*, p. 183.

[27] A. Spinelli, *op. cit.*, p. XVII.

[28] *Ibid.*

For Juliet Lodge, the Draft Treaty 'has become the benchmark against which other documents purporting to advance European integration are measured. It is a blueprint for a new constitution', which clearly follows 'a maximalist (or federalist) approach' to European integration as opposed to 'a minimalist (sometimes termed inter-governmentalist) approach'.[29]

If we, then, measure the Single European Act announcing the Single Market for 1993 against this benchmark it seems to be rather a mini-max mix. Resulting from inter-governmental negotiations, it carefully avoided fuelling expectations concluded from the European Parliament's quest for a European Union. But, surely, governments followed to some extent the way proposed in the Draft Treaty (expansion of the EC's policy scope, majority voting in the Council in matters of the introduction of the Single Market, powers of co-decision for the European Parliament in legislation). This may have maximalist/federal *implications* as Lodge puts it. But this is still far from already being a *federal type of political organization* based on distinct modes of representation and intervention. In constitutional terms, the EC is still a strange animal, leaving the bulk of legislative authority to a council of governments' representatives, i.e. the Council of Ministers, having an executive which drafts but does not implement policies and thus lacks the core characteristic to be or to act as a government, and being equipped with a parliament which may influence legislation drafted and ultimately passed elsewhere, i.e. by the Commission and the Council. This is not to deny the changes in the inter- and intra-institutional relations accounted for in some details by Lodge; but this suggests that most of the changes towards a new dynamic of European integration have occurred in the field of policy objectives, shared by most of the political actors within the EC.

The new drive of the Community has not resulted, I think, from a process set in motion by revitalized EC institutions or from a new commitment of national governments to promote the European Union. Rather it resulted from a notion that the EC offers favourable conditions for a far-reaching techno-economic restructuring generally seen as an imperative for the future development of all national economies. Only when the case of European integration became broadly discussed in terms of a solution to the crises of the seventies and early eighties, when it no longer appeared to be a zero sum affair, and when it could be seen as a logical trans-national extension of basically similar policies pursued in all the member states, only then the new EC process gathered its present momentum. An indication of this interpretation is the fact that neither the Draft Treaty of the European Parliament in 1984 nor the Single European Act which actually amended the European Treaties stirred up much excitement at the time of their announcement. It was the subsequent delivery of Commission papers, official and academic reports on the prospects of a Single Market, presented in terms of incentives for growth, and outlining

[29] J. Lodge, 'The Political Implications of 1992', *op. cit.*, p. 35.

the potentials for increasing the competitiveness of the national economies, which captured the mood of national actors as well as of the actors in the institutions of the EC. The Commission was able to play a much more active and prominent role not because of its new competences but rather because especially Jacques Delors, its President, succeeded in articulating the potentialities and potential advantages of further economic integration and translating the policy objectives which had emerged on national arenas into policy initiatives offered within the framework of the EC. In this he was able to build on some of the reports mentioned above, mainly on the 'Cecchini-Report'.[30]

What has changed in the Community, then, is not so much its basic institutional design or the definition of its main goals but the expectations from further integration. To some extent the present situation resembles that of the sixties when the creation of the EEC had triggered an increase in intra-Community trade and thus promoted a climate of Euro-optimism which in turn had contributed to a relatively smooth process of interest intermediation between the member states. What is celebrated at present as a new stage of European integration could well prove to be just another conjuncture of Community affairs, supported by relatively favourable economic conditions (if compared to the seventies and early eighties) and by a widespread trust in the positive effects of 1992. The political progress of the Community in recent years (extended policy scope and procedural changes) is obvious, but it has not yet been transformed into a structural change towards a new type of supranational organization, already assumed or anticipated by many commentators. Thus 1992 and even more so a political reshaping of the Community have still to be achieved.

Concluding remark

The introduction of the single market and the additional drive for economic and social integration which may follow from it demand policies which are not as technical as they often appear to be. This may explain why they are not left to the Eurocrats but often are dealt with as matters of high politics in top-level bodies of the Council of Ministers. Thus, the decision to introduce the single market has not at all discontinued the bargaining processes within the Community and especially between governments which try to preserve or to promote what is regarded to be in the national interest. The present Euro-fever has not resulted in a consensual type of decision-making, and it is only the general acceptance of the ultimate goal which conceals the fact that the procedural changes within the institutional setting of the Community have not really led to a shift of authoritative decision-making from the Council of Ministers to the Commission and the

[30] P. Cecchini, *The European Challenge*, Wildwood, Aldershot, 1988.

Parliament. Therefore we should be sceptical about the general argument that 1992 will be a matter of centralized decision kept away from national actors. The often-mentioned 50 to 80% of legislation enacted in the member states which will have its origin in EC institutions is not imposed by an external body but is decided in a way in which each member state is participating, especially via its national government.

As a result, there is good reason to assume that the diversity of national politics within the Community will not be overcome in the foreseeable future but will be expressed in a continuing policy of differentiation which will allow a 'diversity of practice'. All governments in the member states are committed to the introduction of the single market but one has not to quote Mrs Thatcher in order to recall the differences in the political objectives for Europe as an economic and social space. If critics who argue that the single market will rather increase than reduce the disparities in the EC prove to be right; if the calculations of the positive effects of 1992 prove to be wrong; if the economic conditions change; then these differences may come to the fore again.

DEFICIENCIES AND REFORM POSSIBILITIES OF THE EC FISCAL CONSTITUTION

DIETER BIEHL*

THE term 'fiscal constitution' is used in the present paper in order to cover all those rules of a constitutional or quasi-constitutional nature that determine the revenue and expenditure decision-making powers of a polity. Fiscal constitution represents a subset of rules that all together determine the (written or unwritten) constitution of a country, or, in our context, of the European Community.

The paper elaborates two basic hypotheses. The first postulates that it is possible with the aid of an enlarged economic analysis based on what may be called economic theory of (fiscal) federalism, to derive criteria or 'principles' in order to assess the quality of constitutions or subsets of them. The second hypothesis states that if a given constitution or subset does not sufficiently comply with these principles, the political decisions taken within its framework will be distorted and therefore will produce results that even by those participating in decision-making will not be considered to be always acceptable.

The paper presents the elements of what may be called a theory of (fiscal) federalism in order to derive evaluation criteria. With the aid of these criteria, the existing EC fiscal constitution is assessed in order to identify possible deficiencies. Starting from these deficiencies, the third part of the paper develops proposals in order to exclude, or at least reduce, new distortions in the political decision-making process for the future.

The main elements of a theory of fiscal federalism

Economic analyses basically represent benefit–cost comparisons. The differences between those analyses stem from differences in the type of problems to be dealt with. In the case at hand, assessing an existing fiscal constitution, both the notions of 'benefit' and 'cost' have to be considerably enlarged in order to be able to deal with the basic elements of a

* The author is Professor of Public Economics at the Johann Wolfgang Goethe-Universität in Frankfurt am Main and Managing Editor of the international journal *Public Finance/Finances Publiques*. He was a member of the MacDougall Committee on the Role of Public Finance in European Integration which reported to the European Commission in 1977.

constitutional system. However, a benefit can also be defined so as to mean cost avoided or reduced to the effect that such an enlarged benefit–cost analysis can also be designed as an enlarged cost analysis. It consists of two main types of cost: resource cost and preference or frustration cost.

Buchanan and Tullock in their seminal book *The Calculus of Consent*[1] have already forged the type of analytical instrument to be used here. In their terminology, 'expected decision costs' are to be distinguished from 'expected external costs'. These terms are modified here so as to cover all that could be subsumed under 'resource cost' on the one hand and under 'preference' or 'frustration' cost on the other. Resource costs are understood in the usual meaning of opportunity costs, i.e. those benefits forgone that could have been obtained if the resources had been used in the next best (or better) utilization. Preference or frustration costs on the other hand take the form of reduced individual utility independent of any change in the use of resources. The term 'frustration cost' which has been coined by Pennock[2] seems to reflect this point of view adequately. He developed the idea that, for example, people who are subject to the decision of a majority, whose preferences differ from those of a minority, will be negatively affected because they have to comply with a set of implicit or explicit values and assessment that are not their own. If the minority had been the majority, they would have taken a different decision which in turn would also have negatively affected the ruling majority.

The two types of cost show a clearly opposite development in a usual two-axes diagram (cf. Figure 1). The horizontal axis represents the number of individuals required to take collective action (N). If one individual only has the right to take that action without having to involve the participation of the other individuals forming the same group, it can be argued that this is a minimum cost decision-making system in terms of *resource cost*. (Imagine that this person represents the famous great, old, wise statesman or a benevolent dictator.) In formal terms, resource costs are a minimum (in the extreme even zero) because no other individuals and no other resources are required in order to make the decision. To the extent that the other individuals have to participate in the decision-making process, resource costs will increase because of the need to send invitations for meetings, distribute and assess information, draw conclusions for decisions, organize a suitable system in order to finance the expenditure, and so on. This is the reason why the resource cost curve starts from zero at point $N = 1$ and increases progressively up to $\bar{N} = $ all.

Preference or *frustration costs* on the other hand are determined by the fact that whenever there is only one individual that takes the decision for the whole collectivity, these others may have to fear that their preferences will be violated so that the one decision-maker model produces maximum

---

[1] J. M. Buchanan and G. Tullock, *The Calculus of Consent*, University of Michigan Press, Ann Arbor, 1962.

[2] J. R. Pennock, 'Federal and Unitary Government: Disharmony and Frustration', *Behavioural Science*, Vol. IV, 1969, p. 147.

preference or frustration cost. To the extent that the other members are participating in the decision-making process and are able to influence this process based on their own preferences, frustration costs will decline up to the point of $\bar{N}$ = all where they are a minimum (in extreme cases even zero). The preference cost curve, therefore, has its maximum at $N = 1$ and declines towards $\bar{N}$. Preference costs depend on the degree of homogeneity or heterogeneity: PC_2 represents a higher degree of heterogeneity than PC_1. The higher the heterogeneity, the higher are the preference costs.

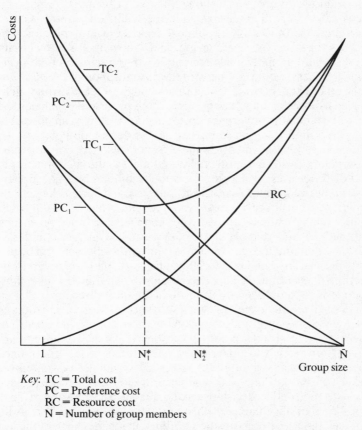

Key: TC = Total cost
     PC = Preference cost
     RC = Resource cost
     N = Number of group members

FIGURE 1   Resources and preference costs dependent on group size.

If an individual (or a group of individuals that have similar preferences) considers these two types of cost and aggregates them for himself to a total cost curve, the result is a U-shaped cost curve of which any economist is fond: with this type of curve there is a clear point of minimal cost and in the approach chosen (individuals required to take collective action) this corresponds to N^*, that is, the number of individuals required to participate in collective decision-making in order to obtain the minimum cost solution.

This type of cost analysis can be applied to many other issues. If, for example, N is considered to represent the number of competences to be distributed, and if the preferences and resource costs linked with competences are represented in the diagram, the optimal number of competences to be attributed to a given level of government can be determined.

Such an approach clearly shows what is meant by an 'enlarged' cost analysis: if in the traditional economic approach only resource costs were considered, centralization of political decision-making processes would always appear as cost minimizing, and, allowing for a plebiscitarian process where all individuals are entitled to participate in the decision-making process, would end up with the maximization of resource cost. If, on the other hand, only individual values and the intensity with which they are negatively affected were considered, the plebiscite case would be the one with minimum preference cost, and the 'dictatorship' case the one with frustration cost maximization. Considering both types of cost simultaneously rules out both of these corner solutions; only intermediate ones would represent potentially optimal solutions. The approach naturally allows us to decompose both resource costs and preference costs in sub-cost functions, whose numbers and forms depend on the problem to be dealt with and the resources and preferences implied.

The results obtained can easily be reconciled with the approaches of other authors, for example, those of Wallace E. Oates who, in his *Fiscal Federalism*[3] characterizes a federal system as 'the optimal form of government' because it combines the advantages of the two polar forms of government: centralized and decentralized. Approaches like those of Albert Breton[4] and Mancur Olson[5] go in the same direction.

It is also useful to enlarge the well known Musgravian notions of allocation, distribution and stabilization. These notions have been coined in order to analyse and separate the problems of public goods provisions, ranging from defence to kindergartens. If there exist public goods or externalities, optimal allocation of resources can no longer be guaranteed by markets, the market 'fails', and a public provision organization is required. This institution and its decision-making rules also need resources so that a second type of allocational problem arises: how much of total available resources should be used for the creation and maintenance of the institutional or constitutional system and how much for providing public and private goods in the traditional sense? As the constitutional system

[3] W. E. Oates, *Fiscal Federalism*, Harcourt Brace Jovanovich, Inc., NY, 1972.
[4] A. Breton, *Economic Theory of Representative Government*, Chicago, Aldine, 1974.
[5] M. Olson, 'The Principle of Fiscal Equivalence: The Division of Responsibility among Different Levels of Government', *American Economic Review*, Vol. 59, 1969, pp. 479 ff.

constitutional system enables a society to produce and manage private property rights and public property rights ('competences'), it is also obvious that a market system for private goods can only be optimal if adequate rights are produced, guaranteed and sanctioned—if necessary. It seems, therefore, to be appropriate to conceive a society as consisting of two hierarchical levels of resource utilization: the higher level being the constitutional system and the lower level the provision system for private and public goods in the traditional sense.

Whereas allocation is oriented towards efficiency, distribution is guided by justice and equity. Justice and equity on the constitutional level imply that political power is distributed in such a way as to obtain division of that power into, for example, executive, legislative, and judiciary institutions, with rules that reduce the danger of one single public monopoly power being concentrated in one of these institutions only. Since Montesquieu, this horizontal division of power has been an essential element of any democratic system. It can, however, be supplemented by a system of vertical division of power that is characteristic of federal or confederal systems, where the state level is divided into two: the supreme or federal level on the one hand, and the state or regional level on the other. Extending the notion of distributional justice and equity so as to cover both the horizontal and vertical divisions of power allows a substantial limitation of monopoly power.

With this enlarged notion of distributive justice and equity, basically the same type of conflict between allocation and distribution can arise on the constitutional level as on the provision level. According to efficiency criteria, a large number of competences may be attributed to the central government level and only a small amount to the state or regional level, whereas distributional justice would require endowing the state or regional level with a sufficiently large number of competences, even at the expense of efficiency, in order to obtain a well designed system of checks and balances.

Stabilization, in turn, in its extended meaning, would not only be geared towards reducing upswings and downswings of economic activity in order to guarantee stable economic growth, but would also include managing the total constitutional and political system so as to minimize political 'cycles' and to secure political stability.

As the 'public' elements of this approach are very high, one has to take into account that the free-rider phenomenon or strategic behaviour would also be a characteristic element. An individual or a group within such a two-level decision-making system could try to hide its true preferences with the aim of convincing the other participants either that an intended decision would cause extremely high costs to him or that the utility he would derive from the decision to be taken is extremely low. To what extent this might allow 'exploitation' of partners would depend on the concrete system to which this type of analysis were to be applied.

In the case of the European Community with the twelve member countries, the probability that a free rider behaviour can be easily and frequently applied seems not to be very high. One of the reasons is that strategic behaviour is most profitable in situations with a large number of anonymous actors and in situations for which only little information about previous behaviour and evaluation of those participating in decision-making is available. Institutionalized negotiating situations like those within the EC Commission, the EC Council of Ministers or the European Parliament are, however, characterized by a low degree of anonymity and a high intensity of information.

The chances for profitable strategic behaviour may also depend on the nature of the decisions to be taken. This, however, is already taken account of by a certain typology of objects of decision-making and majority rules. There exist in almost all democratic systems rules that, for example, current political matters are to be decided upon with simple majorities, whereas more important ones like changes in the constitutional system require larger qualified majorities; and extremely 'vital' decisions may even require unanimity. From the point of view of preference evalua-tion, this implies that the frustration costs of being subject to a majority decision in current affairs are considered to be relatively low. Those of more important legislative decisions are higher, whereas those for which unanimity is required are apparently classified as being extremely high. Only in the last case is the precondition for a very strong strategic position fulfilled, as any actor can apply a veto. However, as experience within an organization like the EC has shown, even where unanimity is required, it is not always possible for each actor concerned to exploit the others by making them pay for his joining the already existing majority. As a consequence, these considerations may complicate the political decision-making system on the constitutional and law-producing level, but are not so strong that they could totally block a decision-making system like the one of the EC in the medium and the long run.

A federalist reference scheme for assessing existing and designing new fiscal constitutions

The many possibilities to make use of the above extended cost analysis can be summarized in six federalist principles. The number of six is naturally arbitrary; any other number of principles or criteria could be derived, depending on the degree of differentiation of the analysis desired or of the problem at hand.

(1) *The principle of optimal centralization/decentralization.* This implies an optimal vertical division of power between government levels, in our case between the European Community, the member states, the states/provinces/regions and local governments. A basic criterion for the allocation of a competence is that the respective public function has to be

given to that level of government which realizes it with the lowest cost. Cost minimization has to be tested with the aid of the congruence principle. This principle is based on the idea that any public good has a certain spatial extension or servicing area. It is, therefore, possible in principle to arrange all public functions according to the size of their servicing areas. The hierarchy then starts from local to regional, national and international/world areas. According to the congruence principle, each function has to be allocated to that level of government, the territory of which corresponds more or less with the servicing area.

In deciding where to allocate a given public function, the so-called subsidiarity principle can also be considered. From the point of view of the cost analysis, this principle can be said to mean that a competence should remain with a lower level government or a smaller governmental unit even if the higher level or larger government would be able to fulfil the public function in question with lower resource costs, but with higher preference costs. Lower resource costs may stem from lower administrative costs, whereas the high preference costs may have their cause in excessive distance from the citizens for whom this function is to be realized, as they do not feel that their preferences are adequately taken into account at the higher or larger government.

(2) *The principle of optimal competence endowment.* Any institutional system can be conceived as representing a certain decision-making capacity. The costs of this capacity are relatively high if both horizontal and vertical divisions of power are to be realized. If, therefore, only one competence were to be given to such an organization, the cost per competence would be very high. If additional competences were attributed to this decision-making unit, the costs per competence would decrease. This can be generalized by stating that any monofunctional (or 'club' in the sense of Buchanan)[6] organization will be a cost-maximizing device, and that the cost per unit can be reduced by endowing a given government with a larger number of competences. If competences are complementary, this would also imply that only 'bundles' or packages of competences should be given to the same government unit.

Another criterion that determines the optimal competence endowment is the expenditure intensity of a public function. If expenditure intensity is extremely high, this may involve the risk that this function can only be allocated to a level of government or a government unit that disposes of sufficiently profitable revenue resources in order to ensure that this extremely expenditure-intensive function does not have to be fulfilled at the expense of other, less expenditure-intensive ones.

(3) *The principle of optimal competence differentiation.* Competences can be allocated as 'full' ones, or as 'partial' ones. Where taxation is

[6] J. M. Buchanan, 'An Economic Theory of Clubs', *Economica*, vol. 32, 1965, pp. 1–4.

concerned a full competence includes legislative competence, the entitlement to receive the revenues from a certain tax source, and the administrative competence to manage and collect the tax in question. If full competences in this sense are allocated without restriction to each level of government, we will end up with a system of tax competition where, for example, each level has its own income tax. The other extreme would be that the full tax competence is given to the highest level only and that this level allocates tax revenues according to his preferences in the form of transfers or grants to the other government levels.

Apparently, the first solution maximizes autonomy and independence of the government levels and government units concerned, whereas the latter solution makes the other levels of government extremely dependent on the decision of the higher level one. If, on the other hand, a full competence is subdivided into its elements and these partial competences are attributed to different levels of government, 'policy interlacing'[7] will result. A more positive aspect is considered if such a solution is labelled as 'co-operative federalism' because allocating partial competences to different levels of government will oblige them to co-operate in order to be able to utilize a given competence.

A full competence can also be subdivided into a frame competence on the one hand and executive competence on the other. In that case, the frame competence can be given to the higher level government in order to obtain some uniformity of public good provision, whereas the executive competences may allow certain room for manoeuvre for the lower level governments.

(4) *The correspondence principle*.[8] The basic argument of the correspondence principle is that both taxpayers and beneficiaries of public expenditures financed by taxes should be adequately represented within a decision-making unit. If taxpayers are in a majority, cost considerations will dominate, with the consequence that public goods provision will be too small or offered with too low a quality, whereas if the beneficiaries dominate, there will be an excess supply of public services. The basic idea underlying the correspondence principle (or what has been called 'fiscal equivalence' by Mancur Olson) is that the benefit principle of taxation is extended from individuals to groups of individuals: if there exists a public good that benefits a clearly separable group of people, then this group should pay for it. The problem that remains to be solved is how to distribute the tax burden among the members of the group. A solution that minimizes preference cost is to endow the group with the right to decide on this. This solution obviously implies that there are no positive or negative externalities so that neither a part of the cost nor a part of the

---

[7] F. Scharpf, B. Reissert and F. Schnabel, *Politikverflechtung: Theorie und Empirie des kooperativen Föderalismus in der Bundesrepublik*, Scriptor-Verlag, Kronberg/Ts, 1976.

[8] W. E. Oates, 1972, *op. cit*.

benefits are exported in form of a spillover. This, in turn, requires that the group cannot be arbitrarily defined but must consist of the people that live within the servicing area of the public good or public function concerned—that is, the congruence principle is realized. If there are spillovers, appropriate instruments like grants or taxes have to be applied in order to internalize these externalities.

(5) *The principle of fair burden sharing.* From the traditional public finance point of view, either the benefit or the ability-to-pay principle can be used in order to realize fair burden sharing. If it is considered fair that the beneficiaries contribute to financing a public good provision proportionately to the benefits derived, tax prices or cost-based fees would be appropriate. In case this is not considered to represent a fair solution—for example, in the case of financing transfers to low income persons or when the persons benefiting from a public service are entitled to receive a subsidy in consuming the service in question—then the benefit principle is to be replaced by the ability-to-pay principle. It normally means that the link with benefits received is cut off (or the benefits cannot be identified and assessed), and people are forced to pay according to their income, their consumption, or their wealth. In designing the adequate tax schedule to be applied, the choice is open between regressive, proportionate and progressive taxation. National tax systems comprise taxes of all of these sorts; total incidence can be more or less progressive according to the mix.

Sometimes, however, the benefit principle can have a much larger application than is usually thought of. In the case of the EC, for instance, the MacDougall Report[9] demonstrated that highly developed and rich regions within national economies contribute to the financing of public services in the less developed and poorer regions of the same economy, so that at first sight this seems also to be an application of the ability-to-pay principle to regions, states or provinces. However, it was shown that the richer regions very frequently also are net exporters of private goods and services whereas the poorer ones are net importers. The reason is that the higher developed regions profit from better resource endowments in a wide sense: they are centrally located and not peripheral regions; they profit from positive externalities of agglomeration and urban settlement systems, they have a sectoral structure that is better adjusted to structural change and, last but not least, they benefit from a much better endowment with public infrastructure. As has been shown by Dieter Biehl *et alia*,[10] it is possible to explain interregional GDP per capita differences with extremely high coefficients of

[9] MacDougall Report, Commission of the European Communities (eds): Report of the Study Group on the Role of Public Finance in European Integration, 2 volumes, Brussels, 1977.

[10] D. Biehl *et al.*, The contribution of Infrastructure to Regional Development, Document, Commission of the European Communities, 2 volumes, Luxembourg/Brussels, 1986.

determination with the aid of a quasi-production function comprising location, agglomeration, sectoral structure and infrastructure as explanatory variables. Under these conditions, it is easy to understand that producers in those well resource-endowed regions are very competitive and are able to outcompete their competitors in the less well endowed regions. As the latter ones, however, are not allowed to protect themselves against this competition, the producers in the highly developed regions profit from the 'open market' situation. As a consequence, the higher income and tax capacity of the more developed regions within a country are to a certain extent the result of these 'gains from trade' that are not due to 'private', but to 'public' competitiveness. If under these conditions the richer regions retransfer to the poorer ones that part of their higher tax returns that is derived from the latter keeping their markets open and accepting the decline of their less competitive producers, this could also be considered to be in line with the benefit principle.

Be that as it may, the principle of fair burden sharing is still important for assessing inter-governmental transfer systems and in case of the EC, also transfers among member states. If the richer member countries were to contribute more to the financing of EC activities relative to their GDP, this would partly represent application of the benefit principle and partly application of the principle of fair burden sharing.

(6) *The principle of 'Finanzausgleich' (fiscal equalization)*. Usually, explicit untied transfers between richer and poorer governments are characteristic features of mature federations, but also of a number of unitary states. Implicit transfers, possibly at a much higher intensity than normally assumed, seem to exist in almost all public finance systems. However, these implicit transfers may not always correspond with the principle of fair burden sharing in the sense that the richer are net payers and the poorer net receivers. The fact that explicit transfer systems in the sense of 'Finanzausgleich' are not very frequent may have to do with the possibility that those untied transfers imply that the donors accept any decision of the receiving entity even if it would go counter to the preferences of the donor. This means that high preference costs are involved for communities with high degrees of heterogeneity, which may explain why there does not yet exist such an untied transfer system within the EC. The only instrument that works in the direction of transferring money from richer countries to poorer ones within the EC is the Regional Fund. However, the distributive effects of, say, the Common Agricultural Policy (CAP) seem to be in the counter direction—from poor to rich agricultural regions. This has to do with the fact that in its early years the CAP was more oriented towards so-called 'northern' products and not so much towards 'southern' ones; this later changed to a certain extent. As CAP expenditure consumes roughly two-thirds of EC funds, its inter-regional incidence dominates the rest of the Community budget. Fortunately, the reform of the structural funds decided in the context of

the budgetary reforms in 1988 strengthened the positive redistributive roles, especially of the Regional Fund.

The British case is the outstanding example of the distorted distribution of EC funds. When Great Britain entered the EC, she brought with her an agricultural policy with a very low degree of protection and, therefore, with a low share of agriculture in GDP and in exports, but with high imports from the Commonwealth. As a consequence, the EC cashed high import levies from these imports, but had not much to pay for British agricultural exports and for dealing with excess production. As private consumption seems to have been high in Britain too, the EC received high amounts of VAT. The net result was that this country became the second biggest net payer in the EC system, despite the fact that its GDP per capita had been below EC average for many years in the past. Clearly, the principles of fair burden sharing and of 'Finanzausgleich' seem to have been violated. But the British case is not the only disturbing one—the mirror image of the British situation is that some of the richer member countries are net receivers despite the fact that their GDP per capita is higher than the British, and that even, according to some estimates, Portugal could become a net payer, too.

The deficiencies of the existing EC fiscal constitution

The British case just mentioned represents one of the findings when applying federalist principles to the EC fiscal constitution and its consequences. The fact that Great Britain is the second largest net payer in the system is the result of a combination of violations of these principles. However, the negative implications go far beyond the British case and affect the EC as a whole.

First, the principle of optimal competence endowment is violated as the CAP clearly dominates the whole EC decision-making and financial system. Given the double digit increases in EC expenditures during the years before 1988, it should have been possible to get a better balance between the agricultural competence and all other competences. Fortunately, since 1985 the CAP share has been decreasing and in 1988, under the German presidency, a bundle of reforms well prepared by the Delors Commission was realised. It can therefore be expected that the CAP share will continue to go down so that the other policy fields of the community can develop more.

Second, the correspondence principle has not been adhered to in several respects. The most important problem is that the EC does not have a tax authority of its own. As a consequence, the EC decision-makers have never been obliged to weigh tax burdens against expenditure benefits and they have not had to defend their policies directly to their voters. As the normal democratic budgetary discipline did not work, it has been necessary to invent artificial rules like the maximum rate increase for expenditure. In addition, the Council of Ministers has been divided so that agricultural ministers have been allowed to serve their clientele by deciding on agricultural expenditure. To the best of my knowledge there is no individual country in which one group of 'spending' ministers is allowed to act in this way. Even the minimum restrictions that at least a sort of cabinet decision-making is applied—that is, to integrate the agricultural ministers with the other spending ministers for regional, social, technology development affairs and, above all, with the finance ministers—has not been realized at the EC level. Another deficiency stems from the arbitrary distinction between compulsory and non-compulsory expenditure categories in the EC budget. There is at first no systematic rationale for this distinction, as CAP expenditure, for example, is considered to be compulsory because it is based on legal texts, whereas the wages and salaries of EC employees are non-compulsory despite the fact that there is a similar legal basis. Another non-compulsory item is regional fund expenditure although there are also clear rules that determine the spending. What is more intriguing, however, is that as a consequence of the very complicated budgetary procedures, it is the Council of Ministers that has a sort of 'last word' in compulsory, and the European Parliament in non-compulsory, expenditure. As a consequence, there has been expenditure-increasing competition between the two parts of the budgetary authority. The Council was the initial victor as it could increase drastically CAP expenditure, though in the years since 1985 the Parliament has succeeded in expanding its share of the budget faster.

Third, there seems also to be a violation of the principle of optimal competence differentiation. The EC disposes of a full competence for CAP and for the external tariffs. As far as the latter is concerned, this seems to be appropriate, as there is no reason to decentralize tariff decision-making. However, it would be advisable to apply a certain decentralization to CAP. To be sure, all that has to do with the agricultural market policy should remain at the EC level. However, there are so many links between regional and environmental policies on the one hand and structural agricultural policy on the other that decentralization should be envisaged here. As has been proposed by an international working group of the Institute for European Policy in Bonn,[11] decoupling price and incomes policy on the one hand and integrating agricultural structural policy, regional policy and environmental policy on the other could be a good combination in order to solve the agricultural problem. The proposal includes, for example, the possibility of paying farmers a remuneration for environmental protection—a possibility that cannot be uniformly applied throughout the EC because preferences are extremely different (the Germans might be ready to pay substantially for that goal

[11] D. Biehl, et al., *Common Agricultural Policy, European Integration and International Division of Labour*, Institut für Europäische Politik, Bonn, 1987.

whereas it is difficult to see that this instrument would be widely used in Greece or Portugal).

The preceding analysis has shown that there are some very important deficiencies in the fiscal constitution of the EC. It remains to be seen what reform proposals could be derived from this analysis.

Reform proposals for the EC fiscal constitution

The Single Act of Luxembourg 1986 demonstrates that there is a new political will to engage in strengthening the European Community despite the fact that the British position again seems to be very sceptical and reluctant. The Act has endowed the EC with some new competences in the fields of environment, technology, professional training and structural policies. It facilitates a reform of the EC fiscal constitution, as it goes in the direction of a better balanced system of competence and endowment. The structural funds that will be doubled between 1988 and 1993 will help to reduce the undesirable distribution effects and contribute to greater convergence.

However, not much has been decided that could help to reduce the violations of the federalist principles by the fiscal constitution. One could even argue that especially the decisions taken in the context of the medium-term financial perspective have rather added to the deficiencies. Admittedly, strong decisions have been necessary to end the budgetary crisis of the EC. The problem is that after 1992, perhaps even earlier, when the 'austerity' period is considered to end, all the distortions still existing within the EC fiscal constitution will show up again and will induce inadequate decisions. It seems necessary to prepare new decisions now in order to avoid this outcome.

The following proposals are meant to start a discussion on these issues, hoping that there will be enough time to weigh the pros and cons so that a well-balanced set of decisions will be available in due time.

First, the EC should be endowed with a tax authority of its own. As already explained, the only way in democratic societies to obtain budgetary discipline is to oblige the politicians to ponder the pros and cons of increasing the tax burden for the European voter at the same time that they consider expenditure increases. The basic elements of this proposal have already been presented elsewhere:[12] a two-stage new revenue source in the form of a progressive surcharge. In the first stage, the member countries are so to speak 'assessed' on the basis of their GNP and their GDP per capita, and the amounts of shares to be paid from each member state will have to be decided. This system is not totally new—it is

---

[12] D. Biehl, 'A Federalist Budgetary Policy Strategy for European Union', in Sir Charles Carter (ed.), *Policy Studies*, *The Journal of the Policy Studies Institute*, vol. 6, part 2, October 1985, pp. 66–76.

already used in order to finance the United Nations. In a second stage, the amounts to be paid according to the principle of fair burden sharing are transformed into a progressive surcharge to be applied to each individual taxpayer, either only to income taxpayers or to income and corporation taxpayers. This would directly confront European decision-makers and their electorate; they could no longer argue that member states are saving so much tax monies because the EC is taking over some expenditure functions. At the same time, national politicians would be freed to defend the EC tax burden even if they did not participate in deciding on EC expenditure.

It could be argued that this progressive surcharge is only a second best solution—why not endow the EC with a uniform European income tax? The answer is that such a tax will certainly be a solution in some distant future, but not for the next 15 to 20 years. The reason is that, given the differences in structures and history of taxation in the member states and considering the strong differences between national income and corporation taxes, it will be extremely difficult to obtain a consensus of how such a European income tax should look. In my judgement, the preference and resource costs are too high for the near future. As long as the member states maintain their differences in income and corporation taxes, they reveal their preferences. If, on the other hand, they use these taxes for financing their national expenditures, then it is worthwhile to consider using the same taxes also for financing EC expenditure. Furthermore, when financial contributions are thought of as appropriate financing instruments for the Community, then it is implicitly accepted that member states finance the EC exactly with their specific mix of peculiar national taxes. And the new fourth revenue source decided in 1988 at the Brussels summit, the GDP levy, will also be financed from that mix of national taxes. To repeat: the progressive two-stage surcharge proposal is not presented as a first best solution, but as one that would allow the EC to acquire a tax authority of its own relatively soon and to reduce the regressivity of the current financing system. Regressivity, however, is not in line with the principle of fair burden sharing because it implies a relatively higher burden for the poorer member countries and a relatively lower burden for the richer ones.

The second proposal is meant to remedy the distorted decision-making system of the CAP. No single group of national spending ministers should be allowed in future to decide on EC expenditure, they will always have to sit in a full Council meeting together with all their other spending colleagues and with, above all, the ministers of finance.

The third proposal aims at abolishing the distinction between compulsory and non-compulsory expenditure. At the same time, the principle of comprehensiveness for the budget should be applied with a view to integrating the not yet included EC expenditure into the budget, for example, the Community development funds. The two parts of the budgetary authority, Council and Parliament, would then have a joint responsibility for this total budget. This requires, however, the introduction of rules that say what can be done if Council and Parliament disagree on important budgetary issues so that a blockade could arise and no budget would be adopted. The solution should consist in introducing first an Intermediation Committee of both institutions charged to find a compromise. This compromise could then be put to the vote in both chambers and would only be rejected if there were a qualified majority against the compromise. The other procedure could be to give one of the two institutions a right of final decision. It should be possible with the aid of this proposal—or with any other that aims at solving the same problem—to abolish the incentives for the spending competition between the Council and the Parliament and to strengthen their joint responsibility for all EC policies.

THE SINGLE MARKET AND EUROPEAN POLICIES FOR ADVANCED TECHNOLOGIES

MARGARET SHARP*

COMMUNITY policies towards advanced technologies were for the first time given legal base in the Single European Act of 1987. Until that time, policies to promote research, development and technology, with the exception of nuclear power (which was covered by the Euratom treaty) and iron and steel (covered by ECSC), were based upon action under Article 235 of the EEC Treaty (Treaty of Rome). This provides general powers for Community action where no specific powers have been granted, subject to unanimous decision of the Council and consultation with the Assembly.

The Single European Act adds to Part III of the EEC Treaty a Title (Title VI, Article 130F) which reads:

> The Community's aim shall be to strengthen the scientific and technological base of European industry and to encourage it to become more competitive at an international level. In order to achieve this it shall encourage undertakings, including small and medium sized undertakings, research centres and universities in their research and technological development activities; it shall support their efforts to co-operate with one another, aiming, in particular, at enabling undertakings to exploit the Community's internal market to the full, in particular through the opening-up of national public contracts, the definition of common standards and the removal of legal and fiscal barriers to that co-operation.

The Single Act also lays down a two-pronged implementation mechanism. First, unanimous adoption by member states of a multi-annual framework programme, laying out the main scientific and technological objectives and defining priorities. Secondly, implementation of that programme through a series of sub-programmes which can be adopted by the Council, after consultation with Parliament and the Economic and Social Committee, by qualified majority voting.

The purpose of this paper is to look behind the formal wording of the Single Act at what has been happening in practice. To do so requires going back in time to developments in the 1960s and 1970s, to examine the unsatisfactory nature of some of these developments, the sea-change in

* Margaret Sharp is a Senior Research Fellow with the Science Policy Research Unit at the University of Sussex. An economist by training, she has written extensively on industrial policy and the development of new technologies in Europe, and was joint author of a recent Chatham House Paper on *European Technological Collaboration*.

policy which took place in the 1980s with the introduction of ESPRIT and other Community programmes, and the degree to which the Single European Act made *de jure* what was already *de facto*.

The ESPRIT programme captured well the spirit of the early 1980s—a spirit, on the one hand, of fear and pessimism as European firms watched US and, particularly, Japanese competitors picking off their traditional markets, and, on the other, of a willingness to change and accept change. There was also, at that time, a vacuum in leadership, which the Community, in the ESPRIT programme, seized, and in so doing provided one of the catalysts to its revitalization and recommitment to the single market. Part of the thesis of this paper is that technology and developments in technology themselves underlay and have provided a considerable spur to these developments.

The other part of the thesis relates to what is decribed as 'the dialectic of 1992'. Community policies for advanced technology are currently proceeding along a twin track. On the one hand is the Framework Programme, with its series of sub-programmes, most modelled on the collaborative, shared-cost basis that proved so effective with ESPRIT. While these have done much to revitalize European firms in the sectors they cover, they have also implicitly encouraged and promoted the substantial concentration that has taken place in most of the new technology sectors. Many of the sectors are now dominated by one or two large firms whose size and global affiliations put them well beyond the control of national competition authorities, arguably also beyond the control of the Community authorities. The other track of Community policy, and arguably the central feature of the single market, is deregulation and liberalization—a policy at times seemingly at odds with the collaborative ethic of the Framework Programme. The paper argues that the two tracks need not conflict, and that 'Fortress Europe' is the wrong interpretation of Community technology policies. On the contrary, it is argued, the two complement each other. Only by maintaining an open, liberalized environment can Europe hope to control its giant firms; yet only by breeding firms of a size to compete with the IBMs or Toshibas of this world can Europe hope to remain competitive in advanced technology sectors. The dialectic is thus resolved.

Early moves towards a European Technological Community

The concept of the European Technological Community has never been far below the surface for those seeking to create a united Europe. It formed an explicit part of the programme for Jean Monnet's Action Committee for a United States of Europe,[1] and was subsequently

[1] The Action Committee for the United States of Europe was founded in October 1955, on the initiative of Jean Monnet, by the Socialist, Christian Democrat and Liberal parties, and non-communist trade unions of six EC countries: Belgium, France, West Germany, Italy, Luxembourg and the Netherlands.

translated into an action plan in Christopher Layton's book, *Europe's Advanced Technologies: A Programme for Integration* (1969). More recently it has resurfaced in Karl Heinz Narjes' (Davignon's successor as Research and Technology Commissioner) call in 1985 for the creation of a Technological Community to be built upon the Community's research and development (R&D) programmes and the various technology initiatives.

There has, however, always been a degree of schizophrenia in such advocacy, with tension between the free marketeers, whose emphasis throughout has been on competition and the diminishing of internal barriers to free competition within the Community, and the mercantilists, who have constantly warned against Europe's increasing dependence on US (and latterly Japanese) technology, and whose vision centred on a more positive and interventionist approach.[2] The Treaty of Rome exacerbated this schizophrenia, in so far as it did not endow the Commission with explicit powers to promote research and development or, for that matter, industry. It provided for a range of policy powers which could be used to determine the regulatory framework and help shape the market environment: competition policy, freedom of movement for capital and labour, the right of establishment, the regulation, and harmonization of state aids. But no general policy framework was established for either industrial or technology policy. This left the Commission to operate only through unanimous decisions of the Council of Ministers and hostage, therefore, to any national interests considered to be of over-riding importance.

The need to operate via consensus among the Council of Ministers helps to explain the stop–go nature of some of the early experiments. DG III, responsible for industrial affairs, was not established until 1967, and then took some time to decide what its proper role should be. Initially it decided on an active stance, encouraging trans-national mergers,[3] but became caught between West German liberalism and the more interventionist philosophy of the French. Attempts in the early 1970s to create an Industrial Policy Committee under the joint auspices of the Council of Ministers and the Commission failed, in effect leaving Community industrial policy in limbo until the end of that decade. Science and technology policy fared little better. The first meeting of the Council of Science Ministers was held in 1967, and in a flurry of activity they commissioned studies of the potential for Community action in six broad

[2] See Jean Jacques Servan Schreiber, *Le Défi Americain*, Paris, De Noel, 1967, for an example of fear of US dependence. Roger Williams, *European Technology: the Politics of Collaboration*, London, Croom Helm, 1973, discusses the emergence of these trends in Europe in the 1960s and early 1970s.

[3] The first major attempt to map out an industrial policy for the Community was the Colonna Report—*La Politique Industrielle de la Communauté* published by the European Commission (COM(70)100—final) in 1970. As indicated, the report rapidly fell foul of wrangling between the French and the Germans and never really had much impact.

areas of technological development—transport, oceanography, metallurgy, environmental issues, data processing and telecommunications—but detailed discussion of proposals was held up by Britain's application for membership. Eventually the initiative led to the establishment in November 1971 of COST (European Co-operation in the field of Scientific and Technical Research), a grouping centred on the Community but comprising, in fact, all nineteen OECD Western European members including Switzerland, Sweden and Austria.

COST has become a useful, if low-key, framework for the preparation and implementation of pan-European projects of applied scientific research, but because of its extensive membership it has tended to shift outside the EC framework with separately negotiated agreements of co-operation for each project. Besides the original six areas identified for development in 1967, it has added four more: meteorology, agriculture, food technology and medical research.[4] In the latter half of the 1980s, the COST framework has been overshadowed by the EUREKA initiative, embracing as it does a similar group of European countries but enjoying high-profile encouragement from some national governments anxious to play down Commission initiatives.

In the computing sector, where Servan-Schreiber specifically warned of the growing power of IBM,[5] European initiatives were particularly slow to get off the ground. Several attempts were made during the 1960s to develop cross-national groupings, but most turned out to be inconclusive. In 1962, for example, Siemens, Olivetti, Elliott Automation (later the core of ICL) and Bull began talks to create a cross-Europe grouping, but these came to nothing. Later, in 1969, the Eurodata consortium—ICL, Bull, Philips, AEG-Telefunken, Saab and Olivetti—was established to tender for the ESRO (European Space Research Organization) computer requirement, but this collapsed under pressure from the German government, largely because Siemens had been left out. The subsequent attempt in 1973 to bring Siemens, Olivetti and CII-Bull together under the Unidata umbrella also collapsed amidst much wrangling on all sides. While hopes for the success of Unidata were still riding high, the Commission had pushed through, in 1974, a Council Resolution backing a medium-term programme on the application, development and production of data processing systems. The hope had been that this would mark the beginning of a major EC programme in computers and electronics. With the failure of Unidata this initiative fizzled out, leaving nothing but a series of small and isolated Commission initiatives and illustrating well the problem of trying to create a coherent

---

[4] For further discussion of COST, see Roger Williams *op. cit.*, 1973, and Margaret Sharp and Claire Shearman, *European Technological Collaboration*, Chatham House Paper No. 36, Routledge and Kegan Paul for the Royal Institute of International Affairs, 1987, pp. 28 and 59–60.
[5] See footnote 2.

programme when the susceptibilities of national champions were at stake.[6]

Even nuclear power, where under the Euratom Treaty there were explicit powers to promote R&D, brought difficulties and disagreements. Four joint research centres were set up—at Karlsruhe, West Germany; Ispra, Italy; Geel, Belgium and Petten, the Netherlands. Areas of research included fast breeder reactors, high-temperature gas reactors, nuclear ship propulsion and nuclear applications to agriculture and medicine. Of these, the quest for a European reactor was potentially the most important but in practice the most neglected, with governments unable to agree a mutually acceptable financial framework within which to pursue the research, or even a research agenda. In this respect developments were the casualty both of mistaken assumptions about the future role of nuclear power (which many in the 1960s saw as central to the future economic prosperity of the industrialized world) and the nationalistic ambitions of the individual power plant manufacturers, whose traditional linkages were with US not European firms and who had, in any case, licensed US nuclear technology and were anxious not to exploit it. Euratom has, however, had an important (if controversial) role in regulating and monitoring the use and transportation of nuclear materials, and in compliance with safeguards.

Of all the new technologies of the 1960s and 1970s, the one success story of European collaboration—aerospace—owed nothing to the EC and much to the determination of governments and their respective national champions to see collaboration through to success. Admittedly, both for aviation and space, economics rapidly ruled out the individual firm from acting alone unless heavily supported by government subsidy (which, of course, happened in the military sectors, but not in civil aviation), and even, in time, inhibited individual governments from acting alone. The lessons culled from, first Concorde, and then Airbus, are of the long, slow haul to collaboration, and of the importance of the industry, not governments, dictating the scope for collaboration.[7] Similar lessons were learned too from the space experience with the European Space Agency (ESA). As a narrow but functionally orientated collaborative framework, it has helped to produce a coherence of objective and purpose in the closely knit space community of policy makers, scientists, engineers and industrialists, and has ensured that, by the mid-1980s, Western Europe had the range of space capabilities sufficient to give it a degree of autonomy.[8]

What lessons then are to be learned from the 1960s and 1970s? Perhaps above all that experience bred cynicism—doubts about the ability of any bureaucracy to 'pick winners' and fears that expensive mistakes at

[6] See Sharp and Shearman, op. cit., 1987, pp. 46–47.
[7] See Keith Hayward, International Collaboration in Civil Aerospace, London, Frances Pinter, 1986.
[8] See Royal Institute of International Affairs (RIIA), Europe's Future in Space: A Joint Policy Report, Chatham House Special Paper, Routledge and Kegan Paul for RIIA, 1987.

the national level would be translated into even more expensive mistakes at the supra-national level where accountability is weakened. There were, however, some positive lessons to be gained from the experience. Indeed, part of the success of the EC programmes of the 1980s lay in the degree to which these lessons have been heeded.

The first was to recognize the need for flexibility—that not all programmes had to conform to a uniform EC pattern with participation from all EC countries, but needed to be tailored to circumstances, with scope for reappraisal and review. The 'variable geometry' that was to become an increasingly important theme of the 1980s was already apparent. Second was the need for functional specificity. Programmes with limited but clear objectives were more likely to meet with success than grandiose programmes which promised the earth but could deliver nothing. Equally, it was crucial that the partners perceived sufficient benefit in the longer term to sustain their commitment through the short run and to provide the incentive to reconcile major differences in outlook and interest. In this respect the Franco–German axis was crucial. Programmes which won support from these two partners were more likely to be successful. Third was the need to align the government and industrial roles into one that was mutually reinforcing. There was little point in governments promoting programmes which were of no interest to the industrial community. In this respect programmes needed to be drawn up in line with the 'grain of the market', not against it.

ESPRIT—a watershed in Community policies

The issue of technological dependence which had underlain early moves towards the establishment of a Community technology policy (and stimulated a rash of national policies) resurfaced in the late 1970s when, emerging from the traumas of oil crisis and recession, and beset by problems of adjustment in older industries such as steel, shipbuilding, even chemicals, Europe suddenly became aware of the very fast advances being made by US and Japanese firms in micro-electronics and associated technologies. European firms had seemed blind to many of these developments and were now suddenly faced by the prospect of US and Japanese competitors picking off markets which they had long regarded as theirs. Many businessmen despaired of their ability to regain lost ground—hence the term 'Europessimism' which came to describe the era.

In fact things were by no means as bad as the pessimists made out. In comparison with the United States and Japan, Western Europe's overall competence in advanced technology sectors (including in that definition sectors such as pharmaceuticals, new materials and aerospace, as well as the information technology (IT) sectors) held up well, with West Germany and Sweden standing out both in terms of their commitment to R&D and in terms of patenting activity. A detailed investigation of patenting activity by country and by sector reveals, however, that across the board, Europe is weak in electronics, showing a poor performance in both capital and consumer goods sectors.[9]

Why should Europe's performance in this sector have been so poor? Since the 1960s it was a sector picked out for its strategic importance. The French, British and West German governments had all pumped sizeable support into it. The French had run a series of *Plans Calculs* and *Plans Compositants* culminating in their grand strategy for the *filière électronique*. The British government, like the French, acted as marriage broker in bringing firms together, on the grounds that size was a key element in competitiveness, but in the 1970s had switched emphasis to a series of more generalized programmes aimed at promoting general capabilities and awareness in micro-electronics.[10] In all three countries lucrative public sector contracts in data processing and telecommunications were steered towards the respective 'national champions'; and in France and Britain the defence sector, as in the United States, was an important public purchaser.

Increasingly, observers began to question whether these policies themselves were not at fault—whether promoting 'national champions' in each individual member state was not diverting European companies from taking advantage of the Community's major asset, its common market of 320 million, and instead fragmenting effort between the various national markets. Increasingly, too, the lack of competition was questioned. Large companies might be necessary to achieve the relevant economies of scale and scope, but such benefits were rapidly negated if the companies concerned made little effort to keep up with new technologies, complacent of their protected position in home markets.

It was against this background that Vicomte Davignon, Commissioner for Industry from 1977 to 1985, and for Research and Technology from 1981 to 1985, set in train moves which were eventually to result in the ESPRIT programme. The model was the Japanese Very Large Scale Integration (VLSI) programme of the mid-70s which had successfully launched the Japanese into making mainstream memory chips. Like this programme it was to be a strategic programme of 'pre-competitive research'—that is research necessary to underpin new developments but not in itself having direct commercial application. But it was not to be a heavy-handed, top-down programme designed by Community bureaucrats, and it was to be collaborative across national boundaries to get the national champions thinking along Community, not national, lines.

Davignon played a vital role in developing the ESPRIT programme. In his evidence to the 1985 House of Lords Select Committee on the

---

[9] For details on this see K. Pavitt and P. Patel, The International Distribution and the Determinants of Technological Activity, *Oxford Review of Economic Policy*, Vol. 4, No. 4, December 1988.

[10] For a general discussion of schemes to promote new technologies see M. Sharp (ed.), *Europe and the New Technologies*, Frances Pinter, London, 1985.

European Communities, he outlined the three factors which had motivated his attempts.[11] In the first place, he had been struck by the 'very distinctive difference in performance' between the industries of USA, Japan and the EC. Second, he had felt that the time had come for Community competence to be upgraded to reflect more accurately the state of the art; and, third, he had become aware of the fact that no real incentive existed for cross-border collaboration. Any EC-level solution therefore needed a new approach to policy development. Until then the Commission had tended to work with research directors or their equivalents, and initiatives had come unstuck because they had been unable to carry them higher up the hierarchy. Davignon determined to liaise with only the very highest levels of company management, to define priorities with them and thus secure their commitment to subsequent programmes.

During 1979–80 Davignon therefore invited the heads of Europe's leading electronics and IT companies to a series of 'Round Table' discussions. The 'Big Twelve', as they came to be known, comprised ICL, GEC and Plessey from Britain; AEG, Nixdorf and Siemens from Germany; Thomson, Bull and CGE from France; Olivetti and STET from Italy; and Philips from the Netherlands. Davignon received a more favourable response than the Commission had received from their lower-level counterparts in earlier years. By September 1980 an outline programme began to emerge. The idea was to develop a European strategic programme based on the collaboration between the major European companies, their smaller counterparts, and universities and research institutes. This would focus on the pre-competitive end of collaborative research, a stance which from the Commission's viewpoint neatly avoided the issue of competition policy. [Under Articles 85 and 86, collaboration for the purposes of pre-competitive research is granted a block exemption; collaboration at the development stage (competitive research) is not allowed.] By May 1982 these had been worked into a full proposal and the Commission's paper 'Towards a European Strategic Programme for Research and Development in Information Technology' was put to the Council, and subsequently to the Versailles European Summit in June 1982. The response was favourable and by December 1982 the Commission had the go-ahead for the first pilot phase costing 11.5m ECUs (£8.5m).

The pilot phase, 1983–4, was a deliberate part of the Davignon strategy. Given the doubts he encountered from the participants in his 'Round Table', in particular over the capacity of the Commission to mount an effective programme which would not become bogged down in bureaucratic delays, his strategy was one of 'toe in the water'—see how the pilot phase goes before making a further commitment. A special task-force,

---

[11] House of Lords Select Committee on the European Communities. ESPRIT (European Research and Development in Information Technologies). Session 1984–85. 8th Report 1985, p. 169.

mainly recruited from industry, was set up to handle applications and to cut through the Brussels red tape. The call for proposals went out in February 1983, and contracts began to be signed in May that year. By September, 38 projects had been launched which were later to be incorporated into the main part of the programme. Over 80 per cent of the first round of contracts went to the twelve 'Round Table' companies (comprising, it has to be said, 70 per cent of the industry).

Encouraged by the success of the pilot phase, the Commission rapidly pushed ahead with its full plans. Those comprised a ten-year programme (1984–93) with an overall budget (50 per cent Community funded; 50 per cent industry funded) of 1.5 billion ECUs (approximately £1 billion). The first five-year phase was to concentrate on the pre-competitive stage of developing the technology in three areas (micro-electronics, advanced information processing and software technology) and two fields of application (office systems and computer-integrated manufacturing). These plans were put to the Council in November 1983, but held up until February 1984 by UK and German reservations over budgetary costs.

The first call for proposals under the full programme went out in March 1984 and met with a huge response. The 201 projects eventually selected for the programme's first phase involved 240 firms (57 per cent of these from firms with less than 500 employees) and 210 research institutions. Three-quarters of the research projects involve collaboration between firms and academic research units. By January 1987, a total of 1.36 bn ECUs (approximately £900m) had been committed, almost the whole of what had originally been seen as a ten-year programme.

An important feature of ESPRIT has been the openness and commitment it has required of the firms linked into it. Project proposals have to be submitted in reply to open invitations. Each project must involve at least two independent industrial partners from separate member states. Costs are generally co-financed by the EC and industry on a fifty/fifty basis. Research results are shared between all the participants in any given project who are free to apply them commercially, and preferential access is then granted to other ESPRIT participants outside that project. These guarantees are the cornerstones of the whole ESPRIT process.

The success of ESPRIT led to immediate demands for a second and yet more expensive programme. Plans for Phase II were, however, delayed by the protracted negotiations of the Framework Programme (see below) and did not get underway until 1988 with the official start of the new programme in February 1989.

ESPRIT II is roughly twice the size of ESPRIT I with a total expenditure over its five-year life of 3.2 billion ECUs, the expenditures being split, as with ESPRIT I, fifty/fifty between the Commission and industry. (The cost to the Community's budget over the five-year period will therefore be 1.6 billion ECUs.) The programme has been streamlined into three main areas of research—micro-electronics, IT processing systems and applications technologies—and there is greater focus on what is called 'demand driven' aspects of the programme, for example greater emphasis on Application Specific Integrated Circuit (ASIC) technology. As with ESPRIT I, considerable emphasis is given to the development of open systems of data-processing such as OSI (Open Systems Interconnect). ESPRIT II also incorporates a number of demonstration projects known as Technology Integration Projects (TIPs) designed to pull together various strands of other work and show how they interlink. For example, work on desk-top workstations is being linked with theoretical work on parallel architectures to offer greater finger-tip capabilities.[12] Although nominally still pre-competitive, there is a good deal in ESPRIT II that in fact comes close to competitive research as those involved in Phase I seek to develop some of the ideas promoted at that stage. Its popularity among manufacturers and research institutions can be gauged from the applications put in during the first half of 1988 for awards under the first tranche of projects for ESPRIT II—the budget was ten times over subscribed![13]

The Single European Act, the Framework Programme and other policies for advanced technologies

Since 1985, ESPRIT has served as a model of other European programmes promoting new technologies. There is not space to go into these in detail, but Table 1 summarizes the most important programmes currently in being.[14] (More are being added all the time.) It is worth noting from Table 1 how ESPRIT dominates in terms of spending, being more than twice the value of the next largest programme—RACE (telecoms). Both ESPRIT and RACE are administered by DG XIII which deals exclusively with electronics and telecommunications and incorporates the rump of the old Task Force set up to administer ESPRIT. DG XII, which deals with science and technology, administers most of the other programmes and is generally regarded as more traditional in its approach (more bureaucratic, but also more laissez-faire compared with an element of dirigisme seen within DG XIII). The largest of the DG XII programmes is BRITE/EURAM whose aim is to upgrade industrial technology and materials. The biotechnology programmes pale to insignificance beside the expenditures on IT and to date have largely funded academic research—indeed one of the criticisms of the programmes is that grants

[12] For a succinct summary of the main components of the current ESPRIT programme see DTIs, *A Guide to European Community Industrial Research and Development Programmes*, DTI, London, October 1988. Ref: EC8 describes the ESPRIT programme.

[13] *Financial Times*, 12 April 1988.

[14] Table 1 has been compiled from a number of sources. The DTI *Guide to EC R&D Programmes*, *op. cit.*, Note 12. Commission of the European Communities, *Research and Technological Development Policy*, European Documentation, Luxembourg, 1988. Commission of the European Communities, Report of the Framework Programme Review Board, Brussels, June 1989.

TABLE 1   THE MAIN EUROPEAN COMMUNITY PROGRAMMES FOR PROMOTING NEW TECHNOLOGIES

Name	Dates	Budget* Cost (MECUs)	Main objectives
ESPRIT European Strategic Programme for R&D in IT	I—1984–88 II—1988–92	800 1530	To promote European capabilities and competitiveness in IT technologies, primarily micro-electronics and systems development.
RACE R&D in Advanced Communications Technologies for Europe	Definition Phase—1985–87 Main Programme—1988–92	21 460	To establish a European competence in broadband communications by developing the equipment, standards and technology necessary for an Integrated Broadband Communications (IBC) system
BRITE/EURAM Basic research in Industrial Technologies/ Advanced Materials for Europe	BRITE I 1985–88 EURAM I 1986–88 BRITE/EURAM 1989–92	100 450	Support for industrial R&D which upgrades technological/materials base of production.
BAP Biotechnology Action Programme	1985–89	75	Support for infrastructure development in biotechnology with particular emphasis on research and training.

BRIDGE Biotechnological Research for Innovation, Development and Growth in Europe	1989–93	100	As for BAP, but emphasis put on larger, more comprehensive projects in areas such as advanced cell culture, molecular modelling etc.
ECLAIR European Collaborative Linkage of Agriculture and Industry through Research	1989–94	80	Industrial applications of advanced biotechnologies in agro-industrial sector, with emphasis on use of agricultural produce as industrial raw material.
FLAIR Food Linked Agro-Industrial Research	1989–94	25	
COMMETT Community Programme in Education and Training for Technology	Phase I—1987–89 Phase II—1990–92	30 30	Co-operation between university and industry in training programmes for innovation (a) through establishment of university/enterprise partnerships and (b) through transnational exchange of students and staff.

Sources: See footnote 14.
* The figures given as budget cost exclude any industrial contribution for the ESPRIT and other programmes which are shared cost programmes. Total expenditures under the various programmes are therefore approximately double the amount of the budget cost quoted.

111

have been too small to attract major industrial participation. (A criticism which the new BRIDGE programme aims to overcome with its emphasis on industrially oriented projects.) More recently, the Commission has begun to embark upon a series of programmes to promote education and training and basic research. COMMETT is the oldest and largest of these, now entering its second phase, but programmes such as SCIENCE (to promote collaborative research and exchanges with the scientific community) and SPES (to promote similar objectives in economics) are as yet very new, and take the Commission into new territory (the promotion of basic research and education). There are also a series of projects aimed explicitly at developing applications of technology—hence AIM (medical technology), DRIVE (automobile and IT), DELTA (educational technology). None at present involve expenditures on a par with those identified in Table 1.

Although the programmes all differ in aims and levels of expenditure, all share four common characteristics:

(i) they are collaborative between organizations and between countries—to qualify, applications must involve firms and/or institutions from two or more Community countries;

(ii) where there are industrial partners (all except the educational programmes), funding is on a shared cost basis with industry meeting 50 per cent of the research costs;

(iii) while the Commission identifies priorities and broad areas of research, actual research projects are chosen by the applicants and hence the programmes are to some degree demand driven;

(iv) each project, once agreed, is subject to a tight timetable, and monitored through a system of programme management. Those dealt with by DG XII (Science and Technology) are subject to peer review assessment prior to project approval.

The basis for these policies is now provided by the Single European Act which, given that ESPRIT I was well underway in 1985 when the Act was first mooted, effectively made legal what was already happening in practice. The Single Act also introduced the notion of the Framework Programme—an overall programme looking five years ahead, clarifying objectives and identifying, with funding provision, general expenditure priorities. The Framework Programme adopted in 1987 related in fact to the years 1987–91 (inclusive) and had been under discussion for nearly two years, the original hope being that it would be agreed by the Council of Ministers in late 1986. British objections to the level of funding (influenced partly by the wish to use this as a counter in the wider budget discussion on the funding of agriculture) held up agreement on the budget

until September 1987.[15] The final sum agreed amounts to 5.6 billion
ECUs, although Narjes' original bid in 1985 was for funding at the level of
10 billion ECUs,[16] with the British holding out for spending at 3.6 billion
ECUs, little above the spending levels of the years 1983–86.[17] Even at the
higher level finally agreed, spending amounts to only 2 per cent of the total
EC budget, whereas agriculture consumes over 70 per cent. It is not
surprising that the recent review of the Framework Programme commissioned, as required, in its third year of operation, was at pains to stress
that the Framework Programme itself needs to be considered in the light
of overall community priorities.[18]

The Framework Programme is summarized in Table 2 which identifies
both broad objectives (e.g. Quality of Life) and more specific programmes. It will be noted that the IT budget (Line 2), at over 2000
MECUs, is very considerably larger than any other, with ESPRIT and
RACE the two main items in this programme. But note also that the
second largest expenditure goes not to the BRITE programme or biotechnology, but to energy, where fusion and fission power together still
consume resources equivalent (almost) to the total ESPRIT programme.
The fusion expenditures under the JET (Joint European Torus) and the
NET (New European Torus) programmes fund research centres at
Culham, near Oxford in the UK, and at other smaller research centres in
France, Italy and FR Germany. The fission expenditures reflect mainly
continuing expenditures on the Joint Research Centres (JRCs) set up in
the 1960s. Attempts to diversify the JRCs into, for example, new materials
and ceramics, have not so far been very successful.[19] The BRITE/
EURAM programme comes third after energy, then the Quality of Life
(mainly environmental R&D) followed by biotechnology and the agro-
industrial technologies and the programmes aimed at encouraging cooperation in science and technology, including the promotion of basic
science. One of the main conclusions to emerge from the recent review of
the Framework Programme was the need to promote what was described
as the 'scientific humus' which included not merely exchange programmes
but funding European centres of excellence. The review board meanwhile
reiterated the commitment of the Community to fund only pre-
competitive R&D and warned against the inevitable shift of the programmes, as they matured, towards more competitive elements of R&D.
This, they argued, should either be funded by industry or, where
continuing assistance was required, by EUREKA.

The relationship between the EC programmes and EUREKA is

---

[15] For a fuller discussion of the Framework Budget, see M. Sharp: The Community and
New Technologies; Chapter 11 in Juliet Lodge (ed.), *The European Community and the
Challenge of the Future*, Pinter Publishers, London, 1989.

[16] See *Financial Times*, 7 March 1985.

[17] See *Financial Times*, 9 April 1987.

[18] See Report of the Framework Programme Review Board, Brussels, June 1989, pp. 4–5.

[19] See Review Board, *op. cit.*, Recommendations 38 and 39.

TABLE 2 SUMMARY OF ACTION LINES IN THE NEW (1987–1991) EC R&D FRAMEWORK PROGRAMME

Action Line	Expected total commitment expenditure 1987–1991 (MECU)	Action Line	Expected total commitment expenditure 1987–1991 (MECU)
1. Quality of life		5. Energy	
1.1 Health	67	5.1 Fission	472
1.2 Radiation protection	60	5.2 Fusion	902
1.3 Environment	292	5.3 Non-nuclear	190
2. Towards an information society		6. S&T for development	67
2.1 Information Technologies (ESPRIT)	1534	7. Exploiting the seabed and marine resources	
2.2 Telecommunications (RACE)	462	7.1 Marine S&T	42
2.3 Applications of IT (including Transport)	105	7.2 Fisheries	25
3. Modernisation of industry		8. European S&T co-operation	
3.1 Manufacturing industry (BRITE)	396	8.1 Stimulation	176
3.2 Advanced materials	205	8.2 Large facilities	25
3.3 Raw materials	65	8.3 Forecasting, assessment, etc.	22
3.4 Standards	188	8.4 Dissemination of results	56
4. Biological resources			
4.1 Biotechnology	121		
4.2 Agro-industrial	88		
4.3 Competitiveness of agriculture	56	Total	5.617 BECU

Source: DTI, A Guide to European Community Industrial Research and Development Programmes.

complex. Originally EUREKA was proposed by President Mitterrand in April 1985 as a counter to the US Star Wars programme when it looked as if the latter might poach Europe's ablest scientists. As it has worked out the EUREKA programme is far from the flamboyant programme envisaged by Mitterrand, and instead constitutes an umbrella mechanism for encouraging firm-to-firm collaboration. It applies to all Western European countries, not just the EC, and it has no central funding but projects 'badged' under EUREKA (to verify that they constitute a *bona fide* collaboration) may qualify for national R&D support funding. By 1989 the total number of projects accepted amounted to over 300 with total project costs (to industry and national budgets) amounting to 6,500 MECU—more than the total Framework Programme.[20] Initially EUREKA was seen as a competitor to the EC programmes—indeed much of the initial British support for EUREKA stemmed from a desire to counter Community ambitions on new technologies. Over time, the two have become complementary with EUREKA concentrating on the competitive end of R&D and the EC programmes on pre-competitive R&D. There remains, however, an inevitable element of overlap between the various co-operative R&D ventures promoted on a European basis. Besides EUREKA, the COST programme still exists (and is funded separately from the Framework Budget) and embraces non-EC states. There are also the various specialist initiatives such as CERN (particle physics), EMBO (molecular biology) and ESA (space) all of which are funded by different groups of countries—variable geometry at its best. As the EC increases its presence in these areas, relationships have become more complex. Indeed, yet another of the Review Board's recommendations was that the Community should avoid duplicating such programmes, but should aim to establish 'synergistic' relationships.[21]

Collaboration, confidence, concentration and the Single Market

ESPRIT has proved a turning point in policies towards advanced technologies in more than one sense. As has already been noted it marked a new departure in style for EC policies with the collaborative, decentralized, project-based programme replacing the top–down style of earlier years. It also, as we have seen, provided a model for a whole new range of Commission-based policies latterly brought under the aegis of the Framework Programme. It even, arguably, stimulated the setting up of a

---

[20] See Statistical Overview of all EUREKA projects obtainable from UK EUREKA Office, Ashdown House, 123 Victoria Street, London SW1. By no means all the EUREKA projects will be completed so this figure undoubtedly exaggerates the size of the programme. The Framework Expenditures, of course, deal only with the EC budget cost and do not include industry based expenditures, whereas the EUREKA figures relate to total project cost.

[21] See Review Board, *op. cit.*, Recommendation 7.

competitor programme—EUREKA—which was fairly rapidly tamed and has become a complement rather than a competitor.

Psychologically, however, ESPRIT has proved far more potent in impact than either its example, or, for that matter, the projects it sponsors would imply. In the first place it proved to be a turning point in the confidence of the European electronics industry. Its collaborative framework perforce brought these firms—the old national champions—together and provided them with a channel for communication. (It was surprising how few of them previously had any regular means of exchanging views and information.) In so doing it also provided a mechanism for arriving at a common view. That common view, around which there proved rapid convergence, was that in the long run there was little protection to be gained from tariffs or other protective devices given that foreign competitors could rapidly circumvent them via inward investment. Moreover, given the swing to neo-liberalism, even long-established public purchasing monopolies, such as telecommunications and defence, were vulnerable. The logic led inexorably to the view that to compete successfully, even *within* Europe, these erstwhile national champions needed to set their sights on global markets and global competitiveness. As Davignon had hoped, ESPRIT proved an important stepping stone in the route from national champion to global competitor. In turn this had the effect of creating an important constituency amongst business pressing for the completion of the internal market, for once these firms had lost their national champion status it was imperative that they maximized the advantage to be gained from the single market. Behind Delors and Cockfield in 1985, therefore, were the leaders of Europe's major firms, impatient for the end to such things as customs' delays at borders, to conflicting national standards in data processing, or arcane rules on property ownership.

ESPRIT, however, has also proved to be a catalyst to a far wider reorganization of European industry, affecting both high-tech and low-tech industries. Collaboration was infectious. Admittedly something of the trend was visible before ESPRIT and the other European collaborative programmes that emerged in the mid-1980s. But the period since 1983–84 has seen a substantial rise in joint ventures and other forms of strategic partnership both within the Community and with firms outside the Community.[22] Collaboration is, however, of its nature, usually temporary. Firms collaborate over R&D for the development of a specific product; once that product is in the market place the collaboration often ends. Successful collaborations frequently result in merger. (As indeed sometimes do unsuccessful collaborations.) It is not therefore surprising to find European industry in the latter half of the 1980s in the midst of the

---

[22] For a fuller discussion of these developments, see Margaret Sharp: *European Technology: Does 1992 Matter?* Papers in Science, Technology and Public Policy, No. 19. Available from SPRU, University of Sussex, Brighton BN1 9RF.

merger boom affecting all sectors of industry—from food processing (Nestlé-Rowntree) to heavy electrical equipment (Asea–Brown Boveri). What the Colonna Report of 1970 tried ineffectually to promote, the cross-country European merger, is now happening seemingly every day.

In the electronics sector, where the national champions policy caused undue fragmentation, we have seen companies like SGS Ates (Italy) link with Thomson (France) in semi-conductor production, countering the collaboration between Philips and Siemens on the mega-project. (A project set up between the two companies in 1982/3 aimed at manufacturing the one megabit and four megabit chips.) Thomson has now bought the UK's Inmos, probably the most innovative new European chip company, while Siemens, through its joint bid with GEC, has taken over the UK's other front-running chip firm, Plessey. In consumer electronics Philips acquired Grundig, but Thomson successively took over Telefunken, Ferguson (the TV branch of the British Thorn–EMI), and the consumer electronics interests of RCA in the US, making Thomson the second largest manufacturer of colour TVs in the world and concentrating European consumer electronics capabilities in the hands of Philips and Thomson. In telecommunications, Siemens acquired Rolm in the US, GTE's (the second largest US telecom equipment firm) overseas interests and, through its link with the GEC/Plessey bid, an interest in the British telecommunications market. The most dramatic moves were, however, from Alcatel (the telecom subsidiary of the French electrical and electronics giant, CGE), which in 1987 took over the ITT interests in Europe, parachuting what had, in 1975, been a comparatively small company in telecommunications equipment into being the second largest in the world after AT&T in the US. The national champions of yesteryear were thus transformed into major European-based multinationals.

Collaboration may have led the way, but there is little denying that major impetus has also come from competition, or more specifically from the threat of competition likely to emerge in the wake of 1992. The nexus is an involved one in which cause and effect are intertwined and it is not always possible to disentangle. Briefly, the logic (and the line of argument in this paper) is as follows. World developments in technology, and particularly IT, led to intensified competition in the 1970s from which the US and Japan emerged as the strongest players; this led to Europessimism which in turn caused Davignon to promote ESPRIT; ESPRIT (combined, it has to be admitted with recovery from a major recession) worked like a dream; it restored the confidence of the European firms in their own abilities; got them working together in unison; and led them to promote, on the one hand, moves towards 1992 and, on the other, further collaborations and mergers. This latter trend was then substantially reinforced by moves towards the single market, with the result that, paradoxically, what was intended to be a major stimulus to competition has ended by promoting a substantial increase in concentration.

The dialectic of 1992

Where does this get us? To outside observers there appears growing conflict between the main objective of the Single European Act—more competition in the internal market—and what have always been seen as the subsidiary objectives, namely the strengthening of the supply-side of the economy. 1992 and the Single European Act are supposed to be all about competition. Consider the following extracts from the Cecchini Report, taken from the section headed 'The Competitive Vista of 1992':

> A dramatically new environment awaits consumers and producers alike in the integrated Community market post-1992. The removal of a whole range of non-tariff barriers—frontier red tape, closed public procurement, a plethora of differing product standards—leads to an immediate downward impact on costs. But this is merely the primary effect. ... Much more substantial gains will be generated by ... a new and pervasive competitive climate. One in which the players of the European economy—manufacturing and service companies, and consumers of their output—can exploit new opportunities and better use of available resources ... For firms the era of the national soft option will be over.[23]

Admittedly, Cecchini is looking to dynamic as well as static gains from increased competition, above all the removal of the inefficiencies that stem too readily from the quiet life of protected monopoly profits. But is this really what is happening? Or is the process being dominated by the other 'track' of the Single European Act—that which seeks to promote competitiveness by the more traditionally mercantilist route of promoting R&D in strategic sectors? Indeed, is the mercantilism dominating the process and creating instead a Fortress Europe?

The existence of the 'twin tracks' of 1992 is apparent in many sectors, with simultaneous pressures towards liberalization and deregulation on the one hand, and towards collaboration and concentration on the other. Amongst advanced technologies, it is best illustrated by developments in telecommunications. The emergence of the RACE programme with its commitment to the integrated broadband network has already been mentioned, a development very much in line with the traditional, ordered public-utility approach to network provision which seeks to exploit the maximum *social* benefit (externalities) to be gained from extensive network provision. Simultaneously, and anticipating the liberalization moves of 1992, there has also been an extensive restructuring and the emergence of three leading equipment firms within Western Europe— Alcatel (CGE), Siemens and the Swedish firm Ericsson—all of whom are collaborating extensively with the RACE and ESPRIT frameworks.

Yet, alongside this strengthening of the supply side, the EC Commission has issued a series of directives, using for the first time powers under

---

[23] Taken from Paolo Cecchini: *The European Challenge: 1992: The Benefits of the Single Market*, Wildwood House for the Commission of the European Communities, 1988, pp. 73–74.

Article 90 of the Treaty of Rome (which empowers the Commission in certain circumstances to take action to prevent undue preferential treatment of public enterprises or similar establishments) which seek to force the pace of liberalization. In the summer of 1988 it issued its first directive setting a timetable for the liberalization of (telecommunications) terminal equipment. In October 1988 came another aimed at opening the public procurement of network equipment to competitive tender. In December 1988 came a directive calling for the liberalization of network use for all except voice services by April 1990. Further measures, dealing with access to the publicly-owned voice networks, are addressed by the Commission in its 'Open Network Provision' directive, a draft of which was issued in April 1989. This lays down rules for tariffs, standards and the use of private networks—issues in the heartland of any telecom authority. The strong stance being taken by the Commission is an indication of the importance they attach to these issues, the 'competitive' track of the Single Act, and the degree to which they wish to force the pace on liberalization and deregulation. (Equally, it has infuriated some member states, notably the French, who are taking the Commission to the European Court over their use of Article 90.)

The 'twin tracks' of the Single Act in many respects echo the tension that has been implicit within the Community since its foundation, between the minimalists who saw competition policy as the only necessary tool of industrial policy and the maximalists who from the start argued for more positive supply-side powers. With the Single European Act the maximalists' stance has been legitimized, but the tension has not been reduced. On the contrary, in many senses it has surfaced with greater intensity, witness the development in telecommunications. Yet it can be argued that the tension is creative rather than destructive—that the twin tracks of the Single Act represent a dialectic whose resolution explains all. Fortress Europe is the wrong interpretation of 1992. The logic is that to be competitive, Europe had to transform its national champions into firms which could compete against all-comers on world markets. This inevitably meant firms of a size and influence beyond the control of the nation state, even beyond the control of the European authorities. To protect such firms—to turn them from national into European champions—risked defeating the whole purpose of the exercise, which was to raise and maintain their competitiveness. 'Control' therefore has to come from the market, from these firms having to compete with their Japanese and US competitors in home markets as well as in foreign markets. Liberalization and deregulation therefore becomes an essential complement to collaboration and concentration—the twin tracks to competitiveness.

To conclude, another quotation from the Cecchini Report seems appropriate:

> In short, strengthening the European competitivity leads, so to speak, to the reconquest of the European market. Failure to meet the demands of competitivity

does not mean that the challenges of the (Single) European market will not be mastered. They will. But not by Europeans.[24]

[24] Cecchini, *op. cit.*, p. 75.

CONFLICTING OBJECTIVES IN EUROPEAN ENERGY POLICY

FRANCIS McGOWAN*

ONE of the surprises of the Single European Market initiative has been its impact upon Community energy strategy. Not only has it rekindled activity in an area where the Commission has had little success in the past, but it has also raised a number of questions about the orientations of policy. For most of the last two decades, Community approaches to energy have emphasized its 'non market' characteristics, and the need for interventionist policies to ensure security and diversity of energy supplies. The dynamic of deregulation and integration which the Single Market proposals have brought to the sector, suggests a rather different logic on how the energy industries should be organized.

As a result, it appears that the Commission has more than one strategy for the energy industries of Europe. One is based on the traditional agenda of energy policy, stressing measures to limit vulnerability to price and supply shocks in most member states. The other is based on the dynamics of market forces and on reorganizing the industries to allow for greater competition and trade.

Not only are these agencies rooted in different perceptions of the priorities for such a policy but they also reflect rather different configurations of power among the different members and institutions of the Community. Whereas the 'traditional' energy policy relies on a balance of power concentrated among the member states, with the Commission confined to a goal-setting and subordinate role, in the new market-based agenda the Commission is more activist, utilizing its powers and position under the Single Act and the founding Treaties of the Community.

The existence of these different agendas therefore raises basic questions not only about the direction of energy policy but also about Community dynamics, particularly the institutional tensions both between the Commission and member states and within the Commission itself. Moreover, it illustrates a more general problem for the Commission in implementing the single market: how can the single market, and the orientation of policy it implies, be grafted on to existing Community policies in specific sectors? The paper begins by outlining the past record of the EC in the energy

* Francis McGowan is a Fellow of the Energy Group at the Science Policy Research Unit, University of Sussex. His paper draws on research published in 'A Single European Market for Energy', a joint Occasional Paper from the Science Policy Research Unit and the Energy and Environmental Programme at the Royal Institute for International Affairs. The author gratefully acknowledges the financial support of the United Kingdom Economic and Social Research Council in carrying out this work.

121

sector. It provides a guide to the way in which the goals of energy have changed and the factors which have shaped their content and progress. The paper focuses on the recent past, taking the period from 1986, when the Community last agreed on its objectives for managing energy supply and demand. The factors which have driven member states and Commission concerns since then include changes in the energy markets, the reorientation of government approaches to the industry and the emergence of the Commission's more activist stance in Community affairs. On this basis the treatment of energy as part of the single market debate is considered.

Having established the two strategies which now exist in Community energy policy, and their rather different lineages, the paper assesses whether these approaches conflict with or complement each other. To illustrate this, the paper takes some examples of energy policy issues where the differences between the agendas are sharpest. These include the encouragement of energy conservation, the development of renewable sources of energy, the support of European coal production and the promotion of nuclear power. The paper then notes what these conflicts illustrate about the tensions between different members and institutions in the Community and considers the potential for reconciling them. The paper concludes by drawing some wider lessons for the single market process from the energy experience.

Energy and the community—in principle and in practice

The importance of energy for the European Community can be demonstrated by the fact that two of the three Treaties on which the Community is based are specifically concerned with the industry: the 1951 European Coal and Steel Community (ECSC) and the 1957 European Atomic Energy Community (Euratom) treaties were devoted to the coal and nuclear sectors. Both treaties, moreover, were in principle geared towards the creation of free and integrated markets: the ECSC sought to abolish all barriers to trade between member states while controlling subsidies and cartel-like behaviour amongst producers; Euratom also paid lip-service to the idea of a common market in nuclear products.[1]

A common market for other energy sectors was by default addressed in the Treaty of Rome which founded the European Economic Community (EEC). While the EEC was oriented towards more or less competitively structured markets, it was also intended to cover more oligopolistic or monopolistic (and often publicly owned) industries such as those covering oil, gas and electricity supply. Accordingly, in addition to being subject to the general provisions of the EEC Treaty on opening up markets, these

---

[1] On the details of the treaties, see Nigel Lucas, *Energy and the European Communities*, Europa, London, 1977.

energy industries' special characteristics were covered by the Treaty's provisions on competition policy, particularly those concerning state enterprises and their conduct.

Early attempts at energy policy

The gap between intentions expressed in the Treaties and the outcomes in terms of policy, however, has been a large one for energy, more so than for most other parts of the economy. The European Commission's attempts to influence the conduct of the sector, let alone to devise a strategy which reflected the ideals of the treaties, have proved to be of very limited success. From the 1950s on, the Commission or its equivalents sought to develop a policy, first for coal and then for energy as a whole. In coal, efforts to impose the principle of a free market on national industries failed (with policy focused on tackling the crisis which beset the European coal industry from the mid-1950s on).[2] In the sphere of energy more generally, initial efforts to create a common policy took place in the course of negotiations for the EEC, but came to nothing. A review of the need for a coordinating energy policy determined that it would be effectively addressed by the existing and proposed institutions.

Following the establishment of the EEC in 1957, the bureaucracies of the different Communities attempted to develop a coordinated policy for a common energy market. The main goal of these efforts was to ensure that energy prices were kept low and thereby to contribute to the Community's industrial competitiveness. However, in the wake of the Suez crisis, and the changing balance of energy supply (as imported oil began to challenge the dominance of domestically produced coal in member states' consumption), there was an additional concern with maintaining secure energy supplies.[3]

Despite the renewed efforts of the Commission, and the new balance of the policy proposed, the member governments effectively rejected any EC management or oversight of the sector. While most governments pursued policies of benign neglect towards the energy sector on a day to day basis, they nonetheless sought to maintain ultimate control of the industry.

Following the merger of the three Communities in 1968, the Commission revised its proposals, codifying them into an explicit strategy. With the publication of the document, 'First Guidelines Towards a Community Energy Policy',[4] the Commission noted the persistence of

[2] For an account of the problem of the European coal industry in the 1950s, see Leon N. Lindberg and Stuart A. Scheingold, *Europe's Would-be Polity*, Prentice Hall, New Jersey, 1970.

[3] An indication of the shift in perception over European energy vulnerabilities can be seen in H. Hartley, *Europe's Growing Needs of Energy—How Can They Be Met?*, OEEC, Paris, 1956. See also Political and Economic Planning, 'An Energy Policy for the EEC', *Planning*, Vol. 29, 1963.

[4] The report is fully discussed in Commission of the European Communities, *Third General Report on the Activities of the European Communities*, Office for Official Publications of the European Communities, Luxembourg, 1968, p. 251.

barriers to trade in energy and reiterated the necessity of a common energy market, based on the needs of consumers and competitive pressures. To this end the Commission suggested three broad objectives: a Commission role in planning as a basis for members' investment strategies; measures to bring about a common energy market (tackling issues such as tax harmonization technical barriers, state monopolies, etc); and measures to ensure security of supply at lowest cost. The balance of the proposed policy, therefore, still favoured moves towards a free market in energy. (Indeed, in many ways, the proposals and the analysis were similar to those which the Commission would present in its Internal Energy Market proposals twenty years later.)

As it turned out, the proposals followed previous Commission efforts in failure, as a mixture of member state inertia and opposition prevented most of the measures getting off the ground. The lack of success may also have been due to the contradictions in the policy, specifically between the goals of ensuring low priced energy and guaranteeing security of supply. As a measure of how this contradiction was resolved, it is significant that the only measures to be adopted in the wake of the Commission's proposals concerned the coordination of reserve oil stocks (following the Arab–Israeli war in 1967) and some requirements for energy investment notification.[5] These actions owed more to growing concern about security of supply than the creation of a common energy market, and presaged a wider shift in Commission and member state perceptions of the priorities of energy policy.

Energy crises and the 'New Strategy'

The reaction to the 1973–4 oil crisis confirmed the change in orientation of energy policy proposals away from markets and towards security. The context for the new emphasis on security of supply was the development of the Community's energy balances and the changes in global energy markets generally. Since the 1950s the member states had become less reliant upon domestically produced coal and more on imported resources, primarily oil. This shift in demand reflected not only the growth in energy demand overall, but also a gradual but absolute decline in energy resources among the then member states. By 1970 over 60% of the Community's needs were imported, leaving it highly vulnerable to the supply disruptions and price increases of 1973–4.

In the wake of the first oil shock, the EC attempted a crisis management role but failed even to provide a united front *vis-à-vis* Arab oil suppliers during their embargo of the Netherlands.[6] Member states pursued their

[5] See the account of energy policy in Dennis Swann, *The Economics of the Common Market*, Penguin, Harmondsworth, 1984, pp. 246 ff.

[6] On the failure of policy-making in this period and the prevalence of national concerns, see R. A. Black, 'Plus ça Change, Plus c'est le Même Chose: Nine Governments in Search of a Common Energy Policy', in Helen Wallace, William Wallace and C. Webb (eds), *Policy Making in the European Communities*, Wiley, London, 1977. See also Terence Daintith and Leigh Hancher, *Energy Strategy in Europe: the Legal Framework*, de Gruyter, Berlin, 1986.

own policies or worked through the International Energy Agency (IEA). Formed in 1974, the IEA overshadowed the Community both in breadth of membership (covering all the OECD countries except France) and in terms of its powers on oil sharing in a new crisis.[7]

Even so, the shock of oil price increases had confirmed the reassessment of how the sector should be treated, in both member states and the Commission: a more interventionist approach was adopted both by those that had hitherto not pursued an explicit energy policy and by those (such as the Commission) that had emphasized the need for a free market in energy. The Commission attempted to develop a more strategic approach to the management of energy supply and demand.

The 'New Strategy' on energy[8] envisaged a number of targets to be met by 1985 for the reduction of oil imports, the development of domestic energy capabilities (notably nuclear power) and the rational use of energy.[9] The policy objectives were only agreed to by member states after considerable negotiations and a weakening of the commitments which the Commission originally intended. While only indicative, the policy was significant as a Community statement on how member states should direct their energy programmes and provided the basis for a handful of directives designed to restrict the use of oil and gas. It also mobilized resources for R&D and promotional programmes, covering conventional and nuclear technologies as well as other sectors such as renewables and energy efficiency.

To the extent that the objectives constituted a policy, they clearly entailed a change in emphasis; the goal of a common energy market was demoted, though it was alluded to in some initiatives such as on promoting more transparent energy prices and at reforming the oil industry's conduct in some member states. Overall, however, policy was concerned with changing the structure of energy balances rather than the structure of energy markets.

The orientation of EC policy prevailed throughout the 1970s and early '80s, reinforced by the second oil shock in 1979–80. Further rounds of energy policy objectives were agreed in 1979 (to be met by 1990) and 1986 (for 1995).[10] The current objectives include: improving the efficiency of final energy demand by 20%; maintaining oil consumption at around 40% of energy consumption and net oil imports at less than

---

[7] J. G. van der Linde and R. Lefeber, 'IEA Captures the Development of European Energy Law', *Journal of World Trade*, Vol. 22, No. 5, October 1988.

[8] A full statement of the new policy is given in Commission of the European Communities, *Bulletin of the European Communities—Supplement*, *No. 4*, Office for Official Publications of the European Communities, Luxembourg, 1974.

[9] See Commission of the European Communities, *Community Energy Policy Objectives for 1985*, Commission of the European Communities, Brussels, 1974.

[10] For an account of the most recent objectives and an assessment of the progress each member state has made with them, see Commission of the European Communities, *The Main Findings of the Commission's Review of Member States' Energy Policies*, Commission of the European Communities, Brussels, 1988.

one-third of total energy consumption; increasing the share of solid fuels in energy consumption; pursuing efforts to promote consumption of solid fuels and improve the competitiveness of their production capacities in the Community; reducing the proportion of electricity generated by hydrocarbons by less than 15%; and increasing the share of renewables in energy balances. There were also more general, or 'horizontal', objectives set relating to pricing, environmental and regional policies.

By the 1980s, therefore, the Commission had succeeded in establishing a place in energy policy-making. However, it was well short of being central to member states' own considerations, let alone dictating the development of a common energy market. It was largely indicative, consisting of information gathering, target setting and enabling activities (the latter had a substantial budget for energy R&D and promotion). The priority of the policy was to reduce vulnerability to energy shocks; its perception of the energy sector was of unstable markets requiring control through policy interventions.

The new energy agenda

In the course of the 1980s, however, the agenda for energy policy began to change. Developments in energy markets, the attitudes of governments towards the energy industries and the overall position of the Commission in Community decision-making contributed to yet another reorientation of Community energy strategy.

Energy markets

Conditions in energy markets, in terms of fuel availabilities and price, have always played a key role in shaping the policies pursued by governments and the attitudes of consumers and suppliers. This has proved just as true when energy prices have been falling as when they have been rising. After the increases of the 1970s, energy prices stabilized and faltered in the early 1980s and continued to weaken until the 1986 oil price collapse. While the immediate causes of the collapse were to be found in disputes among the major oil producers, more fundamental changes were at work.

The 1970s price increases had the effect of boosting exploration for, and production of, energy resources across the world. Furthermore, many countries inside and outside the Community sought to improve energy efficiency and diversify their sources of energy (economic recession of the 1980s also dampened consumption). The combined effect of these changes in both the supply and demand sides of the market was to bring about a surplus of production capacity which forced down prices, not only in the oil sector but, through interfuel competition, in other energy markets as well.

The psychological effect of this shift in energy prices and supply positions was a weakening of the scarcity culture which had prevailed among suppliers, consumers, governments and agencies such as the Commission. As prices fell and markets appeared well supplied so the concerns of policy focused less on supply at any cost and more on the price of supply and the existence of obstacles to the lowest prices.

National policies

This change in market conditions made many energy policies hard to sustain. Indeed, in some cases, governments re-thought their approaches to the sector: the UK is perhaps the most extreme case, where the government made an explicit move to rely on market forces for determining supply and demand. A major plank of that policy was deregulation, with attempts to introduce competition into the supply of gas and electricity, and privatization, with the sale of oil interests and then the gas and (at present) electricity industries.[11] Similar policies were under review in other members of the Community though these were often conceived at a less ambitious level or pursued for rather different reasons. This change in government priorities was not unique to the energy sector: in other utility industries, and in the economy as a whole, the 1980s were a decade where, for many states, the tendency to disengage replaced the tendency to intervene.

Community policies

This trend was also manifest at a Community level, but here the focus was not, at least initially, upon energy. If anything, attempts to reform the energy sector did not begin until the policies had been developed in other sectors, effectively spilling over from them. This was the case with the Commission's plans for the Single European Market (SEM). The overall strategy of the White Paper was to deregulate many aspects of the Community economy where existing controls proved to be an unnecessary barrier to trade. Partly as a reflection of past energy policy failures, however, the Commission did not include energy in the initial agenda for the SEM. While there were some areas where energy was affected indirectly by broader components of the single market programme (such as the proposals for harmonizing indirect taxation regimes and to liberalize public procurement practices), the operating characteristics of the energy industries were not addressed.

The prospects for successful Commission initiatives in these areas were assisted by the changes brought about by the Single Act and in the overall revival in the Community's profile following the nadir of the early 1980s, of 'Eurosclerosis', budget crises and policy inertia. Undoubtedly, the

---

[11] For a fuller account of UK energy policy in the 1980s, see Dieter Helm, John Kay and David Thompson (eds), *The Market for Energy*, Clarendon Press, Oxford, 1989.

single market programme played a major role in restoring confidence in the Community as a forum for European economic restructuring. In that context, it became possible to address even difficult sectors like energy.

The potential for a more fundamental attack on the conduct of the energy sector was also indicated by a number of moves taken by the Competition Directorate of the Commission towards 'utility' industries (those industries which had enjoyed a special status in most economies as a result of their monopolistic operating characteristics and/or their economic and social importance, and which were generally nationally owned and regulated). The directorate sought the introduction of more competitive arrangements in the civil aviation industry and was able to threaten the use of legal powers to this end. In the field of telecommunications it sought to open access for equipment and service sales, using powers under Article 90 of the Treaty of Rome to do so. Not only did these moves demonstrate a willingness to act but also provided a range of mechanisms which could be used in other sectors. The further the policy went in one industry the more likely it would be applied to others.

There were signs of a different policy towards energy prior to the 1992 proposals. From the early 1980s on there were some attempts to regulate national pricing policies and, while the moves failed, they indicated a rekindled Commission interest in the issue. The Commission was also increasingly interested in curbing energy-related subsidy policies. In some member states it sought to control the provision of cheap energy supplies to particular industries (as in the case of Dutch support to its horticultural industry by cheap gas sales). In other cases it scrutinized support for the energy industries themselves (as in the case of certain members' coal support programmes).[12]

The changes in energy balances, in the priorities of member states' policies and in the approach and powers of the Commission, meant that the idea of a market-based energy policy was back on the agenda with a higher profile than for many years. Even the 1995 objectives which were largely flavoured by energy security concerns, included a commitment to an 'Internal Energy Market' (IEM). As the momentum of the single market increased, so did the desirability of applying it to energy.

The Internal Energy Market

The Commission's approach was revealed in 'The Internal Energy Market',[13] a review which set out potential benefits of an IEM and the obstacles which stood in the way of its completion. According to this

[12] On the Commission's investigations of cheap gas supply, see Commission of the European Communities, *Fourteenth Report on Competition Policy*, Office for Official Publications of the European Communities, Luxembourg, p. 152. On the scrutiny of coal subsidies, see Commission of the European Communities, *Fifteenth Report on Competition Policy*, Office for Official Publications of the European Communities, Luxembourg, p. 130.

[13] Commission of the European Communities, *The Internal Energy Market*, Commission of the European Communities, Brussels, 1988.

report, such a market would mean lower costs for consumers (particularly in energy intensive industries), thereby making the European economy as a whole more competitive. It would increase security of supply by increasing the integration of the energy industries; it would rationalize the structure of the energy industries and allow for greater complementarity among the different supply and demand profiles of member states. According to the Commission, the benefits which would stem from this mixture of cost-reducing competition and the achievement of scale economies in a number of industries, would amount to between 0.5% and 1% of Community GDP.

The obstacles to the IEM, in the Commission's view, were to be found in the structures and practices of the various national energy industries. The most important divergences ranged from the different taxation and financial regimes to the restrictive practices which protected energy industries in particular countries from competition. These conditions also prevented the full coordination of energy planning and supplies at the most efficient level. The absence of such cross-Community structures had a particularly diverse effect in the gas and electricity industries (where the Commission believed major economies of scale were possible). Given the special characteristics of these industries (including their monopolistic practices and their public service obligations) it was not clear how far competition would be feasible (as the Commission had to admit). Nonetheless, the Commission's report called for closer scrutiny of the reasons for the existing limitations on access and competition in the utility industries.

The report demonstrated that the Commission was determined to implement an IEM and would examine all barriers to its development. From the time the report was published, the Commission began to put the new agenda into practice. It has introduced directives aimed at improving price transparency, increasing the coordination of investment and encouraging greater trade in electricity and gas, and has presented revised proposals on liberalizing procurement and reforming indirect taxation regimes. The Commission is also investigating the relationship between the coal and electricity supply industries in a number of member states (to ascertain whether the arrangements violate competition principles) and has been examining any member state attempts to reform their energy industries.

While it is not clear how successful the Commission will be, it does appear that it is determined not to abandon the policy initiative. The pace of the debate has not only been helped by changes in Community decision-making procedures (notably the majority voting procedures allowed by the Single Act) but also by the prospect of the Commission using its own powers under the Treaty of Rome to investigate and possibly reform the energy sector. In this respect it is following its strategy, noted above, in other utilities such as air transport and telecommunications (though so far it has not had to test the policy in the dramatic ways it has tackled these sectors).

Which energy policy?

After more than 30 years of limited success the Commission is once again formulating energy policy, and the momentum behind it may mean that it will be more successful than before. Each of the mainstream energy sectors will be affected by the IEM proposals, with the focus on restructuring them towards greater reliance on competitive forces. However, how does this 'new' energy policy agenda relate to the traditional agenda, particularly in terms of the roles of governments, consumers and industries? Where the two are in conflict, moreover, which one is to prevail?

The problem of trying to reconcile an interventionist policy (as required by the 1995 objectives) with the goal of a free integrated market (as required by the 1992 objectives) is not new. From 1951 to 1973, energy policy efforts tried to balance the goal of a common competitive energy market with the need to maintain security of supply. For the next ten years, the security goal predominated, more or less obscuring ideas of a common energy market. Now, the balance between the two agendas is harder to assess, though all factors indicate that there has been a return to a market-led policy. However, while the current debate and the nature of proposals suggest that the IEM appears to be in the ascendant, the 1995 goals remain part of policy.

The Commission apparently sees no problem in reconciling the two agendas: as noted, the 1995 objectives included the achievement of an IEM while recent Commission statements indicate that the goals of 1995 are consistent with the IEM. Indeed, it might be argued (as the Commission seems to believe) that the two agendas are complementary, given their different concerns and their respective 'power bases' (the potential of legislative action to impose the IEM and the provision of financial resources to encourage the achievement of energy policy goals). However, decisions taken in pursuit of one agenda will affect the outcomes in the other one, with potentially contradictory consequences.

In those circumstances it is not immediately clear how the two policies can be reconciled. While one aims to impose the logic of the market-place on the energy industries, the other aims to tackle the market failures which abound in the sector. In its extreme form, the IEM would indicate that the lowest cost source of supply should be obtained, and that this goal should prevail over any other policy considerations, notably that of controlling energy vulnerability. As the following examples demonstrate, this brings the two agendas of energy policy into conflict.

Energy conservation

Energy conservation and diversification has been a major component of the traditional energy agenda and it is to the fore in the 1995 objectives (where member states agreed to improving the efficiency of final energy demand by 20%). Energy saving is generally regarded as the best solution to the problem of managing environmental emissions and improving security of supply. It has been pursued by member states with varying degrees of enthusiasm. Not surprisingly, the keenest have been the Danes and other countries with lower levels of indigenous energy supplies, while countries such as the UK have been among the less enthusiastic. For its part, the Commission has sought to encourage conservation and diversification directly through funds for programmes and R&D as well as through directives against the use of particular fuels (such as oil and gas) in power stations. While the effectiveness of these measures might be debated (it is unlikely that the Community as a whole will be able to meet the 1995 objective), they demonstrate how far the Commission has supported energy efficiency.

However, conservation hardly rates a mention in the IEM proposals. While it is not in principle in conflict with the idea of a single market, many of the mechanisms which are used to achieve it are (such as high levels of taxation on energy products or subsidies to encourage energy efficiency). More generally, if the goal of the IEM is to lower energy costs and prices then energy efficiency measures (which were at their most successful when prices were high) are harder to sustain. This is demonstrated by the experience of countries like Denmark after the 1986 oil price collapse. Taxes were raised higher to sustain the same level of prices. Yet the IEM has aimed to harmonize excise taxes for energy products, with the effect that the rate of taxation in Denmark may have to fall substantially.

Another aspect of how the two agendas clashed has occurred in Spain. The Spanish government was offering subsidies to industrial companies to invest in energy efficient technologies. A Commission investigation found that these aids were in contravention of article 92.1 of the Treaty of Rome controlling subsidies, but permitted a derogation from that policy. The limits of the policy were determined by the Commission, but how far they established a precedent remains to be seen.[14]

Renewable sources of energy

The development of renewable sources of energy (such as wind, wave and solar power) is another goal of the Community under the 1995 objectives. It has, moreover, been supported by substantial commitments from EC R&D budgets (in 1987 it received 84m.ECU or 9.5% of Community energy grants). A number of countries have also supported the development of renewables, particularly in terms of requiring minimum scale projects for utilities to develop. The Commission itself has favoured special conditions for purchasing electricity produced from renewables.[15]

[14] *Agence Europe*, 22 March 1989.
[15] Commission of the European Communities, *Proposal for a Council Recommendation to Promote Cooperation between Public Electricity Supply Companies and Private Generators of Electricity*, Commission of the European Communities, Brussels, 1988.

As with energy efficiency measures, renewables are not explicitly addressed in the IEM proposals, and while there is no conflict in principle, in practice there may be difficulties in promoting them under the new energy agenda. If the IEM does not permit quotas or special terms for particular types of energy production, then it is hard to see renewables (which have generally, at least initially, required subsidy and support to make them competitive) being developed.

There is a more fundamental problem, however, for renewables in a regime dominated by the IEM. As with energy conservation, if the main goal of energy policy is to obtain the lowest possible cost, then the development of scale economies at a plant and at a network level may be regarded as the best option, leaving small scale renewables out of the picture. Integrating renewables into an increasingly centralized system may prove difficult. More generally, experience suggests that the low price conditions which the IEM aims to achieve may squeeze out renewables.

Solid fuels

As part of the traditional energy agenda there has been considerable backing for the development of domestic energy resources as a means of maintaining security of supply within the Community. On this basis (though also, more importantly, for domestic social and political reasons) a number of countries have sustained their national coal industries. The policy has been accepted by the Commission: the energy policy objectives have generally expressed a commitment to this sector. Over the 1980s, however, many of these industries have become uncompetitive as world energy prices have fallen. The maintenance of subsidies is often directly borne by the consumers of the energy resource (or indirectly in the case of electricity industries using national supplies of coal). This burden has prompted complaints from certain industrial consumers as well as from potential foreign suppliers of cheaper energy resources.

Tackling such subsidy programmes is a major component of the IEM proposals. Indeed, the scale of support was a matter of concern to the Commission before the new agenda emerged: the Competition Directorate was seeking a restructuring of many national coal industries in the early 1980s. It is clear that the sorts of vertical arrangements between domestic coal suppliers and the electricity supply industry which have prevailed in countries like Germany, Spain and the UK are not in the Commission's view compatible with the IEM. As the Commission has sought to control these policies, the German coal industry (which is the most subsidized in the Community and therefore the one with the most to lose) has begun a legal case against the Commission, arguing that not only does the Commission have no right to investigate such policies but that the new policy is in contradiction to existing Community energy policy (which, the industry claims, encourages domestic energy production).[16]

[16] *International Coal Report*, No. 227, 14 July 1989, pp. 6–7.

Nuclear power

Much of the pressure for a close scrutiny of member states' coal industries has come from the French government and nuclear industry. They want to export their surplus of electricity generating capacity to neighbouring states. Traditionally, the Commission has shared the French enthusiasm for nuclear power, regarding it as meeting not only the objective of secure energy supplies but also promoting the industrial development of the Community. There is, however, no direct support of nuclear power in the 1995 objectives because of the opposition of some member states. Nonetheless, it is clear that the Commission generally favours the industry (as evidenced by the substantial R&D resources—341m.ECU in 1987, 39% of energy grants—which the Community provides to the sector).

The basis for much of the support of nuclear power has been the apparently low cost of electricity produced from that resource. However, the status of nuclear power has been changing in many member states in recent years. The economic advantages of nuclear power—its traditional benefit—have been called into question. As the real full costs of nuclear power have emerged, there has been a shift from economic arguments to those which stress its role in reinforcing security of supply and aiding the environment.

Surprisingly, the IEM's treatment of nuclear power is rather weak by comparison with other aspects of the energy sector. It focuses primarily on the terms and conditions of nuclear equipment and fuel purchases. If anything, the IEM proposals implicitly maintain the Commission's support for nuclear power. The proposals for a Europe-wide power pool and the Commission's expectations of the resulting savings that would be obtained, are premised on utilizing the surplus of French nuclear capacity that exists.

Subsequently, however, the issue of how nuclear power should be supported by member states has risen to the fore. The difficulties which the economic case for nuclear power has experienced have been such that, in the UK, the government has encountered insurmountable difficulties in including it in their electricity privatization programme. The nuclear component of the industry was droppped from the proposed sell-off, despite various proposals for levies and quotas to protect the sector.

One reason why nuclear power was removed from the sale was the decision of the Commission's Competition Directorate to investigate the plans for protecting the industry. This followed complaints from environmental groups that the government's plans for supporting nuclear power in the private sector were in breach of the Treaty of Rome. These investigations eventually resulted in a strict EC control on the UK's support of nuclear power, limiting aid for eight years. It is therefore the logic of the IEM (specifically the drive against distortions of energy markets), rather than the IEM proposals themselves, which have driven the decision to scrutinize the sector. Ironically, it is the actions of the UK government—which, in seeking to promote 'competition' in nuclear power, was one of the member states most in line with Community thinking—which have provided the Commission with the opportunity to investigate and possibly rule against a national electricity policy.[17]

Each of these cases (involving technologies or policies close to the core of EC energy activities) demonstrates some of the tensions between the 'market failure' perspective of 1995 and the 'myopic' perspective of 1992. When does support in one of these areas, with the aim of securing one of the 1995 objectives, become a restraint of trade or an anticompetitive measure out of step with an IEM? Determining how each is settled will be an extremely delicate task. It might be argued that in each case it will be possible to permit exceptions and give priority to a particular objective. This has been the traditional approach (as in the recent decision by the Commission to permit the Spanish government to subsidize energy efficiency measures). But how will the Commission devise criteria for choosing the priorities, particularly given the likely tensions which specific cases will give rise to, both within the Commission and between the Commission and member states?

How can these actual or potential conflicts in energy policy objectives be explained?

Partly they arise out of the inertia of the established agenda and the relatively dynamic pace with which the new agenda has arisen. In a sense, the old strategy has become less relevant and, though not abandoned, may wither on the vine as other policies in the sector are pursued.

Another explanation is that the conflicts reflect a diversity of perspectives in different parts of the Community and its institutions about energy issues. This is clearest in terms of member states' own positions. Countries' energy policies will depend on their own energy endowments, their political orientations and the priority they give to the sector. Inevitably, any policy that emerges must be a comparison of sorts. More importantly perhaps, any persistence of parallel policies reflects a failure to compromise and to reconcile conflicting positions between the member states.

This was evident in the drawing up of the 1995 objectives. The UK proposed a commitment to nuclear power in those, but in the face of Danish opposition the objective was effectively neutered.[18] It is also very evident in the drawing up of directives to implement the IEM agenda. Moves to open up electricity trade in the Community, supported by Portugal (which wants to import electricity), France (which wants to export its surplus nuclear power) and the UK (which wanted to extend the competitive mechanisms which it sought to introduce in its home market), have been diluted by the opposing interests of the bulk of electricity

[17] *Power in Europe*, No. 58, 14th September 1989, p. 7.
[18] *Agence Europe*, 22 March, 5th June, 14 July 1986.

companies in the Community as well as most governments which have wanted to protect their national autonomy.

These disputes between member states will almost always involve the Commission on one or other side. Within the Commission itself there are likely to be tensions. These stem from the variety of directorates involved in the formulation of energy policy and the variety of characteristics which such a policy entails. In the 1970s, the making of energy policy was largely focused on the energy, external relations and research and development directorates. Now the environmental, competition and possibly regional directorates are also involved. The focus for energy policy has broadened.

In considering how these different issues and directorates line up, it is not unreasonable to assert that the core directorate, energy, rather like other 'sectoral' directorates, is in the position of being 'captured', in the US regulatory sense; the industries it is supposed to oversee in fact determine its outlook. By contrast, cross-cutting directorates such as environment and competition have a very different approach. In the case of the competition directorate, there is a desire to establish how far industry structures and conduct accord with the goal of a competitive and integrated European market. There is a sense in which, as it tackles a sector, it applies the lessons of equivalent measures elsewhere, probably as a result of a mixture of economics and case law.

So far this paper has emphasized the contradictions between the energy policy agendas devised by the Commission. While there may be a host of issues where no conflict arises, it seems that the fundamental differences of perspective between the two agendas must be reconciled. Three solutions are possible.

One solution is that the IEM debate gets bogged down and that things carry on as they are. Countries pursue their own policies with occasional conflicts, largely resolved without recourse to the Commission.

Another possibility is that, in creating a European energy market, a European energy policy will be developed to cope with the market failures that emerge. It would be the Commission that made this decision. In other words, in the process of arbitrating between policy measures the Commission would effectively take control of energy policy.

A final option is that the agendas are swept aside by a more pressing set of concerns. This appears quite likely given the growing importance of environmentalism in the Community. It is an area where the Commission's role has expanded dramatically since the 1970s, particularly in the energy sector. Indeed it has been one of the few areas where the EC played a critical policy role in the energy sector during the early 1980s.[19]

The issue has been raised in the context of the Single Act and the proposals for a single market. The Single Act pinpoints environmental policy as an area where a high level of protection is to characterize

[19] Susan Owens and Christopher Hope, 'Energy and the Environment—the Challenge of Integrating European Policies', *Energy Policy*, Vol. 17, No. 2, April 1989.

Community policies. It is an area where 'harmonization' will remain the principal mechanism of policy. These considerations were reinforced in the White Paper and the way in which the single market has been implemented. Within energy specifically, environmental concerns were addressed in the 1995 objectives. In policy terms there have been a few measures already adopted—most notably the controls on emissions from power plants. Although it has been five years in the making, the directive is robust, setting targets which member states must meet or face legal action.

The policy is now being taken further. As part of the IEM debate, the environmental implications of different options are being closely examined. In addition, the next set of energy objectives (for 2000) will give far more attention to the environment than previous energy policy targets. With renewed concerns over issues such as the 'greenhouse effect', these environmental pressures may become so overwhelming in the next few years that they supplant other issues. The consequences of such a change would be that IEM concerns would become less important. The traditional energy policy objectives would return to the fore, but with rather more force than they have done in the past. It would be wrong, however, to expect that these issues will simply overwhelm all other policy considerations. The intra-Commission talks on environment and the IEM have already exposed major differences (in areas such as nuclear power) between directorates. These differences are likely to be even more marked, even stronger, when they are debated by member states.

It may be that a combination of all three solutions will emerge. Certain highly controversial aspects of the IEM may be neutered and member states will retain autonomy in those areas, leaving the IEM to be applied in less sensitive areas. Where the IEM prevails, the Commission may have to resolve the competing and conflicting claims of, for example, increased competition and supply security, with the environmental impact of policies being the determinant of any decision.

Conclusions

The exact outcome of these conflicts is not yet clear, but it does appear that the Commission will be far more involved in energy policy-making than was previously the case, and its proposals will be harder for the member states to ignore. This outcome implies that there has been a real change in the balance of power in the Community, in no small part due to the overall single market debate. What do the Commission's plans for the IEM, and its conflict with the other energy policy concerns of the Community, reveal about the overall prospects for Community policy-making before and after 1992?

The fact that the roots of the IEM policy stretch back to the origins of the Communities—the first mention of a common energy market was made in the 1950s—only serves to demonstrate that the 1992 programme as a whole is in part an admission of failure. The objective of creating a single market (whether for energy or for the economy as a whole) should have been achieved decades ago.

Similarly the 'success' of the IEM agenda owes much to the favourable circumstances in energy markets and to the balance of forces between state and market in the Community. Would the revived Commission programme, whether in energy specifically or in the economy as a whole, have been possible without some of the reassessment of national economic policies which occurred in member states over the 1980s? It is worth recalling how far the single market programme was in fact a response to the Eurosclerosis of the early 1980s and the perceived failure of the economic policies of the previous decade.

The links between what is happening in the energy sector and policies towards other utility industries have already been noted. The IEM is one illustration of a wider exercise in 'integration by deregulation', a key part of the 1992 programme. It is particularly important in the utility sectors as it implies a much more fundamental reorganization of these industries than in other parts of the economy. In telecommunications and transportation, the Commission is wanting to introduce mechanisms which will not only bring about competition and lower costs, but will also reinforce the economic and physical infrastructure of the Community.

The conflicts which may emerge between the different agendas of energy policy will not be unique to the energy sector. It is likely that, as the 1992 programme is applied to more and more parts of the economy, there will be, in a number of sectors, a similar degree of mismatch between the new proposals and the way in which policy has been pursued in the past. Choosing between the policies will be just as difficult as in the energy sector. As in the energy sector, this will leave the Commission in the critical position of determining how the balance should be struck. It may even be that under the aegis of a deregulatory strategy, the Commission will be able to intervene for much broader policy goals.

The prospect of the deregulatory thrust of policy being sacrificed is a possibility in the energy sector (if a more pressing issue takes political primacy). It could also happen in other sectors, if, for example, the 'costs of Europe 1992' prove politically more unacceptable than the economic 'cost of non-Europe' which has so far driven the single market debate. Deregulation has largely been a phenomenon of the 1980s in Europe, a response to specific circumstances in particular sectors as well as to the overall political climate. Whether it will prove sustainable in the 1990s remains to be seen.

IMPLEMENTING THE INTERNAL MARKET

JIM CAMPBELL, IAN BARNES AND CATHERINE PEPPER*

THE acceptance by the member states of the 1985 White Paper from the European Commission on the completion of the internal market has been presented as a radical and imaginative move by the Community. However, it would be naive to assume that the successful implementation of the White Paper proposals by 1992 will lead to the establishment of a single market. Although the abolition of the barriers to trade identified in the White Paper will clearly assist and enhance trade within the Community, it will not abolish the twelve national markets; the European market will still be fragmented. Nevertheless, the 1992 project can be seen as radical in relation to the nature and behaviour of the Community in the late 1970s and early 1980s. This was a period in which the Community was pre-occupied with internal squabbles, principally over finance and the operation of the Common Agricultural Policy. Apart from the expansion of Community membership and the establishment of the European Monetary System, very little development along the road to greater economic integration seems to be taking place. Indeed, to most observers, the Community appeared to be in imminent danger of disintegrating as a result of these apparently irreconcilable differences between the member states. Against that background the unanimous acceptance of the White Paper is to some extent a remarkable achievement; though it has to be said that a significant proportion of the proposals are intermediate steps which are considered to be politically acceptable. In many cases they were developed prior to 1985 but have never been implemented. In this sense 1992 represents a kind of tidying up operation, an attempt to make up for lost time. However, the publicity and hype which has accompanied these moves has clearly enhanced and heightened awareness of the possibilities and potential for business within a single market. At the same time, and perhaps for the first time in the UK, the general public has begun to appreciate the importance of the Community and the opportunities it offers for improving social standards and raising standards of living. However, it is imperative that both business and individuals realize that the 1992 project is an intermediate step along the road to a single market; it is a means to an end, not the end itself.

At one level, the 1992 project could be seen as an exercise in liberalization writ large, its primary purpose being the opening up of previously

* Ian Barnes is a Principal Lecturer in Economics and Catherine Pepper is a Research Officer at the Humberside Business School, Hull, and Jim Campbell is a Lecturer in Economics at the Glasgow College.

closed or protected markets and the removal of impediments to trade and free competition within the Community. Certainly it can be no co-incidence that the general acceptance of 1992 in principle by the member states took place at a time when the 'economics of the market place' dominated the thinking and policies of governments throughout Western Europe, even where there were nominally socialist governments as in France and Spain. However, a closer examination of the White Paper reveals that, although the benefits of completing the internal market are articulated in the language of economic liberalism, the actual process involves a high degree of regulation in terms of harmonization of various standards. This in turn seems to imply an increase in the power and influence of Brussels. Indeed it was probably the realization that this tension existed which led to Mrs Thatcher's notorious Bruges speech in 1988.

This article is concerned with the problems involved in trying to implement the various measures identified in the 1985 White Paper. Clearly it would be impossible to cover all 279 measures; rather we have chosen to concentrate on three crucial areas in which agreement is essential if 1992 is to become a reality—customs documentation, public procurement and road haulage. By focusing on the specific problems encountered in reaching agreement in these areas we hope to highlight the very real difficulties the Community faces in turning the rhetoric of 1992 into reality. In addition, it will allow us to explore in more detail the apparent contradiction between 1992 as liberalization and 1992 as regulation. We are not concerned here with whether member states have actually incorporated single market directives into their own legal systems, though this in itself is a considerable problem; of the 63 directives which had taken effect in mid-1989, only six had actually been incorporated into the national laws of all twelve member states.[1] Our primary concern is the stage before that, where the member states and the Commission through the Council of Ministers and COREPER attempt to reach agreement on the shape, form and detail of the single market. It is this stage which will determine the extent to which the EC is moving towards a true single market of 320 million people or simply becoming a more integrated free trade area.

Customs documentation

The free movement of goods across borders is regarded as being essential if the Community is to successfully complete the internal market. In an ideal world goods should be permitted to move from one member state to another without the need for customs documentation. Trade flows should be a matter of academic interest, rather than the subject of detailed

[1] *The Economist*, 23 September 1989, p. 79.

bureaucratic monitoring. The reality of the system that is now in place, and will remain in place after 1993, is that all commercial movements of goods will have to be recorded via the Single Administrative Document (SAD). This is a standard document which is in use in all member states and available in all the official Community languages. It is a highly complex form which records details of cross-border transactions in over fifty separate boxes.

Before the 1988 customs reforms, intra-Community trade was governed by the EC Transit System. This was designed to protect the Community tariff wall by ensuring accurate documentation, and to provide a procedure which enabled goods to cross internal frontiers with the minimum of formalities. However, because this system allowed the continuing use of national customs documents for administrative and statistical purposes, the combined effect of the twelve separate administration systems resulted in a formidable bureaucratic barrier to the free movement of goods. For example, forty-six different documents were required to transport goods between West Germany and Italy in order to comply with both EC and national administrative requirements.[2] In addition, many of these documents required the laborious duplication of information to fit the non-standardized formats of national documents. Not only did this create frustration among the business community, but it also imposed considerable costs and delays. Recent estimates have suggested that the overall customs-related administrative cost, borne by Community business, is in the region of ECU 7.5 billion.[3]

It is not surprising, therefore, that customs documentation was earmarked for reform: in 1981 the Commission's Customs Union Service (CUS) adopted the responsibility for simplifying the procedure governing intra-Community trade. It proposed withdrawing customs documentation altogether and replacing it with a standardized commercial invoice, similar to the system operating in the Benelux countries at the time. The main objective it seemed was to try and align the documentation requirements of the Community with those of a single member state. The commercial invoice could be extended to include additional data required by member states or the Community. It was hoped that the system would closely resemble the documentation used for transactions between businesses within an individual country. The introduction of an extended commercial invoice was seen as the intermediate stage that would radically simplify documentation in the short term and facilitate the transition to a barrier-free Europe in the long term. Certainly its use would clearly differentiate between trade within the Community and trade outside it, in terms of the documentation required. However, various problems arose with the commercial invoice which created doubts as to its

[2] House of Lords 17th Report of the Select Committee on the European Communities, 'Internal Market', 1982, p. 301.
[3] P. Cecchini, 'The European Challenge—1992: the Benefits of the Single Market', Wildwood House, 1988, p. 11.

suitability for the Community. The main problems were: firstly, it did not satisfy the member states' appetite for statistical data on commercial transactions across their borders; secondly, the lack of harmonization in technical, safety and health standards as well as the wide variations in indirect taxation meant that it was very difficult to withdraw existing customs documentation altogether. Indeed it was because of the limitations imposed on data collection that the commercial invoice was actually withdrawn from the Benelux countries.

Having rejected the commercial invoice, and with it the alignment objective, the CUS turned its attention to what could be done to try to simplify existing procedures. The most effective means was felt to be the introduction of a single administrative document. This would replace a wide variety of national documents, regulations and procedures operating in each member state. It would be 'single' in that it would cover import, export and Community transit operations and would also be uniform in each member-state. The new document would need to satisfy each member state's administrative and statistical needs, and therefore to some extent the design of the new form developed into an· exercise in standardizing the format of national documents rather than simplifying customs procedures. However this in itself proved to be a far from simple task. Between 1981 and 1985 the CUS was involved in trying to get the member states to agree on which data elements should be included in the new document, the level of detail required, and which existing customs documents should be allowed to remain.

The policy formulation process involved not only national governments and customs departments but also trade associations and other interested parties affected by the proposed changes. The Commission dealt directly with the national governments and customs departments whose responsibility it was to discuss the reforms with the appropriate industries and trade associations. Although it was necessary to involve the various national customs departments and trade representatives in the policy-making process, many of these groups may well have felt threatened by the nature of the reforms. Consequently the consultation process afforded some the opportunity to try and minimize the impact of changes in documentation. In the light of this it is important to consider who was actually involved and how they might be affected by the reforms.

Customs officials: To the customs employee the reform of customs procedures may appear to be a rather ominous development. Reduced paper work and faster clearance times could well result in less need for customs officials at border crossings. Furthermore, the implications of 1992 must do little to reassure them of their future job security. The CUS has stated that it may well be in the interests of national customs officials to play down the effects of the reforms. If major reform is perceived to be such a threat, there must be serious doubts about the commitment of customs officials to the simplification objective.

Road hauliers and freight forwarders: Although road hauliers and freight forwarders suffered greatly from the complexities, costs and delays inherent in customs procedures, they also benefited from the situation. Assuming that their profits were a percentage of the overall price, the more expensive and complex the system for exporting and importing then the greater their fee.

Import and export agents: They also benefited from the inadequacies of customs procedures. While intra-Community trade remained entangled in national bureaucracy, agents would be assured of a market for their specialist knowledge. If, however, a new simplified procedure were introduced, the repercussions in terms of demand for agents might be considerable. Agents in the Republic of Ireland have already suggested to the Commission that they be compensated for a potential loss of earnings caused by the introduction of the SAD.

Large companies: These can gain a considerable advantage over small businesses because they are better able to overcome the difficulties posed by complex customs procedures. Most large companies which are heavily involved in international trade have established specific departments geared to the requirements of customs. Not only does this allow financial savings to be made from the removal of agents' fees, but it is also likely to result in faster clearance times at customs; 'large firms are sometimes able to arrange special customs procedures, such as periodic recapitulative declarations, as well as checks made by customs and other officials in the firm, thus dispensing with the need to present goods at customs offices'.[4]

The SAD was introduced on 1 January 1988, replacing the plethora of national documents previously in existence. It satisfied each member state's administrative and statistical needs and presented the information in a format that was uniform to all. To assess the effectiveness of the SAD it is necessary to consider the extent to which it has reduced the burden of bureaucracy, accelerated clearance times at internal borders, reduced costs, and encouraged greater intra-Community trade.

The SAD has replaced over 200 customs and administrative documents. The Commission has claimed that, 'the new form marks a great step forward in rationalizing the paperwork in transporting goods. This will help save time and money for companies and transporters and make the procedures easier to understand . . .'[5] However, a brief glance at the new document would tend to contradict that claim. Although the number of documents and the need for duplication have been reduced, the problem of complexity has yet to be satisfactorily resolved. It is doubtful that a manager new to exporting could even begin to complete the SAD. If customs documentation is to be truly simplified, a more drastic reduction in the amount of information required is essential. However, in reducing the number of documents customs officers can legally demand, the CUS

---

[4] *Ibid.*, p. 48.
[5] Commission of the European Communities, 'Completing the Internal Market', *European Documentation* 4/1987, p. 34.

has made some progress towards eliminating the bureaucratic and nationalistic barriers raised by border formalities. It seems reasonable to assume that some improvements in customs clearance times would result from this kind of reform. This does not seem to have happened. Neither the Road Haulage Association nor the Freight Transport Association expect clearance times to be faster because of the introduction of the SAD.

Since a major expense for most importers and exporters is the cost of employing agents to handle customs documentation, simplification of the procedures might be expected to remove or at least reduce this burden. So far there is little evidence to suggest that this is likely to be the case, primarily because the SAD has made little progress towards creating a more simplified and comprehensible system. The level of simplification achieved by the reforms has reduced the amount of work required of agents for completing documentation, but not their importance in the overall procedure. Most businesses do not possess the necessary expertise to handle their own customs documentation; therefore they will still need to rely on agents, which means they are unlikely to benefit financially from the changes.

The SAD represents an exercise in standardization, not simplification. Although this is a commendable achievement, the important question is whether it will be sufficient to meet the challenge of 1992 and the expected increase in cross-border trade. The various interest groups involved in the policy formulation process were likely to favour only minor changes in order to protect their own particular interests, and on the whole they got their way. Few people actively engaged in trade see the reforms as anything other than bureaucratic changes introduced for their own sake, and are sceptical about the claims that they make life easier. Although it could be argued that the SAD is only a transitional stage and should be seen as a stepping stone to further reform, it may well act as a block to more radical measures. Introducing minor changes and then claiming they make a real difference is likely to be counter-productive because it raises expectations only to disappoint them, leading to disillusionment and making it more difficult to introduce real change in the future.

The fact that the introduction of the SAD made so little difference is not really all that surprising. The implications of abolishing specific barriers such as customs procedures results in resistance not only from national governments but also from the various groups and interests directly affected by their removal. In addition it needs to be borne in mind that one of the main reasons for the continued existence of customs documentation for intra-Community trade is the lack of harmonization of health, safety and technical standards and the wide variations in VAT rates and excise duties. The problem is that harmonization in these areas can only be achieved if the member states cede a substantial part of their sovereignty and subsume their national interests to those of the Community. Even if the political will to do so existed, there would still remain the problem of vested interests who may feel seriously threatened by such moves. Until these areas are tackled and the fiscal and technical barriers to trade removed, bureaucratic customs procedures will still be required. Unfortunately, the experience of the recent customs reforms does not engender much confidence that the rhetoric of 1992 will ever become reality, particularly when one bears in mind that it took the Community almost seven years to agree on these fairly marginal changes.

Public procurement

One of the main difficulties which the community faces in trying to open up public procurement is the perception that the purchasing policies of the public sector are intrinsically linked with the pursuit of national economic interest. Public purchasing can be used as part of a strategy to encourage innovation and improve the balance of trade and more generally to demonstrate the government's commitment to domestic industry. The failure to purchase from indigenous sources may at best be regarded as a wasted opportunity, or at worst, an act of national betrayal, especially when the sheer size of the public procurement market is taken into account. In 1987 total public purchasing accounted for 15% of GDP of the European Community. However only 0.14% of this business is awarded to companies from other EC countries.[6]

Both central and local government tend to favour their indigenous manufacturers and suppliers in the awarding of public contracts. The European Commission argues that these nationalistic purchasing policies artificially create a barrier to trade within the Community and emphasize the fragmented nature of the common market. Not only does it mean that the public sector pays more for its goods and services but the protected market results in inefficient businesses remaining in existence. In short, current public purchasing strategies represent an inefficient allocation of resources within the Community. A recent study has estimated that the Community could make savings in excess of 20 billion ECU per annum if it adopted a more liberal purchasing policy.[7] In economic terms the policy of discriminating in favour of domestic companies is clearly illogical but the unilateral opening up of markets would be politically dangerous; therefore it requires a multilateral or Community-wide solution.

The Commission's attempts to open up public procurement pre-dates the 1992 project. The first relevant directive was adopted in 1972 and was concerned with the award of construction works contracts. Five years later the Commission extended its remit to include supplies contracts. Certain sectors such as water, energy, transport and telecommunications

---

[6] Cecchini, *op. cit.*, p. 16.

[7] Commission of the European Communities, 'The Economics of 1982: an Assessment of Potential Economic Effects of Completing the Internal Market of the European Community', *European Economy*, 35, 1988, p. 59.

procurement were all excluded from the provisions of the directives on the grounds that there was too varied a mix of public and private ownership in these industries. The directives laid down clear rules of procedure to be adopted in the award of public contracts above a certain value—200,000 ECU for supply contracts and 1 million ECU for works contracts. They involved three basic requirements:

(i) the Community-wide advertising of public contracts to provide firms from throughout the Community with the opportunity to tender; in certain circumstances contracts could be exempted from this requirement;

(ii) the application of 'objective awards criteria', i.e. the award must be made solely on the basis of the lowest price proposed or the most 'economically advantageous' tender;

(iii) the banning of discriminatory technical standards in order to ensure open competition.

By these means it was hoped that the public procurement market would become more open. However, the Commission has encountered great difficulty in getting member states to comply not only with the spirit of the directives but also the letter. Evidence would seem to suggest that member states are continuing to favour local and national suppliers. In 1987, fifteen years after the introduction of the first directives, only 2% of public works contracts were awarded to foreign firms.[8] The implication must be that the original directives have had only a limited impact. Indeed this was the view expressed in a recent Commission report which stated:

> The [1972 'works'] Directive has had some success in bringing about a convergence in the terminology and practices of tendering . . . However, the degree of interpenetration of national markets remains disappointingly low . . . there is no denying that discrimination against foreign firms has persisted because of loopholes in the Directive and the lack of effective policing.[9]

One of the most blatant infringements has been the failure to adhere to the advertising requirements. In 1986, for example, 9,500 tender notices were published in the EC's Official Journal. This was believed to be just a fraction of those that met the financial thresholds of the directives. A closer study of one member state confirmed this suspicion: of the 4,500 public contracts that met with the directives' criteria, only 500 were actually advertised in the Official Journal.[10] A particularly popular method of getting round the directives was to split contracts so that they fell below the financial thresholds, even though this was specifically prohibited under Article 7 of the 1972 directive. The problem was that there was a lack of monitoring arrangements to ensure compliance at both

[8] *Ibid.*, p. 55.
[9] Bureau d'Informations et de Provisions Economiques (BIPE), 1987, p. 3.
[10] House of Lords Select Committee on the European Communities' 12th Report, 'Compliance with the Procurement Directives', 1988, p. 9.

the national and Community level. In addition, tenderers who felt they had been discriminated against had no effective means of redress.

However, the British experience has been that even when contracts comply with the directives the response from non-domestic bidders has been rather disappointing. In 1986 130 Property Services Agency (PSA) contracts were advertised in the Official Journal, but this resulted in only two bids from non-UK companies. Further, out of the 66 contracts advertised by the Department of Transport, only 3 responses came from outside of the UK; while the 80 to 100 health authority contracts advertised have yet to generate any response from another member state.[11]

One explanation for this apparent lack of EC interest in UK public works contracts is the cost involved in establishing a base in another member state, which is necessary because such contracts require considerable planning and coordination at the point of construction. Consequently, close links with the domestic suppliers and distributors are essential if the non-resident contractor is successfully to compete. For these reasons, foreign contractors wishing to operate in another member state will probably take over a domestic operator or set up a new company in the contracting member state. The obvious deterrent to this option is the great expense involved in setting up a new company. More importantly, because public works contracts tend to be 'one offs' by nature, there is no guarantee that once the project has been completed, further work will be available. This means that the value of the contract must be sufficiently large to make tendering worthwhile for the non-national contractor because their costs will be relatively higher than those of indigenous bidders. It is therefore not all that surprising that the level of foreign interest in UK public works contracts is minimal.

Supplies contracts by their nature are rather less of a problem to tender for, since the need for a separate, resident base is far less important. To appreciate the reasons behind the disappointing impact of the supplies directive it is necessary to consider the operating conditions of public purchasing bodies, particularly local authorities. The current economic and political climate has placed increasing pressure on public bodies to be more cost effective in their purchasing. Although on the surface this would appear to encourage the use of open tendering, in practice this tends not to be the case. Firstly, open tendering itself can often be an expensive and time-consuming process. Secondly, the availability of only limited storage space encourages a 'just in time' method of stocking which tends to favour local suppliers. As a result, many public bodies prefer to operate some form of restricted tendering, taking into account a wide range of considerations, including the financial status of the firm, its track record with delivery dates and overall reliability.

As a result of the failure to achieve a free market in public procurement, new directives were proposed by the Commission in 1988 as part of the

---

[11] *Ibid.*, p. 4.

1992 project. The basic aim was to rectify the shortcomings of the earlier directives by, firstly, making the award of contracts more transparent, thereby reducing the opportunities for discrimination; secondly, increasing the Commission's powers of intervention, enabling it to prevent a breach of the regulations; and, thirdly, tenderers who experienced discrimination now had a right to damages. The amendments to strengthen the directive on supply contracts came into force on 1 January 1989, and there has been some progress in incorporating it into national legislation, although Greece and Portugal have until March 1992 to put it into effect. The new directive on public works contracts is unlikely to find its way into all member states' national legislation until at least the end of 1992. The new works directive now includes contracts from bodies who receive more than 50% of their funding from the public sector. It also raises the threshold value for the advertising of contracts from one million ECU to five million ECU. This is an inevitable development given the effect of inflation over time, although it does mean that many works contracts will now fall outside the new tighter rules; and it also increases the opportunity for avoidance through contract splitting.

The hope is that these new directives will encourage open tendering by persuading public bodies to adopt a more realistic and commercial awards procedure, with the emphasis on price competitiveness rather than nationality. As a result they should benefit from price reductions, greater choice and increased negotiating power with suppliers. More specifically, it is expected to improve compliance with earlier EC directives by encouraging companies to make complaints against public authorities who operate restrictive purchasing policies. However, both the Federation of Civil Engineering Contractors (FCEC) and the Confederation of British Industry (CBI) have expressed concern that the Commission's proposals 'pay little regard to, and exhibit little understanding of, the manner in which . . . industry operates and of the tendering process'.[12]

The time and expense involved in evaluating tenders favours the drawing up of a list of approved companies, with a selected number of these being invited to bid. The new proposals, which require the contracting authority to write a report justifying the award decision, can only further increase the burden of bureaucracy. With regard to the provision for damages against public bodies for discriminating in favour of locals, the Association of County Councils has expressed the view that the severity of the punishment far outweighs the gravity of the offence.[13] Even if damages are restricted to the cost of the tender this could be anything up to £1m on a major contract. In reality, however, it seems unlikely that aggrieved tenderers will take action in the courts. The problem is not simply the time and expense involved in taking legal action, particularly in another member state, but the understandable reluctance of contractors

---

[12] *Ibid*., p. 14.
[13] Consultative Committee of Local and Regional Authorities, 1987, p. 2.

to antagonize potential clients. This creates a real problem for the Commission because the level of compliance with the directives is to a large extent dependent on the willingness of aggrieved tenderers to take action against the 'restrictive practices' of public bodies.

Paradoxically, the new directives are an example of a cost-cutting exercise which imposes extra costs, both bureaucratic and judicial. In an attempt to encourage the public sector to adopt a more commercial approach to its purchasing, the Commission has proposed a totally unrealistic awards procedure which in most instances will reduce efficiency. Moreover, it could be argued that the changing economic and financial environment in which the public sector operates, means that purchasing bodies are increasingly aware of the need to obtain value for money. The Commission is therefore trying to achieve what financial restrictions demand anyway. Moreover, these measures are being introduced at a time when some member states, particularly the UK, are pursuing privatization strategies. These policies are likely to make a significant contribution to the opening up of public procurement to non-nationals.

In addition, a number of important sectors, including defence, water, energy, telecommunications and transport, are excluded from the provisions of the new directives. It could be argued that these are the areas in which open procurement would have the greatest impact. Currently there is very little in the way of intra-EC trade within these sectors, because of the economic and strategic importance of many of these industries. As a result there is considerable over-capacity in terms of suppliers; for example, only 20% of the capacity is currently being utilized in the boiler-making sector, 60% in turbine generators and 50% to 80% in loco-motives.[14] Therefore, subjecting these sectors to open tendering would result in considerable restructuring and rationalization, with a significant loss of employment in those areas where the less efficient producers are located. Also, if contracts in the excluded sectors are opened to all, it should be remembered that there will be a real threat from producers outside the Community. Many of the gains from opening up these markets may well be lost if non-EC producers come to dominate in the transition period. Clearly, before these sectors can be liberalized, some sort of regional and industrial policy will be necessary in order to compensate the losers. In the absence of such policies, the Commission, under pressure from the member states, has found it necessary to exclude these important sectors from the attempts to open up public procurement.

---

[14] Commission of the European Communities, 'Public Procurement in the Excluded Sectors', in *Bulletin of the European Communities Supplement* 6/88, 1989.

Road haulage

The successful completion of the single market will result in a considerable boost to intra-EC trade. A significant proportion of this is likely to be transported by road. Currently 62.8% of all goods within the EC are transported this way.[15] However, both international and domestic freight transport have been subjected to a variety of controls and restrictions in terms of prices and entry into the market. The extent of regulation varies from country to country. At one extreme there is West Germany which operates restrictions on capacity and prices, and on the other the UK which operates a relatively liberal regime. The problem for the Community is that there is little point in breaking down the physical, technical and fiscal barriers to trade if the industry mainly responsible for the transportation of trade is itself highly regulated and restrictive. Therefore, a fundamental pre-requisite for the successful completion of the internal market is the liberalization of the road haulage industry within the EC. The achievement of this objective is something which seems to have occupied the Commission's collective mind almost since its inception in the 1950s as part of their search for a Common Transport Policy. Before investigating the Commission's most recent attempts to liberalize road haulage as part of the 1992 project, it might be useful to first of all identify the main sources of regulation within this particular market.

Intra-EC haulage operations are governed by a system of quotas, which means that hauliers require a permit in order to transport goods within the Community. At the moment there are two types of permits: the bilateral permit and the Community permit.

The bilateral permit

Since 1965 a series of bilateral agreements have been annually negotiated between individual member states to determine the number of road haulage licences to be granted to non-domestic carriers. If the journey involves transit through a third country then a permit will be required for that country too; e.g. UK–France–Spain. At present, 54% of the Community's road haulage traffic is regulated by this system.[16] Permits are not required by all EC members: for example, a British haulier can freely enter any of the Benelux countries. Indeed, the operation of this type of system does not automatically mean that competition will be impeded, providing the number of permits made available to hauliers is sufficient to satisfy the demand. However, some member states, most notably the UK's three main European trading partners, France, Italy and West Germany, do impose highly restrictive quotas.

[15] *European Business*, Vol. 1, No. 5 (February 1989), p. 12.
[16] Commission of the European Communities, 'The Official Journal of the EC', 13/6/1985.

The Community permit

In an attempt to overcome some of the effects of these restrictions, the EC introduced the Community permit in 1977, which allows unlimited international journeys within the EC. This type of permit is becoming increasingly important; in 1983 it accounted for 5% of total intra-Community road haulage, and by 1988 this had risen to 16%.[17] The Community is following a policy of making it more widely available, and in 1988 it was agreed that the number should grow by 40% per year. The idea is that it will gradually replace the bilateral system until 1 January 1993, at which time all quotas will be removed.

This represents a major breakthrough in freeing the international road haulage market. It leaves untouched the highly restricted domestic markets, complete liberalization of which will require the introduction of cabotage—that is, allowing non-resident hauliers to carry out domestic operations in another member state. Cabotage is still prohibited in some member states even though this contravenes Article 75 of the Treaty of Rome, which charges the Ministers of Transport with a legal obligation to 'lay down conditions under which non-resident carriers may operate transport services within a member state'.[18] The first proposals for the introduction of cabotage were made by the Commission as far back as 1968; the 1985 White Paper set 1988 as the deadline for its introduction; yet the Council of Ministers has resisted making any real progress until December 1989.

Cabotage is seen by the Commission as being an essential prerequisite for the completion of the internal market. It takes the view that there is little point in removing the barriers to trade if the means of transporting goods is still subject to national restrictions. The absence of cabotage represents an inefficient allocation of resources: it has been estimated that in 30% of international return journeys the vehicle is empty.[19] Ernst and Whinney put the cost of this inefficiency at around £830m.[20] The Commission is therefore very keen to deregulate road haulage and argues that there are real economic benefits to be gained from this, pointing to the recent experience of the road haulage industry within the USA as further evidence for this claim.

In 1980 the Motor Carrier Act was passed in the USA, effectively removing restrictions on road haulage between the various states. One effect was to encourage new firms into the market; between 1979 and 1985 the number of operators rose from 17,270 to 33,548. As a result prices in 1987 were on average lower in real terms than those in 1980. In

---

[17] *Independent*, 21 June 1988, p. 16.
[18] Commission of the European Communities, 'The Official Journal of the EC', No. C 349, 1986.
[19] Commission of the European Communities, 'The Official Journal of the EC', 8 July 1987, para 1.6.
[20] *Financial Times*, 23 October 1989.

addition, during the same period 223,000 new jobs were created. The industry has also become less unionized and there has been considerable downward pressure on wage levels. Competition has become much more intense, with the number of bankruptcies increasing six-fold. It has been estimated that customers have saved £38 million per annum as a result of deregulation.[21] It appears that the main impact of liberalization in the USA has been the encouragement of more competition, which has led to lower prices and a better service for the customer. Deregulation of road haulage in the EC should result in similar benefits for the European economy. However, there is a significant difference between the US and the EC in terms of the operating conditions faced by the various national hauliers in the Community. Cabotage and the removal of quotas will by themselves be inadequate if the full benefits of liberalization are to be realized; it also requires the harmonization of operating conditions.

Taxation, particularly Vehicle Excise Duty (VED), is one area in which there is considerable disparity within the Community. Some member states impose a high VED on hauliers as a way of helping to finance the upkeep of roads, while in others charges are made direct in terms of motorway tolls. At 4% of operating costs the UK's VED is the highest in Europe, closely followed by West Germany. Since taxation is based on nationality, i.e. the country in which the haulier is established, British and West German hauliers are to some extent at a competitive disadvantage to hauliers from countries such as France and Italy, where greater use is made of tolls, because they will face a 'double-cost'. Not only do they suffer from a high VED, but also, when operating in Italy or France for example, they will be subject to road tolls, while the French and Italian hauliers can use the British and West German motorways for free. In addition, there is also a problem concerning tax on diesel, which ranges from 4.42 ECU per 100 litres in Denmark to 24.52 ECU per 100 litres in the UK.[22]

The enforcement of the rules and regulations concerning working conditions is another source of disharmony within the Community. In West Germany an armada of functionaries is responsible for enforcing national regulations; there are 2,500 staff employed solely to police rules such as maximum driving hours, weights and dimensions, compliance with compulsory tariffs, road worthiness tests etc.; as a result 42% of drivers who work longer than they are supposed to are penalized. In contrast, other member states take a more relaxed attitude towards control; the corresponding figure for France and Belgium are just 3% and 1% respectively. Although this might seem a minor point, West German hauliers say their Dutch competitors can cut costs by 7% solely on the

[21] European Conference of Ministers of Transport, *Regulatory Reforms in the Transport Sector*, OECD publications, 1987.
[22] P. Mackie, D. Simon, A. Whiteing, *British Transport Industry and the European Community*, Gower, 1987, p. 82.

strength of being checked less often.[23] It is not surprising therefore that West German hauliers feel themselves to be at a competitive disadvantage to operators from other member states.

A third problem in terms of operating conditions relates to the weight of lorries. In the UK and Eire the maximum axle weight for lorries is 38 tonnes, whereas the Dutch operate 50 tonne trucks. A survey of UK international road hauliers showed that 78% of respondents felt that lower UK gross weights put them at a competitive disadvantage to their European counterparts.[24] The Freight Transport Association has estimated that if only half of the 38 tonne vehicles operating in the UK today were changed to 40 tonnes, British industry could save £76 million a year.[25] However, the discrepancy between Britain's maximum lorry weights and those operating in other member states may to some extent protect the UK's domestic market; smaller loads will make haulage operations in the UK less efficient than those in other countries. This is likely to be less of a problem in the future as the British and Irish governments have both agreed to allow 40 tonne lorries from 1999.

Unless agreement is reached in terms of harmonizing these discrepancies in operating conditions, the liberalization of road haulage could well result in unfair competition. In attempting to achieve harmonization on these issues the Commission faces two major hurdles: the rather cumbersome decision-making process and the power of vested interests—groups who may well feel threatened by the prospect of liberalization. For instance, West Germany operates a highly regulated industry which both limits the number of operators and fixes the tariffs they can charge. This is intended to protect the railways and minimize the adverse environmental impact of trucks. One consequence of this restricted market is that the average West German haulier has between four to five trucks and carries out very little cross-border business, whereas the average Dutch company has fourteen trucks and is heavily involved in international carrying. In fact, Dutch hauliers account for 72% of German–Dutch trade.[26] Not surprisingly, the West Germans have been rather resistant to the notion of liberalizing road haulage. In addition, deregulation of road haulage has profound implications for other transport sectors, such as the railways. The West German government already pays approximately £5 billion in subsidies to its rail network and would have to pay a further £1 billion if its road haulage industry were to compete properly, since road tariffs are fixed at a high level in order to maintain the competitiveness of the railways.[27]

After a great deal of equivocation, the West Germans have finally

[23] *The German Tribune*, 5 July 1987, p. 7.

[24] Transport Studies Group, *Freight Transport in the European Community: Making the Most of UK Opportunities*, Polytechnic of Central London, 1987.

[25] *Freight*, October 1987, p. 15.

[26] *Financial Times*, 10 April 1989, p. 7.

[27] *Ibid*.

agreed to the abolition of quotas by 1993; but in an attempt to minimize the impact they have introduced a new road tax (£2,000 p.a.) which is aimed primarily at foreign lorries using West German roads. Since the Treaty of Rome specifically prohibits such blatant discrimination, this tax has to be applied to German lorries as well. However, rather craftily, the Germans have reduced their Vehicle Excise Duty from £3,500 to £1,500—a saving of £2000 which, coincidentally, is the same amount as the new tax, so in effect the domestic industry will not pay anything extra. The justification for this move is that the abolition of quotas will result in increased foreign traffic on West German autobahns and consequently more damage to the roads, therefore it is not unreasonable to expect foreign hauliers to pay something towards the upkeep of the roads. Although the West Germans have accepted that quotas will have to go, their hauliers remain vigorously opposed to cabotage, which will affect them to a much greater extent. The West German hauliers' trade association, Bundesverband des Deutschen Güterfernverkehrs (BDF), estimates that nearly 50% of all German hauliers will go out of business if cabotage is allowed.[28] The fundamental problem is that West German hauliers are prosperous, protected by strict limits on capacity and price, and basically wish to keep things as they are.

In order for the full benefits of liberalization of road haulage to be realized, operating conditions need to be harmonized, otherwise competition will be distorted. The difficulty is that it is almost impossible to achieve real harmonization because of the power of vested interests and the incremental style of decision-making within the EC. The situation is further complicated by the nature of the road haulage market within the Community. There are twelve highly diverse national markets, each with its own tax system, regulations, controls, infrastructure costs, etc.; consequently, reaching an agreement is not an easy task. In addition, each member state has its own indigenous operators to consider. National hauliers are likely to be fearful of, and therefore highly resistant to, any moves to introduce external competition to their protected domestic markets, particularly when the foreign companies may be subject to different operating conditions and therefore enjoy a competitive advantage.

The Commission has clearly recognized the difficulties it faces in trying to achieve harmonization prior to full liberalization, and has adopted a strategy of pressing ahead with opening up the road haulage market irrespective of progress on operating conditions. As a result it has now succeeded in introducing a limited form of cabotage. In December 1989, despite opposition from the West German and Greek governments, agreement was reached to allow a form of cabotage from 1 July 1990.[29] From this date, 15,000 cabotage permits, valid for two months, will be

---

[28] *Ibid.*
[29] *Financial Times*, 5th December 1989, p. 2.

made available. It is envisaged that the number of permits will increase by 10% per annum. They will be distributed to the hauliers by the various national authorities and will allow non-domestic hauliers to operate in another member state. Hauliers taking advantage of the cabotage permits must observe the national rules on things like driving hours, weights and dimensions, and, where they apply, rates and conditions governing transport contracts. So, for example, if they operate in West Germany they must conform to the fixed tariff system which determines the price they can charge. This to some extent restricts the value of the reform, but is clearly necessary in the absence of agreement on operating conditions. Although this reform represents a significant step towards the Commission's goal of a fully liberated road haulage market, it will only cover 1% of the market and there is no clear indication of what is to happen after 1992.[30]

One problem with the whole issue of liberalizing road haulage is that there seems to be an implicit assumption that liberalization *per se* is a desirable objective. Little thought appears to have been given to the wider implications of such moves for other transport sectors and in terms of the physical environment. As a result of increased competition road haulage tariffs should become cheaper, with serious consequences for the heavily subsidized European rail freight network, making it even less competitive. Furthermore, lower costs will encourage greater use of road haulage, leading to increased congestion. Consequently the efficiency of the transport system will be reduced and greater infrastructure costs will be imposed, particularly in the central areas of the Community. Finally, in an increasingly 'Green Europe', the prospect of additional carbon dioxide emissions and other related costs could well be politically as well as environmentally unacceptable.

Liberalization is not necessarily the best way forward for the road haulage industry; in many respects deregulation is a poor substitute for a comprehensive coordination of the transport systems of the Community. The vested interests who have proved to be a considerable obstacle to liberalization are playing a more positive role than they realize or intended. By opposing liberalization they are to some extent highlighting the need for a transport system which offers benefits to all the citizens of the Community, rather than one which is concerned solely with the promotion of market forces, without fully appreciating the consequences.

Conclusion

It is clear that the Community faces enormous difficulties in trying to turn the rhetoric of 1992 into reality. The three areas highlighted in this article emphasize the fact that the shape of post-1992 Europe is unlikely to be

[30] *Ibid.*

consistent with the notion of 'one market'; the Community will remain an alliance, albeit a more integrated alliance, of sovereign national states. To some extent the 'litmus test' for the success of the 1992 project revolves around the extent to which the Community can make significant progress on customs documentation, public procurement and road haulage. Currently all three emphasize quite vividly the fragmented nature of the market within the Community. If the Community can overcome the forces which maintain the separateness of these areas then it will have gone a long way towards successfully completing the internal market. However, it is clear from the case studies that there are some very powerful forces at work which have effectively limited the impact of policy changes. In many ways it is the national governments who are at the forefront of maintaining the fragmented market within the Community. Despite the introduction of the Single Europe Act, they have the power to prevent changes taking place. Governments in all member states are under pressure from 'vested interests' who fear that the changes implicit in the 1992 project will adversely affect them. In addition, governments themselves are suspicious about any moves to usurp their sovereignty, particularly if they could damage the perceived national economic interest. After all governments tend to be judged electorally on their handling of the economy; they will be rather unwilling to cede control of anything which makes that task any more difficult.

The protagonists of one market are unable to act as counterweights to these pressures and find that the only proposals which stand any chance of being accepted are the 'minimalist' ones. A truly common market would not require any customs documentation at all; the Commission accepts that 'national interest' will not accept that, but will accept a standardized form of documentation: the SAD. The road haulage market in the Community should exist under the same operating conditions: the Commission recognized that agreement between the member states on this matter is fraught with difficulty and heavily influenced by vested interests, and therefore introduced the notion of having a liberalized market with diverse operating conditions. A common market in public procurement would not have any excluded sectors; but again the Commission is pragmatic enough to recognize that these are often areas of strategic economic importance for the national governments. In all three cases the policy solution which would be consistent with the creation of an internal market is not a practical possibility, so the Commission must settle for second best or sometimes third best. Harmonization in this context involves accepting the lowest common denominator; the policy which offends the vested interests and the national governments the least.

In the power struggle to determine the shape of post-1992 Europe the Commission requires allies to offset the considerable spoiling power of the vested interests and the national governments. Since it is the latter who ensure that the Community remains a fragmented market, it is possible that such allies might be found within the ranks of European business. If the '1992 hype' results in more businesses beginning to regard the Community as one market and therefore altering their strategies accordingly, then, when they discover that such a market does not exist post-1992, they may well be inclined to put pressure on their national governments to remove these barriers to trade. In effect these elements of business could act as a counterweight to the not inconsiderable power of the 'vested interests'. This scenario would suggest that perhaps the importance of the 1992 project has less to do with the actual detail of policy, since in reality only minimalist measures will be possible, but rather the extent to which it alters the perceptions of business about the European market. In this sense 1992 is a marketing exercise designed to create the impression that economic integration is an irreversible process. To maintain this impression it is important for the Commission to 'keep the pot boiling', by putting forward schemes and suggestions which are consistent with, and logical extensions of, the 1992 project. The Delors plan for European Monetary Union and the European Social Charter can be seen as part of this process. We are not suggesting that this is a deliberate or conscious strategy drawn up by Machiavellian Eurocrats to overcome the national chauvinism which prevents the Community from becoming a single market. Rather it represents perhaps the only means by which a single market can be achieved. As the three case studies demonstrate, there is a considerable gap between what is the 'ideal policy' for a single market and the actual measures which are being implemented.

INDEX